radio amateurs' examination manual

TENTH EDITION

G. L. BENBOW, MSc, CEng, MIEE, G3HB

RADIO SOCIETY OF GREAT BRITAIN

Published by the Radio Society of Great Britain, 35 Doughty Street, London WC1N 2AE.

Tenth edition 1982

ISBN 0 900612 60 6

Printed in Great Britain by Eyre & Spottiswoode Ltd, Thanet Press, Margate

Preface

The ninth edition of the *Radio Amateurs' Examination Manual* took account of minor changes in the syllabus for 1982–85 and various comments and suggestions received concerning the eighth edition; an introduction to basic mathematics for the RAE was included. This revision was carried out by G. L. Benbow, G3HB, G. Denby, G3FCW, D. L. Hoare, G8FQJ, I. Jackson, G3OHX, and G. C. Oxley, G8MW. The tenth edition incorporates the changes to the UK amateur licence schedule which were announced in March 1982. The opportunity has also been taken to make a number of minor amendments in order to improve the clarity of the text.

The *RAE Manual* is intended primarily as a basis for formal tuition and contains all the information necessary to pass the examination, although the treatment is necessarily brief. It is difficult to recommend a more elementary introduction to basic electronics, if needed, to meet the requirements of individual private students. A visit to the local reference library is therefore suggested! *A Guide to Amateur Radio,* also published by RSGB, provides a useful technical background to the hobby of amateur radio.

The UK licence conditions given in Chapter 10 could be subject to change during the currency of this edition. RAE candidates are therefore advised to check the latest licence conditions prior to taking the examination.

Thanks are due to the City and Guilds of London Institute for permission to reproduce the RAE syllabus and objectives (Appendix 3 of this book) and certain specimen RAE questions which have been included in Appendix 4.

Acknowledgement is also made to the Home Office for permission to reproduce information from the publication *How to Become a Radio Amateur.*

Figs 7.3–7.6 inclusive are taken from *Short Wave Radio and the Ionosphere* by Bennington, 2nd edn, and are reproduced here by permission of *Wireless World.*

G. L. B.

CHAPTER 1

Becoming a radio amateur

Before an amateur radio station can be established and used, it is necessary to obtain a licence from the Secretary of State for the Home Office.

Full details are given in the publication *How to Become a Radio Amateur* which is obtainable, free of charge, from the Home Office, Radio Regulatory Department, Radio Regulatory Division, Licensing Branch (Amateur), Waterloo Bridge House, Waterloo Road, London SE1 8UA.

The necessary requirements are summarized in this chapter and the actual licence conditions, with which the RAE candidate must be familiar, are given in Chapter 10.

Requirements of the Amateur Licence

1. Amateur Licence A

1. Applicants must be over 14 years of age and must provide evidence of British nationality (ie a birth certificate, a valid passport or a naturalization certificate).
2. Applicants must have passed the Radio Amateurs' Examination (RAE).
3. Applicants must have passed the Post Office Morse Test not more than 12 months before applying for a licence.
4. The appropriate fee must be paid before the licence is issued and each year on the anniversary of the date of issue of the licence.

2. Amateur Licence B

This licence does not authorize the use of frequencies below 144MHz or the use of morse telegraphy; otherwise its conditions are broadly the same as those of the Amateur Licence A except that one will not be required to pass the Post Office Morse Test.

Commonwealth or alien citizens who reside in the UK may take the UK examination and obtain our licence. There are certain conditions to be observed and the Home Office will be pleased to answer any written enquiry.

The Radio Amateurs' Examination

The City and Guilds of London Institute, Electrical and Telecommunications Branch, 76 Portland Place, London W1N 4AA, holds the Radio Amateurs' Examination twice yearly, usually in May and December. This can be taken at local colleges and examination centres throughout the country. Applications to sit the examination should be made well in advance so that the college is aware in good time of the need to arrange for this examination to be held there. The intending candidate should therefore think of applying for the May examination not later than the end of January; or the end of September for the December examination.

The regulations, syllabus and objectives for the RAE No 765 can be obtained from City and Guilds of London Institute at the above address for a small charge. The syllabus and objectives are given in Appendix 3 of this book, and specimen questions in Appendix 4.

The examination lasts for 3h.

Paper 1 on licensing conditions and transmitter interference takes 1h, and consists of 35 multiple-choice questions. 23 questions are set on licensing conditions and 12 questions on transmitter interference.

There is then a break of 15min.

Paper 2 takes 1h 45min and has 60 multiple-choice questions. These questions are apportioned as follows:

1. Operating practices and procedures	5
2. Electrical theory	11
3. Semiconductors	9
4. Radio receivers	9
5. Transmitters	9
6. Propagation and antennas	10
7. Measurements	7
	60

Candidates must take both components (papers) on their first entry. Candidates who are successful in one but not both components may carry forward their success and need subsequently re-take only the component in which they were unsuccessful.

Details of colleges and institutions which offer courses leading to the RAE are given in *Radio Communication,* the journal of the Radio Society of Great Britain, and other radio journals, usually in July, August and September each year.

Tuition and examination fees vary from college to college, and such information may be obtained from the college on enrolment.

The Post Office Morse Test

Morse tests can be taken throughout the year at the Post Office HQ in London or at any of the Post Office Coast Stations (located at Highbridge, Somerset; Whitley Bay, Northumberland; near Mablethorpe, Lincs; near Penzance, Cornwall; near Ventnor, Isle of Wight; Broadstairs, Kent; Connel, Argyll; near Stranraer, Wigtownshire; near Amlwch, Anglesey; Stonehaven, Kincardineshire; Wick, Caithness; Ilfracombe, Devon) or at any of the Radio Surveyor's Offices (located at Aberdeen; Belfast; Cardiff; Falmouth; Glasgow; Hull; Edinburgh; Liverpool; Newcastle on Tyne; Southampton). Tests are also held, provided there are sufficient applicants, in March and September of each year, at the Head Post Offices in Birmingham, Cambridge, Derby, Leeds and Manchester.

In the test, 36 words (average length five letters per word) must be sent and 36 words received in two periods of 3min each. Up to four errors are permitted in the copy received and up to four corrections may be made while sending; there must be no uncorrected errors in sending. 10 groups of five figures must be sent, and 10 groups copied, in two periods of 1½min each; a maximum of two receiving errors are permitted in this section and up to two corrections may be made while sending.

At those centres at which tests can be taken throughout the year, tests will be arranged as far as possible to suit the candidates' convenience but the Post Office cannot of course guarantee this.

The application form for the morse test is included in *How to Become a Radio Amateur,* which also contains the postal addresses of the centres and details of the fee payable.

As a pass in the morse test is valid for only 12 months, it is advisable to take the morse test *after* passing the RAE. Exemptions on the grounds of Service or civil qualifications are no longer granted from either of these examinations, and even if the applicant has previously held an amateur licence he must show that he has passed the RAE (which was first held in 1946) and must retake the code test unless he has passed this within the last 12 months.

Fees

The fee, on issue and on annual renewal, for Amateur Licence A and Amateur Licence B is currently (1982) £8.

Too often one hears expressed the erroneous belief that the conditions imposed by the authorities have been devised to discourage the experimenter. Such is very far from the truth: the newcomer can be confident that his or her desire to obtain a licence will meet with courtesy, assistance and every encouragement from the authorities—provided that no special concessions are expected.

Reciprocal licences

There are now agreements between the UK and certain foreign countries whereby citizens of those countries who hold a transmitting licence issued by their own government may obtain a UK licence and vice versa.

Details of such licences are outside the scope of this manual and intending applicants for reciprocal licences should seek guidance from the Radio Society of Great Britain.

The Radio Society of Great Britain

Every reader of this manual is advised to become, if not already so, a member of the Radio Society of Great Britain (RSGB).

The RSGB is the national society for radio amateurs in the UK. The majority of its 30,000 members hold amateur transmitting licences: the others either hope to do so later or are interested primarily in the receiving side of amateur radio. More than 2,000 members live overseas.

The Society acts as the spokesman for the radio amateur and amateur radio in the UK, and is one of the founder members of the International Amateur Radio Union, the world-wide association of the various national societies.

The Society was founded as the London Wireless Club in 1913 but soon attracted members throughout the country. The name "Radio Society of Great Britain" was formally adopted in 1922. For many years its activities have been devoted almost entirely to the many aspects of amateur radio—that is, the transmission and reception of radio signals as a hobby pursued for the pleasure to be derived from an interest in radio techniques and construction, and for the ensuing friendships with like-minded persons throughout the world.

The Society is recognized as the representative of the amateur radio movement in all negotiations with the Home Office on matters affecting the issue of amateur transmitting licences.

The Society maintains close liaison with the Home Office on all matters affecting licence facilities and the frequencies assigned to amateur radio, and sends official representatives to the important World Administrative Radio Conferences of the International Telecommunication Union and other conferences where decisions vital to the future of amateur radio are taken.

The Society helps amateur radio in many ways. Of particular importance is the provision of information on technical matters and on the various activities and events of concern to amateurs. Since 1925 it has published a monthly journal, *Radio Communication,* the oldest and largest magazine in this country devoted to amateur radio. All members receive this magazine by post, without payment other than their annual membership subscriptions.

Anyone over 18 years of age or holding an amateur transmitting licence is eligible to become a Corporate Member of the Society. It is not necessary to be engaged professionally in radio but equally this would not debar anyone from joining. Many members do in fact work in the electronics field, but for very many others radio is purely a spare-time hobby. Those under 18 years old who do not hold an amateur transmitting licence may become Associates. Associates have many of the privileges of full membership but do not vote in the annual Council election or on matters affecting the management of the Society. Associates must apply for transfer to Corporate membership on reaching 18 years of age or immediately they obtain a transmitting licence if under this age.

All applicants, for both Corporate and Associate membership, should be proposed by a Corporate Member of the Society to whom they are known personally. The member simply completes the proposal on the application form and it will be found that he or she will be glad to do this.

The Society however fully recognizes that many new-comers to amateur radio, who are most welcome as members, may not know or be in touch with other members. In such cases, a brief reference in writing should be submitted from a suitable person who can vouch for the applicant's interest in amateur radio. All applications are placed before the Council at its regular meetings.

Full details of the aims, activities and advantages of membership of the RSGB may be obtained from the Radio Society of Great Britain, 35 Doughty Street, London WC1N 2AE. Telephone 01-837 8688.

CHAPTER 2

Electrical theory and calculations

Atoms and electrons

All matter is composed of *molecules,* the molecule being the smallest quantity of a substance which can exist and still display the physical and chemical properties of that substance. There is a great number of different sorts of molecules. Further study of a molecule discloses that it is made up of smaller particles called *atoms* and it has been found that there are over 100 different types of atoms. All molecules are made up of combinations of atoms selected from this range. Examples of different atoms are atoms of hydrogen, oxygen, iron, copper and sulphur, and examples of how atoms are combined to form molecules are (a) two atoms of hydrogen and one of oxygen to form one molecule of water, and (b) two atoms of hydrogen, one of sulphur and four of oxygen to form one molecule of sulphuric acid.

Atoms are so small that they cannot be seen even under the most powerful microscopes. Their behaviour, however, can be studied and from this it has been discovered that atoms are made up of a positively-charged relatively heavy core or *nucleus* around which are moving a number of much lighter particles each negatively charged, called *electrons.* Atoms are normally electrically neutral; that is to say, the amount of positive electricity associated with the nucleus is exactly balanced by the total amount of negative electricity associated with the electrons. One type of atom differs from another in the number of positive and neutral particles (called *protons* and *neutrons*) which make up the nucleus and the number and arrangement of the orbital electrons which are continually moving around the nucleus.

Large atoms, such as those of uranium, are complex, but small atoms, such as those of hydrogen and carbon, are relatively simple, as can be seen in Fig 2.1.

In the case of hydrogen the two atoms (H_2) share their electrons so that at any one instant the first ring is complete, ie it has its full complement of two electrons. The first ring of the carbon atom is complete and the second ring, which is full when it has eight electrons, only has four electrons. These atoms will link together and share their outer electrons forming a *crystal lattice.* The outer electrons are very difficult to dislodge and the resulting substance, in its pure form, is a diamond, which is not only very hard but a good insulator. The type of carbon used for electric motor brushes and for the positive electrode in Leclanché cells is not pure, and does conduct electricity, although not as well as copper.

In the case of copper, the atom has 29 electrons arranged as follows, first ring: 2; second ring: 8; third ring: 18; outer ring: 1. This outer electron is very easily detached and so copper is a very good conductor.

Conductors and insulators

The ease with which the electrons in a substance can be detached from their parent atoms thus varies from substance to substance. In some substances there is a continual movement of electrons in a random manner from one atom to another, and the application of an electrical pressure or voltage (for example from a battery) to the two ends of a piece of wire made of such a substance will cause a drift of electrons along the wire called an *electric current*; electrical *conduction* is then said to take place. It should be noted that if an electron enters the wire from the battery at one end it will be a different electron which immediately leaves the other end of the wire. By convention, the direction of current flow is said to be from *positive* to *negative*.

Materials which conduct electricity are called *conductors.* All metals belong to this class. Materials which do not conduct electricity are called *insulators.* See Table 2.1.

Sources of electricity

When two dissimilar metals are immersed in certain chemical solutions *(electrolytes),* an *electromotive force* (emf) is created by chemical action within the cell so that if the pieces of metal are joined externally to the cell there is a continuous flow of electric current. Such a device is called a *simple cell,* and in a cell comprising copper and zinc rods immersed in dilute sulphuric acid,

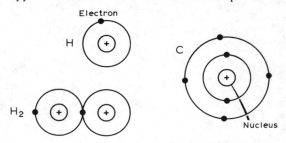

Fig 2.1.   Structure of hydrogen and carbon atoms

Table 2.1
Materials commonly used as conductors and insulators

Conductors	Insulators
Silver	Mica
Copper	Quartz
Aluminium	Glass
Brass	Ceramics
Steel	Plastics
Carbon (graphite)	Air
Certain liquids	Oil

the flow of current is from the copper to the zinc plate in the external circuit; ie the copper forms the positive (+) terminal *(anode)* of the cell and the zinc forms the negative (−) terminal *(cathode)*.

In a simple cell of this type, hydrogen forms on the copper electrode, and this gas film has the effect of increasing the internal resistance of the cell and also setting up within the cell a counter or *polarizing* emf which rapidly reduces the effective emf of the cell as a whole. This polarization effect is overcome in practical cells by the introduction of chemical agents surrounding the anode for the purpose of removing the hydrogen by oxidation as soon as it is formed. Such agents are called *depolarizers*.

Primary cells
Practical cells in which electricity is produced in this way by direct chemical action are called *primary cells*. One of the earliest examples of this type of cell was the Leclanché cell in which the active agents were carbon and zinc, the electrolyte being liquid ammonium chloride. The modern equivalent of the Leclanché cell is the common "torch battery". In this, the black paste surrounding the carbon rod usually contains powdered carbon, manganese oxide, zinc chloride, ammonium chloride and water, the manganese oxide acting as depolarizer by combining with hydrogen formed at the anode to produce another form of manganese oxide and water. The remainder of the cell is filled with a white paste which usually contains plaster of Paris, flour, zinc chloride, ammonium chloride and water. The cell is sealed with pitch except for a small vent which allows accumulated gas to escape.

The emf developed by a single dry cell is about 1·5V, and cells may be connected in series (positive terminal to negative terminal and so on) until a battery of cells (usually referred to simply as a *battery*) of the desired voltage is obtained.

Many other forms of dry cell have been developed. These often have increased capacity for a given size but are generally more expensive. Mercury and alkaline primary cells are now in common use and Fig 2.2 compares them with the zinc-carbon cell.

Secondary cells
In primary cells some of the various chemicals are used up in producing the electrical energy—a relatively expensive and wasteful process. The maximum current available is also limited. Another type of cell, called a *secondary cell, storage cell* or *accumulator,* offers the advantage of being able to provide a higher current and is capable of being charged by feeding electrical energy into the cell to be stored chemically, and be drawn out or discharged later as electrical energy again. This process of charging and discharging the cell can be repeated almost indefinitely.

The most common type of secondary cell is the lead-acid cell such as that used in motor car batteries. It consists of two sets of specially prepared lead plates immersed in a mixture of sulphuric acid and water. Briefly, the action of the cell is as follows.

In the discharged state the active material on each plate is lead sulphate. During the charging process the lead sulphate in the positive plate is changed to lead peroxide and sulphuric acid, and the lead sulphate in the negative plate to a form of lead called *spongy lead* and sulphuric acid. During discharge the reverse process takes place and lead sulphate forms again on both plates. The state of the charge of the cell may be checked by measuring the specific gravity of the electrolyte with a hydrometer since the concentration of sulphuric acid increases during charging and decreases again as the cell is discharged. Typical values of specific gravity are 1·250 for a fully charged cell and 1·175 for a discharged cell. The terminal voltage of a single lead-acid cell when fully charged and left standing is about 2·05V. In the discharged condition the voltage falls to about 1·85V.

Nickel-cadmium secondary cells have an emf of approximately 1·3V, and this emf remains practically constant throughout the discharge cycle. Discharge should not continue after the emf per cell has fallen to 1V.

Mechanical generators
Direct current or alternating current generators are available in all sizes but the commonest types likely to be met in amateur radio work are (i) ac petrol-driven generators of up to 1 or 2kW output as used for supplying portable equipment and (ii) small motor generators, sometimes called *dynamotors,* which furnish up to

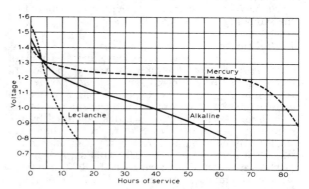

Fig 2.2. Discharge characteristics of alkaline, Leclanché and mercury cells

Table 2.2
Units and symbols

Quantity	Symbol used in formulae	Unit	Abbreviation
charge	Q	coulomb	C
current	I	ampere	A
emf	E	volt	V
voltage	V	volt	V
time	t	second	s
resistance	R	ohm	Ω
capacitance	C	farad	F
inductance	L	henry	H
mutual inductance	M	henry	H
power	W	watt	W
frequency	f	hertz (one cycle per second)	Hz
wavelength	λ	metre	m

Abbreviations for multiples and sub-multiples

G	**giga**	10^9
M	**mega**	10^6
k	**kilo**	10^3
c	**centi**	10^{-2}
m	**milli**	10^{-3}
μ	**micro**	10^{-6}
n	**nano**	10^{-9}
p	**pico**	10^{-12}

about 100W and comprise a combined low-voltage dc electric motor and a high-voltage dc generator so that a high-tension supply may be derived from a 6 or 12V car battery.

Electrical units

Unit of quantity
Since all electrons, whatever kind of atom they belong to, carry the same charge, the amount of electricity associated with the electron could be used as the unit of quantity of electricity. It is, however, too small for use as a practical unit, and a more convenient unit is called the *coulomb*; this is equivalent to the charge on approximately 6×10^{18} (six million million million) electrons. This is analogous to using the litre instead of the molecule as the practical unit of water.

The charge of electricity in coulombs is denoted by the symbol Q.

Unit of current flow
Continuing with the water analogy, just as a flow of water is spoken of as *x litres per second* the flow of electricity can be expressed as *x coulombs per second*. A current of one coulomb per second is called an *ampere* (amp) and the strength of a current is said to be *x amperes*. A current flow is usually denoted by the symbol I. The currents used in radio are often very small fractions of an ampere and for convenience the two small units *milliampere* (10^{-3}A) and *microampere* (10^{-6}A) are used. Thus a current of 0·003 ampere is written as 3 milliamperes. See Table 2.2 for abbreviations.

The relation between the total quantity of electricity

(Q) which has passed a point in a wire, the time of flow (t) and the rate of flow (I) is therefore

Quantity (coulombs) = current flow (amperes)
× time (seconds)

or in symbols

$$Q = It$$

$$\text{hence } I = \frac{Q}{t}$$

Unit of electrical pressure
In order to make a current flow continuously through a circuit, it is necessary to have some device which can produce a continuous supply of electrons. This may be a battery in which the supply of electrons is produced by chemical action or a dynamo or generator in which mechanical energy is turned into electrical energy. As mentioned earlier the battery or generator produces an electrical pressure or *electromotive force* (emf, symbol E) which may be used to force a current through a circuit. The unit of electrical pressure is the *volt,* and voltages are usually denoted in formulae by the symbol V.

Unit of electrical resistance
The ease with which an electric current flows or can be conducted through a wire depends on the dimensions of the wire and the material from which it is made. The opposition of a circuit to the flow of current is called the *resistance (R)* of the circuit. The resistance of a circuit is measured in *ohms* (Ω), and a circuit is said to have a resistance of 1Ω if the voltage between its ends is 1V when the current flowing is 1A. For convenience, because the resistances used in radio equipment may be up to 10,000,000Ω, two larger units called the *kilohm* (1,000Ω) and the *megohm* (1,000,000Ω) are used. Thus 47,000Ω may be abbreviated to 47kΩ. See Table 2.2 for abbreviations.

The utilization of electricity in all branches of electrical engineering depends on the existence of a conductor to carry the electric current and insulators to restrict the flow of the current to within the conductor.

In practice, the conductor is almost universally a single or stranded wire of copper, generally tinned for ease of soldering. For special purposes, aluminium or steel-cored aluminium is used and for some applications the copper may be silver plated.

Many different insulators are in common use, from rubber and glazed ceramic to the modern synthetic materials such as pvc, polythene, polystyrene and ptfe, the last three of which have good insulating properties at very high frequencies.

The direct current circuit

Fig 2.3 is the simplest dc circuit in which a current from a battery flows through a circuit R. The ratio of the

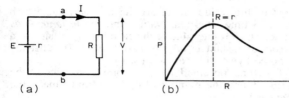

Fig 2.3.   Simple dc circuit

voltage across the circuit to the current which flows through it is constant:

$$R = \frac{V}{I}$$

The constant is known as the *resistance (R)*, and is the opposition to the flow of the electric current, while the relationship is known as *Ohm's Law*; V is measured in volts and I in amperes; R is then in ohms.

It should be noted that in this arrangement the current I also flows through the battery, which has an internal resistance r. Thus the emf of the battery is the total voltage available to drive the current I through a total resistance of $(R + r)$. The emf is thus equal to $(IR + Ir)$. Some voltage is inevitably lost in driving the current through the battery itself. That which is left to do useful work is known as the *potential difference* between the points a and b. The best battery is therefore one with the lowest internal resistance.

The maximum transfer of power from the battery to the load (ie the resistor R) occurs when the value of R is equal to the internal resistance of the battery (r). If the power in the resistor is plotted against the value of the resistor, the graph is of the form shown in Fig 2.3(b).

All materials have the property of resistance; in the case of metals suitable for use as conductors of electricity, eg copper (silver is better but is of course much more expensive), it is very low. Special alloys intended for heating elements are made with a very high resistance. Nichrome for example has a resistance which is about 60 times that of copper. Insulators are materials which have an extremely high resistance and therefore for all practical purposes do not conduct electricity. Some materials, eg germanium and silicon, have a resistance which is higher than that of conductors but is lower than insulators. These are often known as *semiconductors*. The resistance of a conductor is proportional to its length and inversely proportional to its cross-sectional area. It also depends upon the material from which the conductor is made. The resistance of a copper wire 58m long, having a cross-sectional area of

1 square millimetre, is 1Ω at 20°C. Similar wires made from other materials will have resistances as follows:

Silver	0·96Ω	Brass	3·5Ω
Aluminium	1·7Ω	Iron	7Ω
Gold	2·2Ω	Tin	7Ω
Zinc	3·5Ω	Lead	11Ω

Power in the dc circuit
The passage of an electric current through a resistance causes heat to be dissipated in the resistance. Thus electrical energy is converted into heat.

The power dissipated in the resistance is

power (watts) = voltage (volts) × current (amps)

$$W = V \times I$$

By the use of Ohm's Law, the power dissipated in the resistance may be expressed in two other forms

$$W = V^2/R \quad \text{and} \quad W = I^2 \times R$$

Resistors

In series
A discrete component having the property of resistance is called a *resistor*. A number of these can be connected as shown in Fig 2.4(a). This is the *series* connection, and the effective resistance R is

$$R = R_1 + R_2 + R_3 + \ldots$$

In parallel
The *parallel* connection is shown in Fig 2.4(b). The effective resistance in this case is

$$\frac{1}{R} = \frac{1}{R_1} + \frac{1}{R_2} + \frac{1}{R_3} + \ldots$$

$$\text{or} \quad R = \frac{1}{\dfrac{1}{R_1} + \dfrac{1}{R_2} + \dfrac{1}{R_3} + \ldots}$$

The effective resistance of two resistors in parallel is

$$R = \frac{R_1 \times R_2}{R_1 + R_2}$$

The commonest forms of resistor are
   (a) carbon (in the form of a rod)
   (b) spiral carbon track (on glass or ceramic former)
   (c) wire wound (with high-resistance wire)
They are graded according to their *dissipation,* ie the amount of heat they can dissipate safely for a given temperature rise. The smallest resistor commonly available is rated at 0·1W, while certain resistors in the output stage of a transmitter may be required to dissipate 10–20W. The dissipation of every resistor used should be calculated to confirm that it is not being over-heated.

The main application of the resistor in electronic circuits is to create a given voltage drop across the resistor

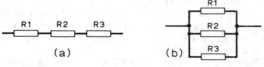

Fig 2.4.   Resistors (a) in series and (b) in parallel

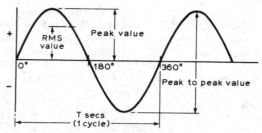

Fig 2.5.   Alternating (sinusoidal) waveform

as a result of a known current flowing through the resistor (by Ohm's Law). A fairly high value of resistor may often be employed to provide a leakage path to earth from a particular part of the circuit. Resistors are commonly used to provide a resistive load which is sometimes used to dissipate the output of an amplifier or transmitter.

The alternating current circuit

In the ac circuit the voltage and current are not constant with time as in the dc circuit; the value of each alternates between positive and negative states.

The ac waveform is shown in Fig 2.5 and is a *sine-wave* or *sinusoidal* waveform. There are two values of the amplitude of this waveform which are relevant:

(a) the peak value
(b) the rms value

The peak value is clear from Fig 2.5 and the root mean square (rms) value is that value which is equivalent in heating effect to a dc supply of the same value. For a sine wave, the rms value is 0·707 times the peak value. The rms value is used to define an alternating voltage, ie the standard 50Hz supply mains are 240V (rms) (the peak value is therefore 340V).

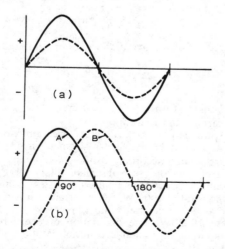

Fig 2.6. (a) Two alternating waveforms in phase, ie they start at the same point in time. (b) Two alternating waveforms with a phase difference of 90°

Two other values of use are the *average* value, which is 0·636 times the peak value, and the *instantaneous* value, which is the value of the current (or voltage) at a particular instant in an alternating cycle. It is usually denoted by small letters ie i (or v).

The time occupied by one complete cycle is the *period T* and the number of cycles in unit time is the *frequency f*. Thus

$$f = 1/T \quad \text{and} \quad T = 1/f$$

Phase difference between waveforms

Phase in this context means "time" or time difference between two waveforms. For convenience, this time difference or phase difference is measured in degrees; one complete cycle of the waveform is taken to be 360° and a half-cycle is 180° etc. Thus the time difference between two alternating waveforms can be defined by the phase angle between them.

Two alternating waveforms are said to be *in phase* when they begin at the same point in time, see Fig 2.6(a). At any other point they are *out of phase*. The term "in phase opposition" is sometimes used to describe a phase difference of 180°. In this case, two waveforms of equal amplitude would cancel each other.

In Fig 2.6(b); A and B are 90° out of phase or the phase difference between A and B is 90°, and it may be said that A leads B by 90°, conversely B lags on A by 90°.

The relationship between the two alternating waveforms of Fig 2.6(b) can be shown on a simple diagram (Fig 2.7) in which the lines OA and OB represent the waveforms A and B and the lengths of OA and OB are proportional to the amplitudes of A and B. The angle AOB represents the phase between A and B, ie 90°. This diagram represents the situation at any particular instant in time; thus the diagram should be imagined to be rotating anti-clockwise at a speed corresponding to the frequency. However, it is the situation at a particular instant which is of interest, ie as represented by Fig 2.7.

Fig 2.7. Simple phasor diagram showing phase relationship between the alternating voltages of Fig 2.6(b)

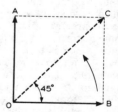

If A and B were two equal voltages of, say, 10V, then the resultant of the two is represented by the line OC and its amplitude would be $\sqrt{(10^2 + 10^2)} = \sqrt{(2 \times 100)}$ or 14·14V and its direction or phase would be leading OB by 45°.

The lines OA, OB and OC are known as *phasors*. The diagram is called a *phasor diagram*.

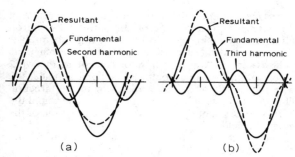

Fig 2.8. Distortion created by addition of second harmonic (a) and third harmonic (b) to fundamental

Distortion of alternating waveforms

Distortion of an alternating waveform is caused by the presence of other sinusoidal waveforms of frequencies which are related to the original frequency (known as the *fundamental*); thus if the fundamental frequency is f then $2f$ is the *second harmonic* and $3f$ is the *third harmonic* etc.

Fig 2.8 shows the distortion resulting from the addition of 30 per cent of 2nd harmonic to the fundamental (a) and 20 per cent of 3rd harmonic to the fundamental (b).

Distortion increases as the number and amplitude of the harmonics present increases; harmonics up to the 12th will result in quite a good square wave.

Inductance and capacitance in the ac circuit

Two new circuit elements have significance in the ac circuit. These are:

the inductor which has *inductance*;
the capacitor which has *capacitance*.

A circuit possesses inductance if it can store energy in the form of a magnetic field. The unit of inductance is the henry (H) and the symbol for inductance is L. A circuit has an inductance of one henry if a current in it, changing at the rate of one ampere per second, induces an emf of one volt. The energy stored in an inductor is $\frac{1}{2}LI^2$ joules, where L is in henrys and I is in amperes.

A circuit possesses capacitance if it can store energy in the form of an electric field. The unit of capacitance is the farad (F) and the symbol for capacitance is C. A circuit has a capacitance of one farad if a charge of one coulomb sets up a voltage of one volt across it. The energy stored in a capacitor is $\frac{1}{2}CV^2$ joules, where C is in farads and V is in volts. The farad is an impractically large unit and the practical unit is the *microfarad* or μF (0·000001 farad).

Note that no energy is stored in an inductor if there is no current flowing. In a capacitor, however, there need be no movement of charge and the energy stored is static. A good-quality capacitor can maintain a considerable, perhaps lethal, voltage across its terminals, long after it was charged up.

If the effect of resistance is temporarily ignored, the opposition to the flow of an alternating current is the reactance (X).

Inductive reactance X_L is the reactance due to an inductance and

$$X_L = 2\pi f L$$

X_L is in ohms when f is in hertz and L in henrys. Hence inductive reactance increases as the frequency increases.

Similarly, capacitive reactance X_C is the reactance due to a capacitance and

$$X_C = \frac{1}{2\pi f C}$$

X_C is in ohms when f is in hertz and C in farads. Hence capacitive reactance decreases as the frequency increases. (Note that $2\pi f$ is often written as ω in mathematical formulae.)

In a series circuit which contains X_L and X_C the effective reactance is

$$X = X_L - X_C \quad \text{or} \quad X = X_C - X_L$$

because the effects of inductive and capacitive reactance are equal and opposite.

If resistance is now taken into account as well as reactance, the total opposition to the flow of an alternating current is called impedance (Z) where $Z = \sqrt{(R^2 + X^2)}$. Ohm's Law now holds, ie

$$Z = V/I$$

It is very important to remember that, although resistance and reactance are both measured in ohms, resistance and reactance must never be added arithmetically. They must always be added vectorially by taking the square root of the sum of the squares, ie

$$Z = \sqrt{R^2 + X^2}$$

The following relationships should be noted:

Inductors in series: $L = L_1 + L_2 + L_3 + \ldots$

Inductors in parallel: $\dfrac{1}{L} = \dfrac{1}{L_1} + \dfrac{1}{L_2} + \dfrac{1}{L_3} + \ldots$

Mutual inductance (which will be discussed later) is assumed to be zero.

Capacitors in series: $\dfrac{1}{C} = \dfrac{1}{C_1} + \dfrac{1}{C_2} + \dfrac{1}{C_3} \ldots$

Capacitors in parallel: $C = C_1 + C_2 + C_3 + \ldots$

Magnetism

Permanent magnets

A magnet attracts pieces of iron towards it by exerting a magnetic force upon them. The field of this magnetic force can be demonstrated by sprinkling iron filings on a piece of thin cardboard under which is placed a bar

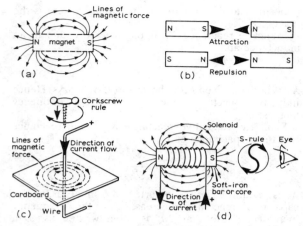

Fig 2.9. (a) Magnetic field produced by bar magnet. (b) Attraction and repulsion between bar magnets. (c) Magnetic field produced by current flowing in straight wire. (d) "S" rule for determining polarity of electromagnet

magnet. The iron filings map out the magnetic field as in Fig 2.9(a).

It is seen that the field is most intense near the ends of the magnet, the centres of intensity being called the *poles,* and *lines of force* spread out on either side and continue through the material of the magnet from one end to the other.

If such a magnet is suspended so that it can swing freely in a horizontal plane, it always comes to rest pointing in one particular direction, namely towards the earth's magnetic poles, the earth itself acting as a magnet. A compass needle is simply a bar of magnetized steel. One end of the magnet is called the *north pole* (N), which is an abbreviation of "north-seeking pole", and the other end the *south pole* (S) or "south-seeking pole". It is an accepted convention that magnetic force acts in the direction N to S as indicated by the arrows on the lines of force in Fig 2.9(a).

If two magnets are arranged so that the north pole of one is near the south pole of another, there is a force of attraction between them, whereas if similar poles are opposite one another the magnets repel one another; see Fig 2.9(b).

Magnets made from certain kinds of iron and nickel alloys retain their magnetism more or less permanently, and find many uses in radio equipment such as loud-speakers, polarized relays, headphones and cathode-ray tube focusing arrangements.

Other types of iron and nickel alloys, eg soft irons, are not capable of retaining magnetism, and therefore cannot be used for making permanent magnets. They are effective in transmitting magnetic force, however, and are used as cores in electromagnets and transformers.

Electromagnets

A current of electricity flowing through a straight wire creates a magnetic field, the lines of force of which are in a plane perpendicular to the wire and concentric with the wire. If a piece of cardboard is sprinkled with iron filings, as shown in Fig 2.9(c), they arrange themselves in rings round the wire, thus illustrating the magnetic field associated with the flow of current in the wire. Observation of a small compass needle placed near the wire indicates that, for a current flow in the direction illustrated, the magnetic force acts clockwise round the wire. A reversal of current reverses the direction of the magnetic field.

The *corkscrew rule* enables the direction of the magnetic field round a wire to be found. Imagine a "right-handed" corkscrew being driven into the wire so that it progresses in the direction of current flow; the direction of the magnetic field around the wire is then in the direction of rotation of the corkscrew.

The magnetic field surrounding such a straight wire is relatively weak, but a strong magnetic field can be produced by a current if, instead of a straight wire, a coil of wire or *solenoid* is used: moreover the field can be greatly strengthened if a piece of soft iron or other magnetic material, called a *core,* is placed inside the coil. The extent by which the strength of the solenoid magnet is increased by the introduction of the core is called the *permeability* of the core material. Permeability is really the ratio of the number of lines of force (or flux density) in the magnetic core to the flux density in a vacuum (ie no magnetic core). The difference between a vacuum and an air core is so small that it is ignored. As it is a ratio, strictly it should be referred to as *relative permeability* μ_r, but the word "relative" is often omitted colloquially.

Fig 2.9(d) shows the magnetic field produced by a solenoid, which is seen to be very similar to that of a bar magnet, as shown in Fig 2.9(a). A north pole is produced at one end of the coil and a south pole at the other. Reversal of the current reverses the polarity of the electromagnet. The polarity of a solenoid can be deduced from the *S rule,* which states that the pole which faces an observer looking at the end of a solenoid is a south pole if to him the current is flowing (ie from positive to negative) in a clockwise direction. See Fig 2.9(d).

The strength of a magnetic field produced by a current is directly proportional to the current, a fact made use of in moving coil meters. It also depends on the number of turns of wire, the area of the coil and the permeability of the core.

Interaction of magnetic fields

As with the attraction and repulsion of permanent magnets, there can be interaction between the fields of electromagnets or between a permanent magnet and an electromagnet, and in just the same way the interaction is manifest as a force causing relative motion between the two. This interaction forms the basis of several types of electromechanical devices which are used in radio, such as loudspeakers, earphones and moving-coil meters.

The principle of the loudspeaker is shown in Fig

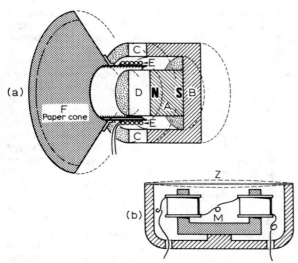

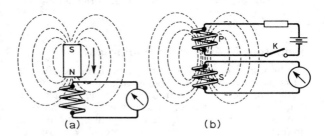

Fig 2.10. (a) Principle of moving-coil loudspeaker. (b) Principle of earphone

2.10(a). A strong permanent magnet A forms part of a soft-iron magnetic circuit BCD which has a narrow annular gap between the circular pole-pieces C and D; a strong radial magnetic field is thereby produced in this gap. Speech-frequency currents are passed through the coil E which is free to move in the annular gap and is fixed to a cone F. Interaction between the magnetic field in the gap and that due to the current flowing in the coil causes the coil to move backwards or forwards according to the strength and polarity of the speech signal: the cone therefore vibrates in sympathy with the speech currents and causes sound waves to be produced.

The principle of the earphone is shown in Fig 2.10(b). A permanent magnet M is situated close to a circular diaphragm Z made of magnetic material. The permanent magnet's field holds the diaphragm in a state of stress. Around the arms of the U-shaped magnet are two coils wound with many turns of fine wire through which speech currents are passed. The magnetic field due to the speech current flowing in the coils adds to or subtracts from the field holding the diaphragm in a state of stress, causing it to vibrate in sympathy with the speech signal and emit corresponding sound waves. If there were no permanent magnet, the diaphragm would be attracted on each half-cycle of audio frequency current, giving rise to severe distortion.

Electromagnetic induction

If a bar magnet is plunged into a solenoid, as indicated in Fig 2.11(a), the moving coil microammeter connected across the coil shows a deflection. The explanation of this phenomenon, known as *electromagnetic induction*, is that the movement of the magnet's lines of force past the turns of the coil causes a voltage to be induced in the coil which in turn causes a current to flow through the meter. The magnitude of the effect depends on the strength and rate of movement of the magnet and the size of the coil. Withdrawal of the magnet causes a reversal of the current. No current flows unless the lines of force are moving relative to the coil. The same effect is obtained if a coil of wire is arranged to move relative to a fixed magnetic field. Dynamos and generators depend for their operation on the principle of electromagnetic induction.

If a pair of coils of wire is arranged as shown in Fig 2.11(b), when the switch K is open there is no magnetic field from the coil P linking the turns of the coil S, and the current through S is zero. Closing K causes a current in the coil P which produces a magnetic field. This field, as it builds up from zero, induces a voltage in S and causes a current to flow through the meter for a short time until the field due to P has reached a steady value, when the current through S falls to zero again. The effect is only momentary and is completed in a small fraction of a second. The change in current in the circuit P is said to have *induced* a voltage in the circuit S. The fact that a changing current in one circuit can induce a voltage in another circuit is the principle underlying the operation of transformers.

Self-inductance

If a steady current is flowing through a coil, there is a steady magnetic field due to that current. A current change tends to alter the strength of the field, which in turn induces in the coil a voltage *(back emf)* tending to oppose the change being made. This process is called *self-induction*. A coil is said to have *self-inductance,* usually abbreviated to *inductance*. It has a value of one *henry* (H) if, when the current through the coil changes at a rate of 1 A/s, the voltage appearing across its terminals is 1 V. Inductance is usually denoted by the symbol L in formulae. As the inductance values used in radio equipment may be only a very small fraction of a henry, the units *millihenry* (mH) and *microhenry* (μH) (0·001 and 0·000001H respectively) are commonly used.

The inductance of a coil depends upon the square of the number of turns, the cross-sectional area and the permeability and length of the magnetic path. If the

Fig 2.11. Electromagnetic induction: (a) relative movement of magnet and coil causes a voltage to be induced in coil; (b) when current in one of a pair of coupled coils changes in value a voltage is induced in second coil

turns on a stiff coil are prised apart, the magnetic length is increased. Thus

$$L \propto \frac{\mu_r A T^2}{l}$$

The inductance of a coil of a certain physical size and number of turns can be calculated to a fair degree of accuracy from formulae or it can be derived from coil inductance charts.

Mutual inductance

A changing current in one circuit can induce a voltage in a second circuit (see Fig 2.11(b)). The strength of the voltage induced in the second circuit S depends on the closeness or *tightness* of the magnetic coupling between the circuits; for example, if both coils are wound together on an iron core, practically all the lines of force or magnetic flux from the first circuit link with the turns of the second circuit. Such coils are said to be *tightly coupled* whereas if the coils are both air-cored and spaced some distance apart they are *loosely coupled*.

The mutual inductance between two coils is measured in henrys, and two coils are said to have a *mutual inductance* of 1H if when the current in the primary coil changes at a rate of 1A/s the voltage across the secondary is 1V. Mutual inductance is denoted in formulae by the symbol M.

The mutual inductance between two coils may be measured by joining the coils in series, first so that the sense of their windings is the same, and then so that they are reversed. The total inductance is then measured in each case.

If L_a and L_b are the total measured inductances, L_1 and L_2 are the separate inductances of the two coils and M is the mutual inductance, then

$$L_a = L_1 + L_2 + 2M$$
$$L_b = L_1 + L_2 - 2M$$
$$L_a - L_b = 4M$$
$$\text{ie} \quad M = \frac{L_a - L_b}{4}$$

The mutual inductance is therefore equal to one quarter of the difference between the series-aiding and series-opposing readings.

Inductors used in radio equipment

An inductor consists of a number of turns of wire. However, within the framework of this simple definition there is an extremely wide range of inductance values and types of construction. For example, an inductor required as a tuning coil at vhf might have an inductance of $0.5\mu H$; this would probably be one or two turns of 2mm wire, self-supporting. At the other extreme, a smoothing choke in a power unit would have an inductance of, say, 30H and consist of 1,000–2,000 turns wound on a paxolin bobbin with a laminated iron

core. If this choke were designed to carry a current of 500mA, it might weigh about 6kg and occupy a 15cm cube in volume. Specialist low-frequency applications may require inductance values up to 500H.

The form of construction depends basically on the inductance value required. The number of turns of wire necessary to give the inductance depends on the permeability of its core. Air has a permeability of 1 but there are magnetic materials which have a very much higher permeability. Hence to achieve a reasonably high inductance without having to wind many thousands of turns of wire on an "air" core, many fewer turns are wound on a magnetic core appropriate to the particular frequency involved.

The commonest magnetic core is made up of laminations, normally 0.3mm thick of silicon iron. Laminations are available in a vast range of shapes and sizes and are insulated on one side so that when they are assembled in a core they are insulated from each other. This reduces the power loss due to eddy currents induced in the core. The commonest shape of lamination is a pair, one being T-shaped and the other U-shaped, so that they fit together when assembled into the paxolin bobbin which carries the winding.

This type of core is standard for low-frequency chokes and power transformers. Thinner laminations of different types of iron are available for use at frequencies in the audio range.

Radio-frequency coils are usually air-cored, either self-supporting or wound on low-loss plastic or ceramic formers. The number of turns is often quite small, with inductance values up to about $20\mu H$.

Larger values of inductance up to 1–2mH at frequencies from about 100kHz upwards may be wound on dust iron or ferrite cores.

A dust-iron core is a core of very finely divided iron alloy moulded in an insulating medium. Being moulded, different shapes and sizes can be made cheaply. Often a brass-threaded rod is moulded into a small cylindrical core. The position of the core within the coil can then be adjusted to vary the inductance value to tune the coil to a specific frequency. This is known as *slug tuning*.

The more modern ferrite cores are non-metallic materials of high resistivity, and therefore low eddy-current loss, and so can be used at higher frequencies.

These moulded cores are often in two similar halves as a "pot" core. The winding is put on a small plastic bobbin which goes inside the two halves and so is surrounded by the ferrite material. Ferrite materials are also moulded in the form of a ring or *toroid* (a "toroidal" core). Such cores ensure that the magnetic flux is nearly all contained within the windings, ie there is practically no stray field.

Capacitors used in radio equipment

Capacitance may be defined as the ability of a conductor to store an electric charge. A device in which this effect is enhanced is called a *capacitor*. In its simplest form, the capacitor consists of two parallel plates as

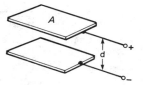

Fig 2.12. Parallel-plate capacitor. The capacitance is proportional to area A and inversely proportional to spacing d

shown in Fig 2.12. The material between the plates is known as the *dielectric*; in this case the dielectric is air.

The capacitance of such a capacitor is proportional to the area of the plates and inversely proportional to the distance between them. It also depends upon a property of the dielectric known as the *permittivity* (the dielectric constant). As in the case of permeability, referred to earlier, permittivity is a quantity referred to the vacuum (or air) state. It is hence a ratio or relative property.

Typical relative permittivities are

air	1
paper	2 approximately
polythene, rubber etc	2·3 ,,
mica	5 ,,
ceramics	10 and upwards

The dielectric material determines the maximum frequency at which a capacitor may be used, eg paper up to 20MHz or so, some ceramics and plastics (polythene or polystyrene) up to 150–200MHz, and mica even higher.

The capacitor exists in many forms and is classified by the material used as the dielectric. The range of capacitance commonly available is from 1pF to at least 5,000μF. As capacitors have the property of being able to store a charge of electricity, they must be capable of withstanding a voltage difference between the plates. Thus the larger the plates and/or the smaller their separation, the greater is the charge that the capacitor holds for a given voltage across its plates. Ultimately, if the voltage between the plates is too high the capacitor will flash over or break down. The safe working voltage is therefore an important property of a capacitor. Capacitors are made with working voltages from 6V to many thousands of volts.

It is clear from its form of construction that a capacitor presents an open circuit to a direct current but it appears to pass an alternating current because of the build-up and decay of charge on one plate and then the other as the direction of flow of the alternating current changes.

A good-quality capacitor holds its charge for several days or more. In the majority of cases the charge is insignificant, but precautions have to be taken to ensure that high-value, high-voltage capacitors are discharged when the equipment is switched off.

Mica capacitors are normally made up to a value of 0·01μF and may be used up to very high frequencies (vhf). They consist of a stack of plates interleaved with layers of mica, which are clamped together, dipped in wax or potted in resin. In the silvered-mica type, the plates are made by spraying a very thin layer of silver onto the mica dielectric.

Paper capacitors consist of layers of special paper and thin foil wound together in the form of a tube, the dimensions of which determine the capacitance. These are generally known as *tubular* capacitors. Paper capacitors are made in capacitances up to about 16μF and up to very high working voltages. High-value, high-voltage capacitors consist of many smaller paper capacitors in series and parallel to achieve the required value, and are therefore bulky. Paper capacitors are normally used up to a frequency of about 20MHz; above this frequency the internal losses increase rapidly.

Ceramic capacitors are made by spraying silver "plates" on to both sides of a ceramic cup, disc or tube. The ceramic used has high permittivity so that a high capacitance is obtained in a small volume. They are made in relatively low working voltages (500V maximum) and are most commonly used as bypass capacitors at vhf.

The feed-through capacitor is a form of ceramic capacitor in which one plate is a threaded bush on the outside of a ceramic tube (the dielectric), and the other plate a stiff wire through the centre of the tube. This type is used for feeding through power supplies into a screened box; thus it combines a feed-through insulator with a bypass capacitor.

Electrolytic capacitors have plates of aluminium or tantalum foil and have a semi-liquid conducting compound, often in the form of impregnated paper, between them. The dielectric is a very thin insulating layer which is formed by electrolytic action on one of the foils when a dc polarizing voltage is applied to the capacitor. As the dielectric is very thin, very high values of capacitance can be put into a small space. The capacitance value can be 50,000μF or more and at the lower values the working voltage can be quite high, eg 16μF 600V, 100μF 450V. There is a small leakage current through an electrolytic capacitor and it must be emphasized that generally they are polarized, ie one terminal is positive and the other is negative. Although electrolytic capacitors can withstand a small ripple (alternating) current, this polarity must be strictly observed otherwise the capacitor may explode.

Electrolytic capacitors may be connected in series to increase the working voltage, ie two 100μF 450V capacitors in series are equivalent to a 900V capacitor, but the effective capacitance is only 50μF. It is essential to connect a resistor across each capacitor in order to equalize the voltage appearing across each. The resistors also provide a discharge path for the capacitors when the apparatus is switched off. A 100kΩ 3W resistor is generally adequate.

The main application of the capacitor is to provide a low-impedance path (generally to earth) for an alternating current of a particular frequency, eg as a "smoothing" capacitor (16–5,000μF) in a power supply or a bypass (decoupling) capacitor at audio or radio frequencies in a receiver or transmitter.

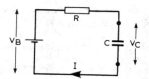

Fig 2.13.   Simple RC circuit

Time constant of RC circuit

The charge Q (in coulombs) in a capacitor is the product of the voltage across the capacitor and its capacitance, ie

$$Q = CV$$
$$\text{hence}\quad C = Q/V \quad\text{and}\quad V = Q/C$$

(C is in farads and Q is in coulombs)

If a capacitor of C farads is connected to a dc source of V volts via a charging resistor of $R\ \Omega$, the instantaneous current on switch-on is $I = V/R$ (see Fig 2.13). (The capacitor has no back emf associated with it at the instant of switch-on and so behaves as a short circuit.) The capacitor charges exponentially, and the *time constant* is the time taken for the capacitor to charge to 63 per cent of the supply voltage.

$$\text{Time constant (in seconds)} = C\ (\text{F}) \times R\ (\Omega)$$

For all practical purposes, the current reaches zero and $V_C = V_B$ after a time equal to $5 \times CR$ seconds. It should be noted that the current is a maximum when the voltage across the capacitor is zero. These voltage and current relationships are shown in Fig 2.14.

Capacitance and inductance in ac circuits

Capacitance
When a sine wave of voltage V is applied to a circuit containing capacitance only (Fig 2.15(a)), the relationship between the current and voltage is shown in Fig 2.15(b). This is another simple phasor diagram. The

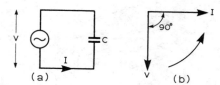

Fig 2.15.   (a) Sine wave of voltage V applied to a capacitor. (b) Phasor diagram showing relationship between current and voltage in the circuit

current through the capacitor is said to *lead* the voltage across it by 90°.

Inductance
When a current flows in a perfect inductor (Fig 2.16), ie one which has zero resistance or distributed capacitance, the rate of change of current at B is zero and a maximum at point C as shown in Fig 2.17(a). Between A and B, the current is increasing in a positive direction, hence the back emf is negative-going (Fig 2.17(b)). The back emf is zero at D when the rate of change of current is zero. The waveform of the back emf is shown in Fig 2.17(b). The applied voltage required to overcome the back emf and to keep the rms value of current steady must be equal and opposite to

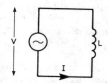

Fig 2.16.   Sine wave of voltage V applied to an inductor

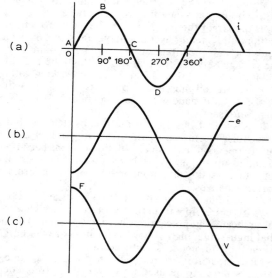

Fig 2.17.   (a) Current, (b) back emf and (c) applied voltage in Fig 2.16

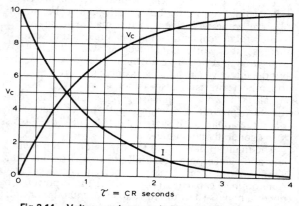

$\tau = CR$ seconds

Fig 2.14.   Voltage and current in Fig 2.13 after switch-on

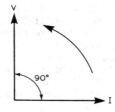

V

90°

I

Fig 2.18. Phasor diagram for Fig 2.16

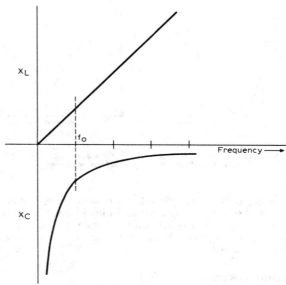

Fig 2.20. How the reactance of a capacitor and an inductor vary with frequency

the back emf, Fig 2.17(c). The current reaches a maximum value at B, one quarter of a cycle (90°) after the applied voltage reaches a maximum, point F.

Thus the current through the inductor lags the applied voltage by 90° as shown by the phasor diagram, Fig 2.18.

Tuned circuits

The parallel and series arrangements of an inductor and a capacitor to form a *tuned circuit* are shown in Fig 2.19(a) and (b) respectively.

Fig 2.20 shows how the reactance of a capacitor, $X_C = 1/2\pi fC$, and an inductor, $X_L = 2\pi fL$, vary with frequency.

At a frequency denoted by f_0, the value of X_L is equal and opposite to the value of X_C. The reactances therefore cancel out and only the circuit resistance needs to be overcome. The circuit is then said to be in *resonance*.

$$X_L = X_C$$

$$2\pi fL = \frac{1}{2\pi fC}$$

$$fL = \frac{1}{(2\pi)^2 fC}$$

$$f^2 L = \frac{1}{(2\pi)^2 C}$$

$$f^2 = \frac{1}{(2\pi)^2 LC}$$

$$f = \frac{1}{2\pi \sqrt{LC}}$$

$f = f_0$ and is called the *resonant frequency*.

There are losses associated with all tuned circuits because the components are not perfect, and these losses are assumed to be resistive. In a series circuit containing R, L and C, the opposition to current flow is the impedance Z.

$$Z = \sqrt{R^2 + (X_L - X_C)^2}$$

At resonance, $X_L - X_C = 0$ and hence

$$Z = \sqrt{R^2}$$

$$= R \text{ ohms}$$

In the case of the parallel-tuned circuit, a current known as the *circulating current* flows through L and C. This can be quite large even though the current taken from the driving source (the *generator*) may be very small.

If at any instant the current flowing into the inductor from point A (Fig 2.21) is equal to the current flowing from the capacitor, I will be zero. A resonant parallel circuit will have a high impedance. This particular value is called the *dynamic resistance*; it is a fictitious resistance and exists for alternating currents of the resonant frequency. Its symbol is R_D.

In a series-tuned circuit, the impedance is a minimum at resonance (and is equal to the resistance of the circuit). As the series-tuned circuit accepts maximum current at resonance, it is sometimes known as an *acceptor circuit*. See Fig 2.22(a).

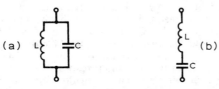

Fig 2.19. Arrangement of capacitor and inductor to form tuned circuit: (a) parallel-tuned circuit; (b) series-tuned circuit

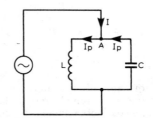

Fig 2.21. The parallel-tuned circuit

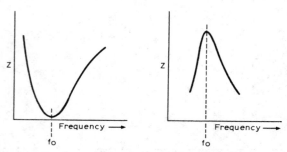

Fig 2.22. Impedance/frequency characteristics of (a) series-tuned circuit; (b) parallel-tuned circuit

In a parallel-tuned circuit, the impedance is a maximum at resonance. The parallel-tuned circuit is often called a *rejector circuit* because, having a high impedance at resonance, it rejects current at this frequency. See Fig 2.22(b).

Magnification factor (Q)

At the resonant frequency of a tuned circuit, the voltage across the inductor (or the capacitor) can be considerably higher than the voltage applied to the tuned circuit from an external source (eg from the rest of the circuit, whatever that may be).

The magnification factor (Q) of a tuned circuit is the ratio of the voltage across the inductor (or capacitor) to the voltage across the effective resistance of the circuit. Thus if the current at resonance is I, and R is the series resistance at a frequency f

$$Q = \frac{IX_L}{IR} = \frac{2\pi fL}{R} = \frac{\omega L}{R}$$

similarly

$$Q = \frac{IX_C}{IR} = \frac{1}{2\pi fCR} = \frac{1}{\omega CR}$$

The resistance of a coil can be much higher than its resistance to dc. At high frequencies, current tends to flow near the surface of a conductor. This is called the *skin effect*. It becomes very significant at frequencies over 100MHz and is the reason for the use of silver-plated coils etc in equipment working at 144MHz or higher.

The dynamic resistance of a tuned circuit (R_D) can be expressed in terms of the Q as

$$R_D = \frac{L}{CR}$$

hence, since $Q = \omega L/R$

$$R_D = \frac{Q}{\omega C}$$

As a capacitor generally has quite low losses when correctly used, the Q of a tuned circuit is determined by the coil. The range of Q obtainable is roughly 100–400, depending on the type and form of the inductor. A good-quality tuned circuit will have a value of R_D of about 50,000Ω. The dc resistance is usually very low.

The ability of a tuned circuit to differentiate between a wanted frequency and an adjacent unwanted frequency is dependent upon the Q. That is, the *selectivity* depends on Q; ie good selectivity requires high Q.

It will therefore be seen that the magnification factor or Q of a tuned circuit is very important.

L/C ratio

The resonant frequency of a tuned circuit is fixed by the product of inductance and capacitance, ie $L \times C$. There is hence an infinite number of values of L and C which will tune to a given frequency.

The choice of the ratio of L and C is determined by practical considerations according to the particular use.

For instance, in receiver tuned circuits, in order to achieve a high value of dynamic resistance (required for high gain) the L/C ratio is high. The limitation here is that there is always a minimum value of capacitance inherent in any circuit (this is the *stray capacitance*).

In some applications, it may be required to swamp completely the stray circuit capacitance, in which case the L/C ratio is low.

The optimum choice of L/C ratio is sometimes difficult. As a compromise, it is convenient to assume that the value of C is 1·5pF per metre of wavelength; thus to tune to 30MHz (ie 10m) a capacitance of about 15pF would be reasonable.

If there are no losses in a tuned circuit the energy stored in the capacitor transfers to the inductor and so on, thus

$$\tfrac{1}{2}CV^2 = \tfrac{1}{2}LI^2$$

$$CV^2 = LI^2$$

$$\frac{V^2}{I^2} = \frac{L}{C}$$

or

$$\frac{V}{I} = \sqrt{\frac{L}{C}}$$

since

$$\frac{V}{I} = Z$$

hence

$$Z = \sqrt{\frac{L}{C}}$$

Resonance curves and selectivity

Fig 2.23 shows how a tuned circuit has maximum response at the resonant frequency; this is known as a *resonance curve*. The width of this curve, ie $(f_h - f_l)$, is known as the *bandwidth* of the tuned circuit and is defined at the level where the response has fallen to $1/\sqrt{2}$ or 0·707 of the maximum response.

The relationship between bandwidth and Q is

$$Q = \frac{f_r}{f_h - f_l} = \frac{f_r}{2\Delta f} \quad (f_r = \text{resonant frequency})$$

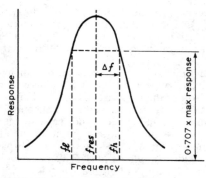

Fig 2.23. Resonance curve of parallel-tuned circuit

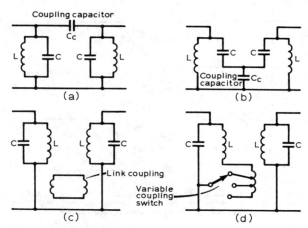

Fig 2.25. Various arrangements for coupling tuned circuits. (a) Top-capacitance coupling; (b) bottom-capacitance coupling; (c) link coupling; (d) variable inductive coupling, suitable for use in variable-bandwidth i.f. amplifier transformers

From this it is seen that the lower f is, the lower Δf is, ie the bandwidth is less and selectivity is greater for a given value of Q. Similarly, the bandwidth is inversely proportional to Q; ie the higher the Q, the smaller the bandwidth.

The effect of several tuned circuits in cascade, eg in successive stages of an amplifier, is to reduce the overall bandwidth, ie increase the selectivity. This is particularly apparent in the region known as the *skirts* of the selectivity curve where the bandwidth is greatest. In the majority of cases, the design aim is to increase the effective overall selectivity, but in some instances it is necessary to decrease the selectivity or increase the bandwidth. This is achieved by a *damping resistor* connected across the tuned circuit; the lower the resistor, the greater its effect, but in practice a considerable amount of damping is given by a resistor of about 4,700Ω.

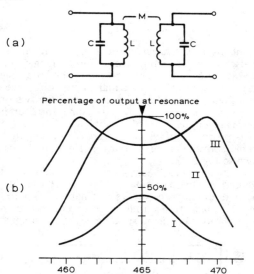

Fig 2.24. Inductively-coupled tuned circuits. Curves shown at (b) represent various frequency-response characteristics of coupled circuit shown at (a) for different degrees of coupling

Coupled circuits

Pairs of mutually-coupled tuned circuits are often used in receivers and transmitters. The effect of varying the degree of coupling between two parallel-tuned circuits resonant at the same frequency is shown in Fig 2.24.

When the coupling is loose, the response from one circuit to the other is as curve I. As the coupling is increased to what is known as *critical coupling*, the output at resonance increases to curve II; here the mutual coupling between the coils is $1/Q$ of the inductance of either coil. Further increase *(tight coupling)* results in the formation of the double-humped characteristic shown in curve III, where the output at resonance has decreased.

Two tuned circuits are often mounted in a screening can, the coils generally being wound the necessary distance apart on the same former to give the required coupling. The coupling is then said to be *fixed*. Other means of achieving the required degree of coupling are shown in Fig 2.25. Some of these, particularly (d), permit the degree of coupling to be varied.

Transformers

The basis of transformer action is a current induced in one circuit by a change in current flow in another circuit, for instance as shown in Fig 2.11(b).

Transformers perform many vital functions in electrical and radio engineering; for example, the transfer of electrical energy from one circuit to another and, implied in the latter, the transformation of an alternating voltage upwards or downwards.

If in a transformer the number of turns on the primary winding is n_p, the number of turns on the secondary winding is n_s, the voltage across the primary is V_p and the voltage across the secondary is V_s then

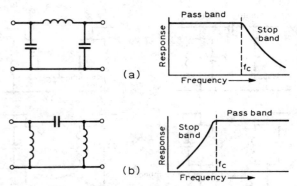

(a)

(b)

Fig 2.26. (a) **Single-section low-pass filter configuration and its response curve.** (b) **Single-section high-pass filter configuration and its response curve**

$$V_s = \frac{n_s}{n_p} \times V_p$$

The term n_s/n_p is called the *turns ratio,* which may be less than or greater than unity; thus the transformer may *step down* or *step up.*

If primary impedance is Z_p and secondary impedance is Z_s then

$$Z_p = \left(\frac{n_p}{n_s}\right)^2 Z_s$$

$$\text{or } \frac{Z_p}{Z_s} = \left(\frac{n_p}{n_s}\right)^2$$

The relationship between the currents in the primary and secondary windings is similarly

$$I_p = \frac{n_s}{n_p} \times I_s$$

When no load is connected to the secondary winding of a transformer, ie I_s is zero, the current taken by the primary is called the *magnetizing current* and in a well-designed transformer is very small.

Power transformers are normally wound on a bakelite bobbin through which a laminated silicon iron core is assembled, as in the case of the iron-cored inductor.

Filters

Filters, or to give them their full name *wave filters,* are passive networks of capacitors and inductors which exhibit certain characteristics as the input frequency is varied.

The filters of most interest in amateur radio are
(a) *Low-pass filters.*
   A low-pass filter passes all frequencies below a specified frequency but attenuates frequencies above it.
(b) *High-pass filters.*
   A high-pass filter passes all frequencies above a specified frequency, but attenuates frequencies below it.

The specified frequency referred to is the *cut-off frequency* (f_c). The configuration of the simplest form ("single section") of each filter is shown in Fig 2.26 which also shows the general shape of the characteristics.

Two or three (or occasionally more) single-section filters may be connected in cascade to increase the rate of the fall-off of the response in the stop band. Further improvement may be achieved by connecting a series arrangement of inductance and capacitance ("half sections") across the input and output of the filter.

The combination of a low-pass and a high-pass filter in series yields a *bandpass filter.* This passes a band of frequencies. By appropriate design this band can be very narrow and have steep edges. Although not strictly a wave-filter, a *T-notch filter* has uses in amateur radio. This provides a tuneable and very sharp *null,* ie a large attenuation over a narrow frequency band.

Filters have a number of important applications in amateur radio. Low-pass filters are used to attenuate unwanted television frequencies in the output of the hf bands transmitter (transmitter–antenna matching unit connection). Another use is to limit the audio bandwidth of a telephony transmitter to the minimum necessary for intelligible communication.

The high-pass filter is commonly used in the antenna down-lead (coaxial cable) of a television receiver in order to attenuate frequencies in the range of the hf amateur bands, principally 14 and 21MHz.

The design of filters can be exceedingly complex but the RAE candidate is not expected to be able to do this and is referred to the *Radio Communication Handbook* for further information.

Mixing

The *mixing* or *heterodyne* process is one in which two signals are mixed to produce two new signals, one of which is equal in frequency to the sum of the original frequencies and the other equal to the difference between them. The undesired product and the two original frequencies are rejected by some form of filter which is generally a tuned circuit.

This process is often called *frequency changing, frequency conversion* or *frequency translation* and is shown in Fig 2.27.

The mixer has many uses in communication engineering. In particular, it is the basis of the superheterodyne receiver (see Chapter 4) and the single sideband transmitter, where frequency conversion to various bands must be achieved by mixing.

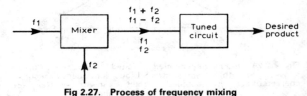

Fig 2.27.   Process of frequency mixing

Owing to non-optimum characteristics in the mixer element, spurious products harmonically related to the two original frequencies (f_1 and f_2) are often produced. The suppression of these is particularly important in an ssb transmitter. The reader is referred to *Radio Communication Handbook* for further information.

Tolerance and effect of temperature on components

These are important aspects of all electronic components, particularly resistors and capacitors.

Tolerance

The tolerance on the value of a component is a measure of how accurate its value is. For example, a resistor of nominal value 10,000Ω, and a tolerance of ±10 per cent, may have an actual resistance between 9,000Ω (ie 10,000 − 10 per cent) and 11,000Ω (ie 10,000 + 10 per cent).

The usual tolerances on the values of resistors and capacitors are ±20, ±10, ±5, ±2 and ±1 per cent.

Temperature effects

Generally the value of a component increases as the temperature increases. A constant known as the *temperature coefficient* is a measure of this increase, and thus (for most items) the temperature coefficient is positive.

There are a few exceptions, eg ceramic capacitors having a negative temperature coefficient can be made. Certain nickel-iron alloys used for resistance wires have an almost-zero temperature coefficient. Carbon and other semiconductors have a negative coefficient.

Thermistors are specially designed resistors having a very large change in value with temperature. They have a resistance of typically 4,000Ω at 20°C, falling to about 100Ω at 100°C.

Preferred values

The three common ranges of basic "preferred values" for components are listed in Table 2.3. The preferred values which are normally available are multiples of the basic values between 1 and 10^7, for example 4·7Ω, 47Ω, 470Ω, 4·7kΩ, 47kΩ, 470kΩ and 4·7MΩ (20 per cent tolerance) resistors. The manufacture of preferred values only is general for resistors, but less so for capacitors, particularly above 1μF.

The piezo-electric effect

Certain crystalline substances (quartz in particular) have the property of developing an electric charge on their surface when a mechanical stress is applied. Conversely they exhibit mechanical strain when these surfaces are electrically charged. This is known as the *piezo-electric effect* (piezo electricity).

The naturally-occurring crystal of quartz is hexagonal, up to 7cm in diameter with pointed ends and can be 10–15cm long. See Fig 2.28(a). The natural

Table 2.3
Preferred values

20% tolerance	10% tolerance	5% tolerance
10	10	10
—	—	11
—	12	12
—	—	13
15	15	15
—	—	16
—	18	18
—	—	20
22	22	22
—	—	24
—	27	27
—	—	30
33	33	33
—	—	36
—	39	39
—	—	43
47	47	47
—	—	51
—	56	56
—	—	62
68	68	68
—	—	75
—	82	82
—	—	91

quartz crystal may be *cut* in various directions, which are defined according to the relationship to an axis of the natural crystal; for example, the *X* cut is perpendicular to the *X* axis etc (see Fig 2.28(b)). Thus the commonest cuts are *X, Y* and *Z* cuts but there are other standard cuts made at particular angles to these axes and known as *AT, BT, DT* etc.

The end product of cutting a natural crystal of quartz is always known as a *crystal,* and such a crystal has very important applications as a frequency-control device and in specialist types of filter circuits.

The crystal takes the form of a thin plate or bar (up to about 7cm long) the thickness or dimensions of which determine the resonant frequency. The roughly-cut crystal is very carefully ground between optically-flat plates to the required dimensions.

It may be mounted between spring-loaded optically-flat plates (the *holder*); sometimes there is a

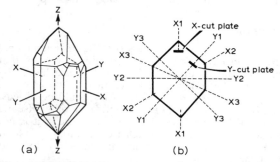

Fig 2.28. (a) Double-terminated natural quartz crystal indicating relationship between X, Y and Z axes. The crystal usually has one pyramidal termination and a rough end where it has broken from the parent rock. (b) Various X and Y axes as viewed along a direction parallel to the Z axis and examples of positions of X-cut and Y-cut plates

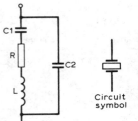

Fig 2.29. Equivalent circuit of piezo-electric crystal. Typical values for a 400kHz crystal are: C_1 = 0·04pF, C_2 = 6pF, L = 3·5H; Q = 25,000 or higher. C_2 represents capacitance of electrodes and holder. The circuit symbol for a crystal is on the right

Circuit symbol

very small air gap between the crystal and one plate. Alternatively, the crystal may be supported by wires soldered to plates formed by the process of sputtering gold onto the crystal surfaces. Generally, in the latter case, the crystal is mounted in a vacuum.

A crystal may be cut to operate at its fundamental frequency (about 15MHz maximum, at which the thickness may be only about 0·3mm). It may also be cut to operate on a harmonic, ie a crystal marked "50MHz" is probably a 10MHz crystal operating at its fifth harmonic, sometimes known as an *overtone* crystal.

The most significant parameter is the temperature coefficient which varies widely according to the cut, ie

X cut	− 25 parts/million per degree Celsius
Y cut	+ 80 parts/million per degree Celsius
BC cut	− 20 parts/million per degree Celsius
AT cut	0 parts/million per degree Celsius

The equivalent circuit of a quartz crystal in its holder is given in Fig 2.29. C2 represents the capacitance of the crystal holder. For a crystal cut to resonate at about 400kHz such as is used in a crystal filter, the approximate values of the equivalent circuit are

$$C_1 = 0·04\text{pF}; C_2 = 6\text{pF}; L = 3·5\text{H}$$

The equivalent Q of a crystal is in the region of 25,000 to 40,000.

It is seen that the quartz crystal in its holder is equivalent to a tuned circuit and as such may be substituted for the tuned circuit in an oscillator (see Chapter 3).

Screening

It is often necessary to restrict the magnetic field around an inductor to prevent coupling between that inductor and another one close to. This is achieved by enclosing the inductor in an earthed metal can, this being known as *screening*. The can should be at least 1½ times the coil diameter from the coil, otherwise the Q of the latter will be degraded. Generally, it is not necessary to screen coils which are separated by at least three coil diameters or which are tuned to different frequencies.

Similarly it is often required to screen one part of a circuit from another, eg to prevent feedback from the output of a high-gain amplifier to its input, or to prevent an unwanted strong signal getting to the input of an amplifier.

Aluminium and preferably copper are satisfactory screening materials at radio frequencies, but a high-permeability alloy such as mu-metal is necessary at audio frequencies.

Formal definitions of the more important electrical quantities

Definitions of units are now agreed and accepted internationally as the "Système International des Unités". Consequently they are known as *SI units* and the more important electrical ones follow.

Ampere (A): unit of electric current. The ampere is the constant current which, if maintained in two straight parallel conductors of infinite length, of negligible cross-section and placed at a distance of 1m apart in a vacuum, will produce a force between them equal to 2×10^{-7} newton/m length.

Watt (W): unit of power. The watt is equal to 1 joule/s.

Coulomb (C): unit of electric charge. The coulomb is the quantity of electricity transported in 1s by 1A.

Volt (V): unit of electric potential. The difference of electric potential between two points of a conducting wire carrying a constant current of 1A, when the power dissipated between these points is equal to 1W.

Ohm (Ω): unit of electrical resistance. The resistance between two points of a conductor when a constant difference of potential of 1V applied between these two points produces in this conductor a current of 1A, the conductor not being the source of any electromotive force.

Farad (F): unit of electrical capacitance. The capacitance of a capacitor between the plates of which there appears a difference of potential of 1V when it is charged by 1C of electricity.

Henry (H): unit of electrical inductance. The inductance of a closed circuit in which an electromotive force of 1V is produced when the electric current in the circuit varies uniformly at the rate of 1A/s.

Calculations

A number of sample calculations involving resistance, capacitance, inductance, reactance and resonance follow, and these are typical of the calculations which are necessary in the design of receiver and transmitter circuits. The mathematics involved in this type of calculation are explained in Appendix 5 with particular reference to the multiple-choice questions likely in the RAE.

Example 1. A current of 50mA flows through a resistor of 1·5kΩ. What is the voltage across the resistor?

By Ohm's Law

$$V = I \times R$$

$$V = \frac{50}{1,000} \times 1,500$$

$$V = 75V.$$

Example 2. In a stage of a receiver, 12V are applied across a potential divider of 3,300Ω and 2,700Ω. What is the current through the resistors?

By Ohm's Law

$$I = \frac{V}{R} = \frac{12}{3,300 + 2,700}$$

$$I = 0.002A.$$

Example 3. Resistors of 33kΩ and 27kΩ are connected in series. What is the effective resistance?

$$R = R_1 + R_2$$
$$R = 33,000Ω + 27,000Ω$$
$$R = 60,000Ω.$$

Example 4. Resistors of 100Ω and 150Ω are connected in parallel. Find the effective resistance.

$$\frac{1}{R} = \frac{1}{R_1} + \frac{1}{R_2}$$

$$\frac{1}{R} = \frac{1}{100} + \frac{1}{150}$$

$$\frac{1}{R} = \frac{6}{600} + \frac{4}{600} = \frac{10}{600}$$

whence by cross-multiplying

$$600 = 10R$$
$$R = 60Ω.$$

Alternatively, the value of two resistors in parallel can be found by dividing the product of their values by the sum.

$$\frac{150 \times 100}{250} = 60Ω.$$

Example 5. In the smoothing circuit of a power supply, capacitors of 8μF, 4μF and 2μF are connected in parallel. What is the effective capacitance?

Effective capacitance = 8 + 4 + 2 = 14μF.

Example 6. Capacitors of 220pF, 470pF and 0.001μF are connected in parallel. What is the effective capacitance?

Before addition can be effected, the values must first of all be expressed either in picofarads or in microfarads. Since there are 1,000,000pF to 1μF,

$$0.001μF = 1,000,000 \times 0.001pF$$
$$= 1,000pF$$

Therefore the effective capacitance is

$$220 + 470 + 1,000 = 1,690pF.$$

Conversely, $220pF = \dfrac{220}{1,000,000} = 0.00022μF$

and $\qquad 470pF = \dfrac{470}{1,000,000} = 0.00047μF$

so that the effective capacitance is

$$0.00022 + 0.00047 + 0.001 = 0.00169μF.$$

Example 7. Two capacitors of 0.001μF and 0.0015μF respectively are connected in series. Find the effective capacitance.

$$C = \frac{C_1 \times C_2}{C_1 + C_2}$$

$$= \frac{1,000 \times 1,500}{1,000 + 1,500}$$

$$= \frac{1,000 \times 1,500}{2,500}$$

$$= 600pF.$$

Example 8. Two inductors of 10 and 20μH are connected in series; two others of 30 and 40μH are also connected in series. What is the equivalent inductance if these series combinations are connected in parallel? Assume that there is no mutual induction.

The 10 and 20μH coils in series are equivalent to (10 + 20) = 30μH.
The 30 and 40μH coils in series are equivalent to (30 + 40) = 70μH.
These two equivalent inductances of 30μH and 70μH respectively are in parallel and are therefore equivalent to one single inductance of

$$\frac{30 \times 70}{30 + 70} = 21μH.$$

Example 9. What power is consumed by a transmitter taking 1.5A at 12V?

$$W = V \times I \text{ watts}$$
$$= 12 \times 1.5 = 18W.$$

Example 10. What is the input power of a transmitter stage running at 24V, 2.5A?

$$W = V \times I \text{ watts}$$
$$= 24 \times 2.5 = 60W.$$

Example 11. Find the power dissipated by a 15Ω resistor when it is passing 1.2A.

$$W = I^2 \times R = 1.2^2 \times 15 = 21.6W.$$

Example 12. The current at the centre of a given λ/2 antenna is found to be 0.5A. If this antenna has a radiation resistance of 70Ω, find the radiated power.

$$W = I^2 \times R = (½ \times ½) \times 70$$

$$= \frac{70}{4} = 17.5W.$$

Example 13. A transmitter output stage is running at 20V, 3A. It is found to produce a current of 0.9A rms in a load resistance of 50Ω. Find (a) the input power, (b) the output power, (c) the efficiency of the stage.

(a) input power $= W_i = $ dc volts × dc amperes
$= 20 × 3 = 60$W.

(b) output power $= W_0 = $ (load current)^2 × load resistance
$= 0.9 × 0.9 × 50 = 40.5$W.

(c) efficiency $= \eta = \dfrac{\text{output power}}{\text{input power}}$

$= \dfrac{40.5}{60} = 0.675.$

or $\eta = 0.675 × 100 = 67.5$ per cent.

Example 14. What is the reactance of a 15H smoothing choke at a frequency of (a) 50Hz, (b) 400Hz?

(a) $X_L = 2\pi fL$
$= 2\pi × 50 × 15$
$= 4,700$Ω (approximately).

(b) At eight times the frequency, X is eight times as great, ie 37,600Ω.

Example 15. A medium-wave coil has an inductance of 150µH. Find the reactance at a frequency of 500kHz.

$X_L = 2\pi fL$

$= 2\pi × 500 × 1,000 × \dfrac{150}{1,000,000}$

$= 470$Ω (approximately).

Note how the frequency in kilohertz must be multiplied by 1,000 to bring it to hertz, and how the inductance in microhenrys must be divided by 1,000,000 to bring it to henrys.

Example 16. What is the reactance of a 2µF smoothing capacitor at a frequency of (a) 50Hz, (b) 400Hz?

(a) $X_C = \dfrac{1}{2\pi fC}$

where f is the frequency and C the capacitance in farads.

$X_C = \dfrac{1}{2\pi × 50 × \dfrac{2}{1,000,000}}$

$= \dfrac{1,000,000}{2\pi × 100}$

$= \dfrac{100,000 × 3.2}{200}$

(taking $10/\pi = 3.2$)

$= 1,600$Ω.

(b) At eight times the frequency, X is one-eighth of the above value, ie 200Ω.

Example 17. A coil has a resistance of 3Ω and a reactance of 4Ω. Find the impedance.

$Z = \sqrt{(R^2 + X^2)}$

$= \sqrt{3^2 + 4^2}$

$= \sqrt{9 + 16} = \sqrt{25}$

$= 5$Ω

∴ impedance $= 5$Ω.

Example 18. Given a series circuit with a resistance of 60Ω and a capacitor with a reactance (at the working frequency) of 80Ω, find the impedance of the circuit.

$Z = \sqrt{(R^2 + X^2)}$

$= \sqrt{60^2 + 80^2}$

$= \sqrt{3,600 + 6,400}$

$= \sqrt{10,000}$

$= 100$Ω

∴ impedance $= 100$Ω.

Example 19. Suppose the coil of Example 17 were connected (a) across 15V dc and (b) across 15V ac (of frequency at which the reactance was 4Ω). Find the current in each case.

(a) At dc the reactance is zero and only the resistance opposes the passage of current. By Ohm's Law

$I = \dfrac{V}{R} = \dfrac{15}{3} = 5$A.

(b) At ac Ohm's Law may still be used, provided Z, the impedance, is used in place of R, the resistance.

$I = \dfrac{V}{Z} = \dfrac{15}{5} = 3$A.

Example 20. In the series circuit of Example 18, suppose the circuit were connected (a) across 240V dc and (b) across 240V ac (of frequency at which the reactance was 70Ω). Find the current in each case.

(a) A capacitor blocks the passage of direct current, therefore the current is zero amperes.
(b) Ohm's Law holds, provided Z (the impedance) is used in place of R (the resistance).

$Z = \sqrt{60^2 + 70^2} = 92.2$Ω

$I = \dfrac{E}{Z} = \dfrac{240}{92.2} = 2.6$A.

Example 21. Find the capacitance required to resonate a 10H choke to 500Hz.

For resonance $2\pi fL = \dfrac{1}{2\pi fC}$

whence

$$C = \frac{1}{4\pi^2 f^2 L} \text{ farads}$$

or

$$C = \frac{1,000,000}{4\pi^2 f^2 L} \text{ microfarads}$$

and inserting the given values

$$C = \frac{1,000,000}{4\pi^2 \times 500 \times 500 \times 10} = \frac{10}{100 \times 10}$$

$$= 0.01\mu F.$$

Example 22. A coil of $100\mu H$ inductance is tuned by a capacitance of 250pF. Find the resonant frequency.

For resonance

$$2\pi f L = \frac{1}{2\pi f C}$$

whence

$$f = \frac{1}{2\pi \sqrt{LC}}$$

$$f = \frac{1}{2\pi \sqrt{\dfrac{100}{10^6} \times \dfrac{250}{10^{12}}}} = \frac{1}{2\pi \dfrac{\sqrt{100} \times \sqrt{250}}{\sqrt{10^{18}}}}$$

$$= \frac{10^9}{2 \times \pi \times 10 \times 15.8} = \frac{1,000 \times 10^6}{992}$$

$$= 1 \times 10^6 \text{Hz (approximately)}$$
or 1MHz (approximately).

Example 23. What value of inductance is required in series with a capacitor of 500pF for the circuit to resonate at a frequency of 400kHz?

From the resonance formula

$$f = \frac{1}{2\pi \sqrt{LC}}$$

the inductance is

$$L = \frac{1}{4\pi^2 f^2 C}$$

Expressing the frequency and the capacitance in the basic units ($f = 400 \times 10^3$Hz and $C = 500 \times 10^{-12}$F)

$$L = \frac{1}{4\pi^2 \times (400 \times 10^3)^2 \times (500 \times 10^{-12})}$$

Taking $\pi^2 = 10$, this becomes

$$\frac{10^{12}}{4 \times 10 \times 16 \times 10^4 \times 10^6 \times 500}$$

$$L = \frac{1}{3,200}\text{H}$$

$$= 310\mu H \text{ (approximately)}.$$

Example 24. If the effective series inductance and capacitance of a vertical antenna are $20\mu H$ and 100pF respectively and the antenna is connected to a coil of

$80\mu H$ inductance, what is the approximate resonant frequency?

The antenna and coil together resonate at a frequency determined by the capacitance and the sum of the antenna effective inductance and the loading coil inductance.
At resonance

$$f = \frac{1}{2\pi \sqrt{LC}}$$

Here the relevant values of inductance and capacitance expressed in the basic units are

$$L = (20 + 80) \times 10^{-6}\text{H}$$
$$C = 100 \times 10^{-12}\text{F}$$

Therefore

$$f = \frac{1}{2\pi \sqrt{(100 \times 10^{-6}) \times (100 \times 10^{-12})}}$$

$$= \frac{1}{2\pi \times 10^{-7}}$$

$$= 1.6\text{MHz (approximately)}.$$

Example 25. An alternating voltage of 10V at a frequency of $5/\pi$MHz is applied to a circuit of the following elements in series : (i) a capacitor of 100pF, (ii) a non-inductive resistor of 10Ω.
   (a) What value of inductance in series is required to tune the circuit to resonance?
   (b) At resonance, what is the current in the circuit?

(a) For the calculation of the inductance, the resistance can be ignored, since it has no effect on the resonant frequency, which is given by

$$f = \frac{1}{2\pi \sqrt{LC}}$$

Rearranging

$$L = \frac{1}{4\pi^2 f^2 C}$$

Expressing the frequency and the capacitance in the proper units ($f = 5 \times 10^6/\pi$Hz; $C = 100 \times 10^{-12}$F)

$$L = \frac{1}{4\pi^2 \left(\dfrac{25 \times 10^{12}}{\pi^2}\right) \times 100 \times 10^{-12}} \text{ henrys}$$

$$= \frac{1}{10,000}\text{H}$$

$$= 100\mu H.$$

(b) At resonance, the inductive and capacitive reactances cancel out and the circuit has a purely resistive impedance of 10Ω. The current I through the circuit at resonance can then be calculated directly from Ohm's Law: $I = V/R$. Since $V = 10$V and $R = 10\Omega$

$$\text{current at resonance } I = \frac{10\text{V}}{10\Omega}$$

$$= 1\text{A}.$$

CHAPTER 3

Solid-state devices

Solid-state devices are based on *semiconductor* materials which have a resistivity greater than the usual conductor, but less than the usual insulator. The most common elements in this category are silicon and germanium.

The silicon (Si) atom

Fig 3.1.   The silicon atom

A simplified representation of a silicon atom is shown in Fig 3.1. Around the positive nucleus there are three rings (orbits or shells) containing negatively charged electrons. The sum of the negative charges balances the positive charge on the nucleus. The first ring contains two electrons and will not accept any more. Similarly the second ring contains eight electrons, but the third ring has only four electrons, and these join with the four electrons in the outer rings of adjacent atoms to form a crystal lattice. The outer electrons are not very far away from the nucleus and are not free to move from the lattice. This pure silicon crystal is therefore a good insulator, but at high temperatures the electrons can become detached from the lattice and a large current can flow.

The germanium (Ge) atom

The germanium atom has 32 electrons, the rings having two, eight, 18 and four electrons. The four electrons in the outer ring, as in the case of the silicon atom, merge with those of adjacent atoms to form a crystal lattice. Because the outer electrons are one ring farther away from the nucleus, they can become detached more easily than in the silicon crystal, and thus at high temperatures a larger current can flow than in the case of silicon.

Semiconductor materials

The manufacturing process of solid-state devices is complex: it requires the refinement of silicon and germanium to an extremely high purity and then the introduction of a small but closely controlled amount of an impurity.

N-type material

In the manufacturing process, atoms having an outer ring containing five electrons are introduced into the crystal lattice. This is known as *doping* and elements used in this way are called *impurities*. Phosphorus (P) and arsenic (As) are two such elements. The lattice now appears to be negative because there is now a surplus electron. The result is known as *n-type* material.

P-type material

If the impurity has only three electrons in its outer ring, eg boron (B) or aluminium (Al), then a gap will be left in the lattice which could be filled by a free electron. Such a gap is called a *hole*. The lattice appears to be positive because an electron is missing, and the result is known as *p-type* material. The doped material of both n- and p-type material is electrically neutral because each of the individual atoms present is itself electrically neutral.

The pn junction

A *diode* consists of a small piece of p-type material fused to a small piece of n-type material. Because the n-type and the p-type materials have different characteristics as described above, there is a diffusion of "holes" in one direction and electrons in the other across the boundary or junction between the two materials.

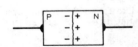

Fig 3.2.   The junction diode

An excess negative charge builds up in the p-type material and an excess positive charge in the n-type. Thus a potential difference is created and this opposes further diffusion across the junction. This potential difference is called the *barrier potential*. The region where the positive and negative charges build up is called the *depletion* layer and is only about 0·001mm in thickness: see Fig 3.2.

If a battery and an ammeter are connected as in the circuit of Fig 3.3, electrons will be attracted by the positive pole of the battery, forced round the circuit and into the n-type material. A conventional current *I* will flow. The junction is said to be *forward biased*. If the battery is reversed, electrons will be detached from the n-type material, making it more positive, and forced into the p-type material, making it more negative. Practically no current will flow after a small initial surge. The junction is said to be *reverse biased*. This device is known as a *junction* diode and it may be made from silicon or germanium.

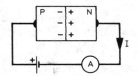

Fig 3.3.   **The forward-biased junction diode**

Characteristic curves of junction diodes are shown in Fig 3.4. In germanium junction diodes, a current begins to flow after a forward voltage of approximately 0·1 V is reached, ie just greater than the barrier potential. A very small reverse current may flow. The silicon junction diode needs a forward voltage of approximately 0·5 V before it begins to conduct.

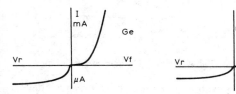

Fig 3.4.   **Characteristics of germanium and silicon junction diodes**

Junction diodes are used for the rectification of alternating voltages in power supplies and for the demodulation of signals in radio receivers.

By changes in the manufacturing process, junction diodes of somewhat different characteristics can be produced. Two such diodes are the zener diode and the varactor (Varicap) diode.

Zener diode

In normal diodes, large voltages may be applied to reverse bias a diode junction and very little current flows. It is possible to construct a diode in which this small current will flow only up to a certain voltage, but if this amount of reverse bias is exceeded a large current will flow (Fig 3.5).

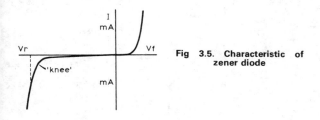

Fig 3.5.   **Characteristic of zener diode**

These diodes are called *zener* or *avalanche* diodes and may be designed to have *zener voltages* (the reverse bias when large currents begin to flow) of between 3V and 150V. Such diodes are useful in power-supply circuits where they can be used to provide a voltage reference which is substantially constant.

Varactor diode

The depletion layer stores energy in the form of an electric field, ie it has the property of capacitance. In the *varactor* diode, special doping can cause the depletion layer to have a large value of capacitance. The width of the depletion layer can be altered by a change in the reverse bias on the diode, and thus the capacitance across the junction may be varied (Fig 3.6).

Fig 3.6.   **Variation in capacitance of a varactor diode**

The varactor diode is therefore equivalent to a variable capacitor, the capacitance of which may be altered by changing the small voltage applied to it. The change in capacitance which can be achieved depends on the diode type and varies from 1–4pF to 15–105pF. It presents a convenient method of altering the resonant frequency of a tuned circuit. Varactor diodes are also used as frequency multipliers in transmitters operating at very high frequencies.

The bipolar transistor

Two pn junctions can be fabricated as shown in Fig 3.7. Here there are two regions of n-type material, one on each side of a very thin wafer of p-type material. The wafer of p-type material is known as the *base,* b, and the n-type regions are known as the *emitter,* e, and the *collector,* c. The whole device is known as a *bipolar transistor.*

Fig   3.7.   **The   npn   bipolar transistor**

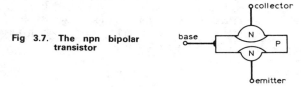

This arrangement could be considered as two pn junctions mounted back-to-back, each junction capable of being biased separately to produce the characteristics described earlier. However, if both junctions are biased simultaneously, different conditions will apply. The lower (emitter-base) junction in Fig 3.8 is forward biased, and hence presents a low resistance, while the upper (base-collector) junction is reverse biased and so presents a high resistance. The forward bias on the emitter-base junction allows a large current (flow of electrons and therefore negative) into it. These electrons would normally flow into the base, but because the base is very thin most of the electrons are captured by the collector which is positive with respect to the emitter. Not all the electrons are captured and those that remain give rise to a very small base current.

A typical value of the base current (I_B) is 5μA when the collector current (I_C) is 1mA. As the emitter-base junction is forward biased, a very small increase in the base voltage (ie the bias voltage), say from 500mV to 520mV, may cause an increase in collector current from 1mA to, say, 2mA, and an increase in base current from 5μA to 10μA.

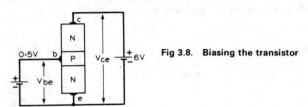

Fig 3.8.   Biasing the transistor

Thus amplification of current has occurred, and in the example quoted above, the current *gain* is 200 (ie 1mA/5μA). This gain is denoted by the symbol h_{FE} (or β) in the manufacturer's literature.

In order to obtain voltage or power amplification, a load resistor is needed in the collector circuit.

If, in the arrangement of Figs 3.7 and 3.8 the material types are interchanged, ie pnp instead of npn, the above discussion still holds provided that the polarities of the supplies are reversed.

Solid-state devices are now manufactured by far more sophisticated methods, but the principles remain the same. Many different transistor characteristics are quoted in the manufacturer's data. Three of the most significant are:

(i) *Current amplification factor* (α) is a measure of how much current in the emitter circuit gets into the collector circuit, or the ratio of a small change in collector current i_c to the small change in emitter current i_e which has caused it. α is very nearly equal to unity and is seldom less than 0·98.

(ii) *Current gain* (β) is the ratio of the change in collector current to the change in base current which has caused it. It may be shown that

$$\beta = \frac{\alpha}{1 - \alpha}$$

In practice, values of β lie between 50 and 500. Values of β for silicon transistors tend to be higher than for germanium.

(iii) *Transition frequency* (f_t) is a measure of the highest frequency at which a transistor can amplify. It specifies the product of the current gain and the bandwidth of the transistor, and is also the frequency at which the gain is unity. Transistors are normally used up to a frequency which is about 10–15 per cent of f_t.

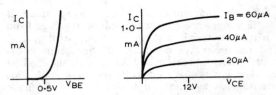

Fig 3.9.   Characteristics of small-signal transistor

The curves in Fig 3.9 are those of a small silicon transistor of the type which may be used in the first stage of an audio or intermediate frequency amplifier. Note that the change in V_{CE} has little effect on the value of I_C.

A larger silicon transistor which could be used in the first stages of a transmitter is the Mullard BFY50 (Fig 3.10). This transistor handles a much larger current and is capable of an output power of a few watts if its case temperature is kept low.

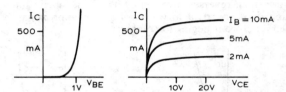

Fig 3.10.   Characteristics of large-signal transistor

Large transistors for audio amplifiers may have a base current of some 80mA, giving a collector current of 3A.

The symbols for transistors are shown in Fig 3.11. The small arrowhead shows the direction of conventional current flow.

Germanium transistors were developed before silicon transistors because they are easier to manufacture—germanium has a lower melting point than silicon. In general, germanium transistors are pnp and silicon transistors are npn, although there are exceptions. A germanium transistor has a larger base current and leakage current than a comparable silicon transistor. The maximum safe working temperature for a germanium device is about 75°C compared with 150°C for a silicon device, and consequently silicon transistors are preferred for most applications.

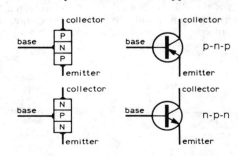

Fig 3.11.   Transistor symbols

The power that a transistor can dissipate depends on how cool the junction can be kept. The temperature of the case and hence the junction of a transistor may be kept low by mounting the transistor on a *heat sink* to increase the effective dissipating area of the case. For instance, without a heat sink, the BFY50 will handle 0·8W if the ambient temperature does not exceed 25°C. If the case temperature can be kept below 100°C, the dissipation can rise to approximately 2·8W. In its simplest form, a heat sink may be a piece of aluminium, say 5cm by 5cm by 2mm, but at the other extreme it may be a 15cm length of a complex extruded aluminium section.

Field-effect transistor

The *field-effect transistor* (fet) consists of a bar or channel of n-type material with a ring of p-type material diffused around it, as indicated in Fig 3.12.

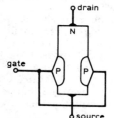

Fig 3.12.   The field-effect transistor

The n-type part is called the *channel* and the p-type ring is called the *gate* (g). The ends of the channel are called the *source* (s) and the *drain* (d). The symbol for the device is shown in Fig 3.13(a). The channel can be made of p-type material, in which case the symbol is as Fig 3.13(b).

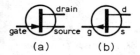

Fig 3.13.   FET symbols

(a)   (b)

Operation of a junction fet

The gate is reverse biased, thus the gate current is very small and the gate/source impedance is very high. In an npn (or pnp) transistor the current consists of negative electrons moving in one direction and positive "holes" moving in the opposite direction. In an fet with a channel of n-type material, only electrons form the current. For this reason, the fet is known as a *monopolar* device. The family is called the *junction* or *junction gate* fet as the input signal exerts control via a reverse-bias pn junction as just described.

Because the gate is negative, electrons are repelled and the width of the depletion layer increases as the reverse bias is increased. The voltage between the gate and source is small, say, 2V; whereas the voltage between the gate and drain is comparatively large, say, 2V + 12V = 14V. For this reason the depletion layer is widest near the drain terminal (Fig 3.14). Increasing the reverse voltage at the gate will eventually cause the

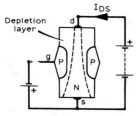

Fig 3.14.   Configuration and operation of a fet

drain current to fall to zero. The voltage required to do this is called the *pinch-off* voltage; see V_{pinch} in Fig 3.15. Electrons flow from source to drain along the channel. As the reverse gate bias is increased the width of the channel is reduced, causing the current I_{DS} to decrease. If an alternating voltage is applied between gate and source, a varying current will flow in the channel.

Typical values for a 2N3823 fet are shown in Fig 3.15.

Because there is practically no current flowing at the gate, due to the reverse bias, the input impedance is very high. One may say that the bipolar transistor is *current operated* and that the fet is *voltage operated*.

Applications of solid-state devices

It must be appreciated that solid-state devices are extremely small and cannot dissipate any significant power. Power transistors need to be mounted on heat sinks, and consequently great care in design and use is necessary because, having virtually no overload capacity, they can be very easily destroyed.

Junction diode

The junction diode may be used as a rectifier (Fig 3.16).

The silicon diode has now generally replaced the germanium diode as a rectifier at mains frequency in power supplies. See Chapter 6.

The diode may also be used as a demodulator at rf or i.f. The diode in this case is usually either the germanium junction or *point-contact* types. The point-contact diode is the modern version of the old "catswhisker" form of detector.

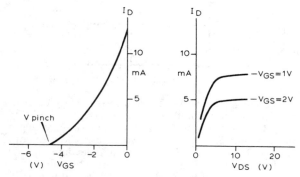

Fig 3.15.   Characteristics of a 2N3823 fet

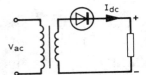

Fig 3.16. Use of the junction diode as a rectifier

Fig 3.17 indicates the use of a diode as the demodulator (detector) in radio receivers. The germanium junction diode is generally used in this application, but at uhf and higher frequencies, the point-contact type is more effective.

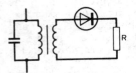

Fig 3.17. Use of the junction diode as a demodulator

Zener diode

The basic arrangement is shown in Fig 3.18. The resistor R_r is chosen so that when the load resistor R_L is carrying its normal current, the voltage drop across R_r will ensure that the diode is operating just beyond the "knee" of its characteristic (Fig 3.5). If the output voltage tends to rise due to a reduction in load current, the diode will take more current from the supply and so keep the output voltage reasonably constant.

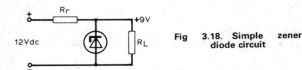

Fig 3.18. Simple zener diode circuit

Varactor diode

The effective capacitance of C1 in Fig 3.19 is in series with the capacitance of the diode, and is connected across the LC circuit. The circuit may therefore be tuned by altering the voltage applied to the diode.

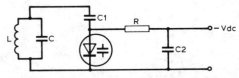

Fig 3.19. Tuning an LC circuit with a varactor diode

The change of diode capacitance is much greater in the forward direction than in the reverse direction (Fig 3.6). However, in the forward direction large changes in diode current occur—this would not allow smooth control. Resistor R and capacitor C2 decouple the dc control circuit from the tuned circuit. The value of R may be 220kΩ and the value of C2 1,000pF to 0·1μF, depending upon the frequency of the tuned circuit.

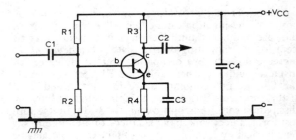

Fig 3.20. Common-emitter amplifier

The transistor as a small-signal amplifier

Small-signal amplifiers are so called because their inputs are measured in microvolts or millivolts, as opposed to large-signal amplifiers which can have inputs of several volts. These latter are normally power amplifiers.

A typical simple small-signal amplifier is shown in Fig 3.20. This is known as the *common-emitter* circuit because one terminal of both input and output circuits is connected to the emitter. This may not appear to be the case but the impedance of C3 is so small at the operating frequencies that the emitter is virtually connected to the chassis. In a similar way the impedance of C4 virtually connects the positive dc line to chassis.

A signal is applied between base and emitter via C1. As the base voltage increases (the positive half-cycle of the signal waveform), the collector current also increases. This causes the voltage at the collector to fall. The voltage between collector and chassis falls with a rise in the voltage between base and chassis, ie there is a 180° phase inversion.

Forward biasing

If the transistor is silicon, eg a BC108, then it will need a forward bias of about 0·7V between base and emitter. Forward biasing should be such that the signal swings on the straight part of the characteristic shown in Fig 3.21. This bias is provided by the potential divider R1 and R2. Three points need to be considered when choosing the values of R1 and R2.

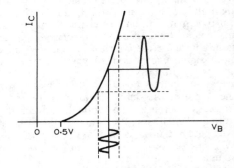

Fig 3.21. Forward biasing of transistor

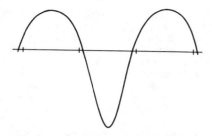

Fig 3.22.   Output waveform of the amplifier of Fig 3.20

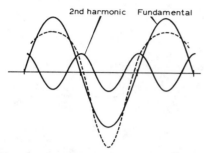

2nd harmonic   Fundamental

Fig 3.23.   The waveform of Fig 3.22 can be considered as the sum of the fundamental and the second harmonic waveforms

(i) If the values of the resistors are too low, they will seriously affect the input impedance. Because current flows between base and emitter the base-emitter resistance may only be approximately 1,000Ω. R1 and R2 are both effectively in parallel with this base-emitter resistance and should have values as high as possible.
(ii) If R1 has too high a value then there will be too large a variation of the voltage across it as the base current changes. (As a rule of thumb, make the current flowing in the resistors 10 times the bias current.)
(iii) The total value of the potential divider resistance $(R_1 + R_2)$ should be kept as high as possible so as to reduce current drain on the power supply.
   The input impedance of this amplifier can vary between, say, 500Ω and 1·5kΩ. The output impedance can be typically 1kΩ to 10kΩ. Values for R1, R2, R3 and R4 could be 100kΩ, 33kΩ, 4·7kΩ and 470Ω respectively. When such an amplifier is used at audio frequencies the values of C1 and C2 will need to be comparatively large, say 1μF. The value of C3 could lie between 10μF and 100μF. If the value of C3 were to be deliberately reduced (or if C3 were to be omitted), then the voltage between the emitter and chassis would vary in step with the signal applied to the base. If the base voltage goes more positive, then an increase in base current will be followed by an increase in emitter current. The voltage at the emitter end of R4 will then go more positive with respect to chassis, ie the emitter voltage *follows* the base voltage. This effect is called *current negative feedback* (see later).
   The output wave shape is slightly distorted. If this distortion is exaggerated a curve such as that in Fig 3.22

will result. Combining two sine waves in which one is the second harmonic of the other, as in Fig 3.23, will produce approximately the same curve.

Cut-off and bottoming
If too large a signal is applied between the base and emitter of the small-signal amplifier shown in Fig 3.20 then the output will be very distorted. On the negative half-cycle the base current will cease to flow because the base-emitter voltage will have fallen below 0·5V. This is called *cut-off*.
   On the positive half-cycle the collector current will increase and cause a large voltage drop in R3, but this voltage drop obviously cannot exceed the supply voltage V_{CC}. In this case the transistor is said to *bottom*. The output voltage as seen on an oscilloscope may appear as in Fig 3.24, and it will be rich in harmonics.

Fig 3.24.   Output waveform of the amplifier of Fig 3.20 when it is overloaded

Transistor operating conditions—Class A operation

Fig 3.25 shows the circuit of a small-signal amplifier. Resistors R1 and R2 are the potential divider providing forward bias for the base-emitter junction. R3 is the collector load. Let the characteristics of the transistor be as in Fig 3.26.

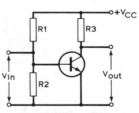

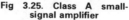

Fig 3.25.   Class A small-signal amplifier

Fig 3.26.   Class A operation

   The base bias has been fixed so that a steady collector current of 3mA flows. The voltage at the collector terminal will be V_{CC} minus the voltage drop in R3. The small signal applied to the input will cause the output voltage to vary. This is Class A bias, and the signal is applied to the "straight" part of the curve. Collector current flows at all times and the output voltage fluctuates as in Fig 3.27.

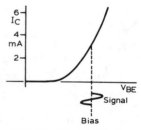

Fig 3.27.   Output voltage of the circuit in Fig 3.25

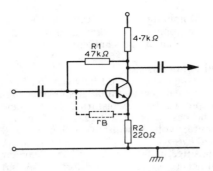

Fig 3.28. Amplifier with two forms of negative feedback

Because the characteristic curve is not a straight line, some distortion occurs, again predominantly second-harmonic.

Negative feedback

Distortion in an amplifier can be reduced by using negative feedback. Fig 3.28 shows a simple amplifier having two forms of negative feedback. The base bias is applied through R1. A positive-going signal on the base results in a negative-going signal at the collector; this reduces the forward bias. More feedback (lower forward bias) will occur during the peaked half-cycles of Fig 3.27, and less feedback during the rounded half-cycles. This reduces distortion and is called *voltage negative feedback*.

Consider now the effect of resistor R2. The emitter current will cause the emitter to be $I_E \times R_2$ volts positive to chassis. A positive-going signal on the base will cause the emitter to go more positive, thus reducing the signal voltage between the base and the emitter. This is *current* negative feedback.

Both forms of feedback help to reduce distortion introduced by the amplifier's solid-state devices, and also to increase the input impedance. As an example let $I_B = V_{BE}/r_B$, where r_B is the input resistance in the absence of R2. The effect of R2 is to decrease V_{BE} and therefore to decrease I_B; the input "sees" an apparently higher value of r_B. A disadvantage of using negative feedback is that the amplifier gain is reduced.

Bypassed emitter resistors, as in Fig 3.20, are included to prevent "thermal runaway". As the temperature of a transistor rises its internal resistance falls, and this allows more current to flow. The extra current will cause a further rise in temperature, and this could go on until the transistor is destroyed. The rise in current through the emitter resistor reduces the fixed forward bias, and so prevents a dangerous rise in transistor current. Silicon transistors are not so susceptible as germanium transistors to thermal runaway.

Class B operation

The circuit in Fig 3.25 can be operated so that no collector current will flow in the absence of a signal. Collector current only flows during the positive half-cycles of the signal (Fig 3.29). The output is very distorted and contains both even and odd harmonics.

Because the characteristics of semiconductors can alter with changes in temperature, Class B amplifiers are generally biased a little forward of the cut-off point, and a small collector current therefore flows when no signal is present. Fig 3.29 shows how the characteristic alters with an increase in temperature. A fall in temperature will shift the characteristic from A to C with a severe increase in distortion. By using a *push-pull* circuit the distortion can however be reduced to an acceptable level.

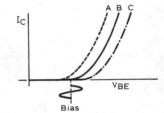

Fig 3.29. Class B operation and change of characteristic due to temperature

Push-pull operation

Fig 3.30 is a simplified circuit of a push-pull audio amplifier. When a change of current occurs in the primary winding of T1 due to the application of a signal to the base of the first transistor, equal and opposite voltages will appear at the ends of the centre-tapped secondary winding. The current in one half of the output transformer primary, T2, will increase; while the current in the other half will decrease. Resistors R1 and R2 determine the base bias on the output transistors; this bias is normally set so that the push-pull transistors are operating just before the Class B state.

In push-pull operation, the second harmonic is virtually eliminated, but third and higher odd harmonics are still present.

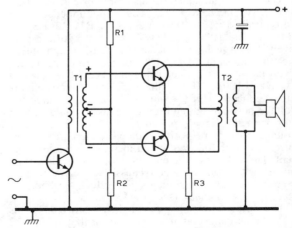

Fig 3.30. Class B push-pull circuit

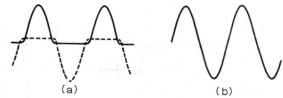

Fig 3.31.   Output waveform of the amplifier of Fig 3.30

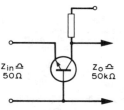

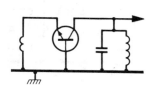

Fig   3.35.   Common-base circuit arrangement

Fig   3.36.   Common-base tuned amplifier (signal path only shown)

Cross-over distortion

In Class B push-pull amplifiers the collector currents add to give a fairly good waveform (Fig 3.31). If the bias is not sufficient to reach the cut-off point then the two half-cycles add together to give a distorted waveform. This waveform (Fig 3.32) is rich in the third harmonic.

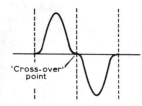

Fig   3.32.   Distortion of waveform caused by incorrect bias

'Cross-over' point

Common-base circuit

This arrangement is shown in Fig 3.35. The input impedance is very low but the output impedance is high, and so the collector can be connected directly to a tuned circuit. The basic signal-path circuit is shown in Fig 3.36. Note that in Fig 3.36 (and also Figs 3.38, 3.39 and 3.40) extra components would be required to form a practical circuit.

Common-collector circuit

The common-collector circuit shown in Fig 3.37 is better known as the *emitter follower*. The large capacitor C (in the power supply) effectively connects the collector to chassis. The input impedance is high, and it can provide a high degree of isolation between two stages. Consequently it is often used as a buffer between an oscillator and a mixer or a frequency multiplier. Emitter followers are prone to self-oscillation, and care must be taken to check that they are not oscillating and so causing interference.

Class C operation

There is no forward bias in the circuit of Fig 3.33 and therefore current will only flow in the collector circuit during the peaks of a positive-going signal (points A and B of Fig 3.34). Severe distortion takes place, but current is only taken from the supply in pulses. The input signal must be comparatively large. Class C amplifiers are used at radio frequencies and normally have a tuned load.

Fig   3.37.   Common-collector circuit arrangement

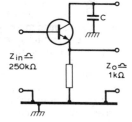

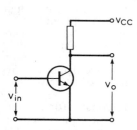

Fig 3.33.   Class C amplifier

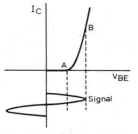

Fig 3.34.   Operation of the Class C circuit

A crystal microphone (impedance 250kΩ) would be coupled to a common-emitter amplifier (input impedance 1kΩ) by means of a common-collector amplifier.

Collector loads in amplifier circuits

The transistor is generally used as voltage amplifier or a power amplifier. This implies that a load across which the voltage or power can be developed must be provided, and this is generally located in the collector circuit.

The impedances existing in the various circuit arrangements must be taken into account when considering the form of the output load. In small-signal audio amplifiers, the collector load is usually a resistor. Large-signal amplifiers (af) can be connected directly to loudspeakers having impedances in the range 15–120Ω, or alternatively an output or modulation

Transistor circuit configurations

The transistor amplifier which has been discussed so far in this chapter is the common-emitter circuit. This is the most-used arrangement but two other circuit arrangements of the bipolar transistor are possible. These are the *common-base* and *common-collector* circuits.

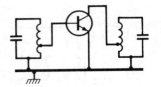

Fig 3.38. Tapping down the base and collector connections (signal path only shown)

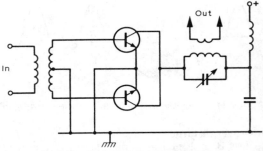

Fig 3.40. Push-push frequency doubler

transformer may be used to match the low output impedance to the required load or transmitter.

At radio frequencies, the dynamic resistance of a tuned circuit is of the order of 50kΩ. This resistance will match the output impedance of the common-base circuit (Fig 3.36). However, this tuned circuit would be severely damped if connected directly as the load of a common-emitter amplifier where the input and output impedances are about 1kΩ and 5kΩ respectively. To achieve a good match, the inductor of the tuned circuit may be tapped about one-third of the way along the winding (Fig 3.38). This will give an impedance transformation of nine times, and the tuned circuit is therefore loaded not with 5kΩ but 9 × 5kΩ or 45kΩ which is approximately equal to the dynamic resistance.

The transistor as an oscillator

Fig 3.39 is a basic circuit of a voltage amplifier having a tuned circuit as its load. The gain of the amplifier is therefore a maximum at the resonant frequency of the tuned circuit. Coil L1 is connected between the base and the junction of the biasing resistors.

If the amplifier is fed with an input signal of a frequency equal to the resonant frequency and the coupling between L1 and L, C is increased, the voltage fed back to the base increases. This voltage may be in phase (positive feedback) or out of phase (negative feedback) with the input voltage, according to which way round the coil is connected.

In the case of positive feedback, as the coupling is increased, some of the output is added to the input voltage, is amplified by the transistor and appears across the tuned circuit.

As soon as the proportion of the output voltage fed back in this manner and amplified is sufficient to overcome the circuit losses, continuous regeneration takes place and the input voltage may be disconnected. The amplifier is therefore now acting as an oscillator.

The conditions required to maintain oscillation are: (i) the feedback must be positive; (ii) the feedback must be sufficient to overcome all the circuit losses.

There are many ways of arranging the feedback in an oscillator, eg coupling between output and input tuned circuits, a single coil having a tapping point which is taken to the emitter; in another arrangement the tap on the coil is replaced by two capacitors across the tuned circuit, the junction of the capacitors being taken to the emitter.

Oscillators are often named after the originator, hence the terms *Colpitts* oscillator, *Clapp-Gouriet* oscillator, *Hartley* oscillator, *Vackar* oscillator etc. In general, there is little to choose between most of the circuits which have been published; in amateur radio the most commonly used circuits are the Colpitts and Clapp-Gouriet oscillators.

Frequency multipliers

As a result of non-linearity of the characteristics of a transistor, the output may not be sinusoidal, ie the waveform of the collector current is distorted and contains the fundamental and harmonics.

If a tuned circuit resonant at, say, the second harmonic is used as a collector load, a certain output voltage at twice the input frequency is obtained.

A feature of the push-pull amplifier is that even harmonics are virtually eliminated, but odd harmonics are still present. Thus a push-pull amplifier stage makes an effective frequency tripler and can give significant output if required. A frequency multiplication of five times is rarely required.

Fig 3.40 shows an interesting doubler (or quadrupler) circuit. This is the push-push arrangement in which the bases of the two transistors are connected in push-pull but the collectors are in parallel. The transistors used in this and in any push-pull circuit should be matched in characteristics.

Other solid-state devices

Many other forms of solid-state devices have been and are being developed, and it is obviously impossible to discuss all these in a manual of this size.

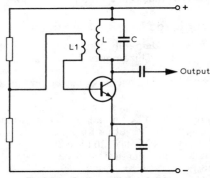

Fig 3.39. Basic oscillator circuit

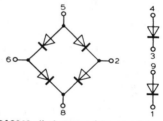

Fig 3.41. Circuit symbols for MOSFETs

The metal-oxide semiconductor field-effect transistor (mosfet) is a specialized device which is becoming common in vhf (and hf) receivers. It is basically a fet with the gate insulated from the channel, hence it is sometimes known as an *insulated-gate* field-effect transistor (igfet). The input impedance is very high indeed.

Some MOSFETS are made with two gates and are thus known as *dual-gate* MOSFETS. The additional gate may be used for the application of the local oscillator injection voltage in the mixer stage of a vhf superheterodyne receiver or for the application of the agc (automatic gain control) voltage. The circuit symbols for single- and dual-gate MOSFETS are shown in Fig 3.41.

The dual-gate MOSFET shown in Fig 3.41 can be easily damaged by static charges applied to the gate (by, for instance, careless handling or from a soldering iron). The oxide thickness is only about 60 millionths of a millimetre and a voltage of some 30V can cause breakdown. In order to protect this insulating layer, diodes can be formed on the transistor substrate as shown diagrammatically in Fig 3.42. This is the *gate-protected* MOSFET. Any handling instructions supplied with MOSFETS and other devices should be carefully followed.

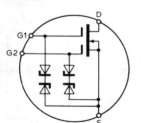

Fig 3.42. Gate-protected mos field-effect transistor

Integrated circuits

Integrated circuits (ICs) result from the extension of transistor fabrication techniques to the formation of complete circuits onto a single n- or p-type silicon substrate (known as the *chip*). The substrate may be typically 4 by 5 by 0·3mm and may be packaged in a medium-sized transistor can or a plastic case, which may measure 2·5 by 0·7 by 0·3cm and have a number of metal tags for connection purposes on the long edges.

There is an almost infinite number of circuit configurations possible in an ic, from two or more diodes to hundreds of diodes and transistors with the appropriate numbers of resistors and capacitors. Resistors cannot be formed to exact values, but two or more can be formed to have the same value. Large inductors and capacitors have to be connected externally, together with, of course, variable resistors and variable capacitors.

The advantages of the integrated circuit are the obvious one of extremely small size and also that the characteristics of similar types of diode and transistor are practically identical, remaining matched as the temperature increases.

It must be realized that an integrated circuit operates in exactly the same way as if the circuit was built up using discrete components, but its extremely small size permits many circuit refinements to be added at little or no increase in overall size. Particular circuit arrangements are often used to offset the impracticability of forming high values of capacitors.

Consequently it will be noted that equipment which is based on ICs inevitably tends to be complex, but it is compact. The cost of integrated circuits has fallen rapidly and many types now cost less than 25p.

Diode arrays

The circuit of a typical diode array (the RCA CA3019) is shown diagrammatically in Fig 3.43. The applications of this would include mixing, modulating and detecting. The similarity of the characteristics of the diodes in the bridge circuit is particularly important in all applications.

Fig 3.43. CA3019 diode array (the numbers refer to the pin connections)

Digital integrated circuits

Digital logic ICs were the first to appear. Digital logic is concerned with devices which have only two states, "on" and "off", and which thus are the electrical equivalent of switches. Digital ICs are the basis of the computer and are finding increasing use in the peripherals of amateur radio such as keyers, frequency counters, synthesizers and control systems.

Linear integrated circuits

This family of ICs is so called because they operate in the linear mode rather than the on-off state of the digital ones. Most of the circuits used in amateur radio (amplifiers, oscillators, mixers etc) fall into this category, and consequently it is the linear ic which tends to be of more interest.

Two or three circuit configurations only will be considered. The basic circuit used for a large variety of requirements is the *differential* amplifier. Consider a simple voltage amplifier: Fig 3.44. The emitter resistor will cause current negative feedback (see p30) and the voltage gain will be much reduced. A large bypass capacitor (shown dotted) could reduce the feedback but such capacitors cannot be formed on the small chip.

Now add a transistor as in Fig 3.45, and let R1 be

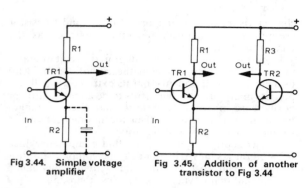

Fig 3.44. Simple voltage amplifier

Fig 3.45. Addition of another transistor to Fig 3.44

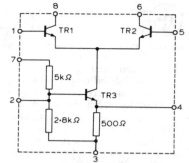

Fig 3.48.   CA3028 integrated circuit

equal to R3. The characteristics of TR1 and TR2 are identical, because they have been formed under the same conditions. For simplicity, biasing arrangements are not shown.

With no signal applied, the collector currents in TR1 and TR2 will have the same value, and a voltage will be present across R2. A positive signal applied to the base of TR1 will cause its emitter current to increase, thus increasing the voltage at the emitters of TR1 and TR2. This reduces the forward bias on TR2 and causes the current through it to decrease. The current through R2, which is the sum of the emitter currents of TR1 and TR2, will remain steady and therefore the emitter voltage of TR1 will remain constant. The effect is to reduce negative current feedback and TR2 appears to act as a large capacitor connected across R2. Because no coupling capacitors are used, the circuit can amplify down to a frequency of zero hertz, ie dc.

With the addition of C1, to connect the base of TR2 to chassis, the circuit is re-drawn in Fig 3.46. Because the output from the collector is not being used, TR1 could be regarded as a common-collector amplifier, while TR2 acts as a common-base amplifier. This basic configuration is usually shown as in Fig 3.47. Let both transistors be biased so that they are working on the linear portion of their characteristic curves. If a signal is applied to both bases, so that when one is positive-going the other is negative-going, then the two output signals will also be equal and opposite.

Any interfering signal, such as mains hum, will affect both bases and tend to make both emitter currents

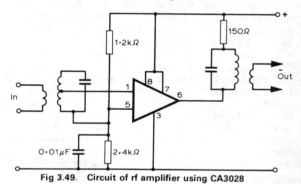

Fig 3.49.   Circuit of rf amplifier using CA3028

increase or decrease, thus causing negative feedback and a reduction in amplification of the interfering signal. By making R2 much larger a greater reduction of interfering signals could be achieved. The disadvantage of this would be that a high supply voltage would be needed to get the required collector current. This problem is overcome by using a transistor in place of R2. In effect a high resistance has been inserted but the current through it will be constant in spite of changes in its collector voltage: see Fig 3.48. An ic using these principles is the CA3028, and an rf amplifier using it is shown in Fig 3.49.

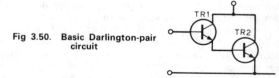

Fig 3.50.   Basic Darlington-pair circuit

Bias to the bases (1 and 5) is provided by the potential divider; pin 5 being connected to the common line (pin 3) through the 0·01μF bypass capacitor. The input to base 1 is tapped down the coil so that the relatively low impedance of TR1 does not damp the tuned circuit.

Darlington pair

Two transistors can be connected in cascade as in Fig 3.50. TR1 acts as a common-collector amplifier and TR2 as a common-emitter amplifier. An increase in the

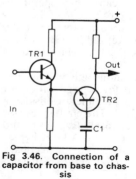

Fig 3.46. Connection of a capacitor from base to chassis

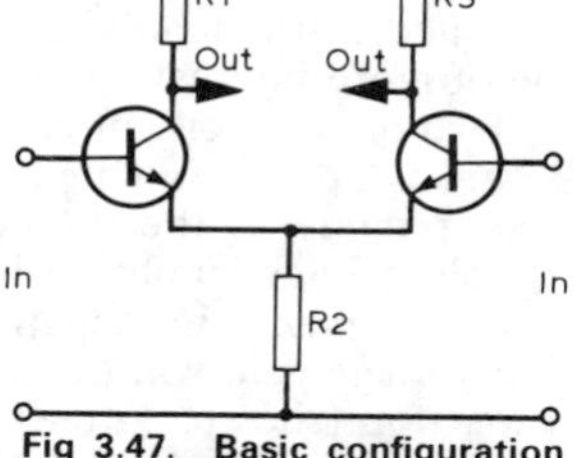

Fig 3.47. Basic configuration of differential amplifier

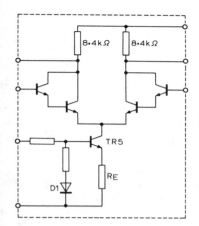

Fig 3.51. Integrated circuit based on Darlington pair

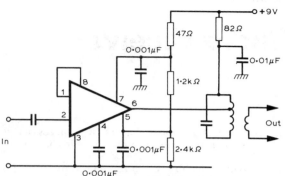

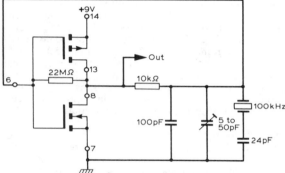

Fig 3.54. CA3028 ic used as a cascode amplifier

base current of TR1 is followed by an increase in the base current of TR2, but because the emitter current of TR1 is nearly equal to its collector current a large current amplification takes place. The overall current gain is practically equal to the product of the individual transistor current gains.

The input resistance of TR2 is an un-bypassed emitter resistor for TR1: the input resistance of the combination is therefore comparatively high.

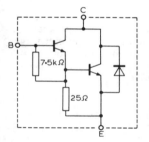

Fig 3.52. Power regulator based on the Darlington-pair connection (B, C and E are the base, collector and emitter of the equivalent single transistor)

Fig 3.55. 100kHz crystal oscillator using part of Motorola CD4007 ic

is shown diagrammatically in Fig 3.52. The two biasing resistors make this arrangement depart from being a true Darlington pair. The diode offers protection in case of reversed connections and surges.

Cascode circuit

This amplifier provides significant amplification of radio frequencies with good stability, and the basic circuit is shown in Fig 3.53. Transistor TR1 operates as a common emitter amplifier, the input impedance being fairly low. TR2 operates as a common-base amplifier: its input impedance is very low and its output impedance comparatively high. Practically no positive feedback takes place between the output of TR2 and the input of TR1. The CA3028 can be used as a cascode amplifier (see Fig 3.54).

This combination of high gain and high input resistance is used in a Motorola ic, the basic circuit of which is given in Fig 3.51. The input resistance R_{in} is 70kΩ. The output resistance R_{out} is 9kΩ.

The resistor R_E is made up of several resistors in series, with suitable tapping points. The diode D1 is formed on the chip near to TR5. A rise in temperature will cause TR5 to conduct more readily. This temperature rise also causes D1 to conduct more readily, ie its resistance is reduced, thus reducing the forward bias and stabilizing the circuit.

Darlington-pair transistors are often used in power-regulation circuits. Lambda Electronics type PMD12K

CMOS devices

Complementary-symmetry metal-oxide semiconductor (cmos) devices are now widely used. They have very much higher impedances and generally consume lower power at lower supply voltages. Fabrication of npn and pnp bipolar transistors on one chip (substrate) is difficult, but if FETs rather than bipolar transistors are formed it is comparatively simple and cheap, and both logic and linear devices are manufactured. Fig 3.55 is the circuit of a 100kHz calibration oscillator using a third of a CD4007 integrated circuit.

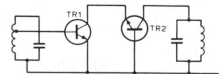

Fig 3.53. Basic cascode circuit (signal path only shown)

CHAPTER 4

Radio receivers

Before discussing radio receivers, it is necessary to explain certain terms used to define their characteristics.

Sensitivity is the ability of a receiver to receive weak signals. The sensitivity of a receiver is normally quoted as being that level of signal which produces a standard ratio of signal-to-background noise, eg $1\mu V$ input to give not less than 10dB signal-to-noise ratio. This means that a $1\mu V$ signal will be such that the level of the signal is about three times the level of the noise with the antenna removed and the receiver correctly terminated. The sensitivity of a communication receiver can usually be varied by means of an rf gain control. For broadcast receiving equipment the sensitivity is often quoted as the input voltage modulated at 30 per cent which produces 50mW power at the loudspeaker terminals.

Selectivity is the ability of a receiver to receive one signal and disregard others on adjacent frequencies. On crowded amateur bands it is necessary for stations to operate on frequencies very close to each other. In order to be able to receive the desired signal with the minimum amount of adjacent channel interference, a receiver with a high selectivity must be used. Selectivity may be quoted, for example, as follows: 2·5kHz at 6dB down; 4·1kHz at 60dB down.

Bandwidth. A receiver with high selectivity is said to have a narrow bandwidth. In the above example, the receiver has a bandwidth of 2·5kHz at 6dB down.

Frequency stability is the ability of a receiver to remain tuned to the desired signal. If a receiver is not stable it is said to *drift*. Stability is determined by the design and construction of the oscillator stage in a receiver.

Automatic gain control (agc) is the automatic control of the sensitivity of a superheterodyne receiver by the strength of the signal to which the receiver is tuned. For weak signals, the sensitivity needs to be high, but for strong signals a low sensitivity suffices. AGC is useful when there is fading on a signal; the sensitivity is varied in accordance with the signal to produce an almost constant audio output level.

Tuned radio frequency receiver

The tuned radio frequency (trf) receiver has limited characteristics; in particular, its rather low selectivity means that it does not have a great deal of application in present-day amateur radio. Nevertheless it is a useful beginner's receiver, particularly as a constructional project. It is useful also as a basis for the study of more complex circuits. Fig 4.1 is a block diagram of a three-stage trf receiver.

RF amplifier

The principal purpose of the rf amplifier stage is to select and amplify the required incoming signal. In a trf receiver it also prevents the antenna from affecting the operation of the following stage, and reduces the risk of radiation by the antenna of the signal generated by the detector stage when it is operating in an oscillating condition.

The rf amplifier increases the sensitivity and selectivity of the receiver. Further improvement may be obtained by the addition of another rf amplifier stage, but high amplification may cause instability unless the shielding of the input and output stages is well-nigh perfect.

Detector

The detector stage in a trf receiver has two functions. First, it converts the rf signal to an audio frequency signal. Second, it provides feedback near the signal frequency in order to permit the reception of continuous-wave telegraphy (cw). The detector circuit normally used in a trf receiver also provides selectivity and amplification at radio and audio frequencies.

AF amplifier

This stage amplifies the af output from the detector and feeds a loudspeaker or headphones. The circuit normally includes a gain control to vary the level of amplification.

Typical circuit

Fig 4.2 shows the circuit of a three-stage trf receiver. TR1 is an rf amplifier, the gate circuit of which is tuned to the required signal frequency. The antenna is inductively coupled to the input circuit. Bias is achieved by the gate resistor and the resistor in the source circuit of the field-effect transistor. The latter resistor is bypassed for rf by a capacitor.

The output from the stage is taken from the drain of

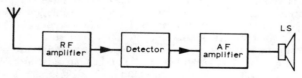

Fig 4.1. Block diagram of three-stage trf receiver

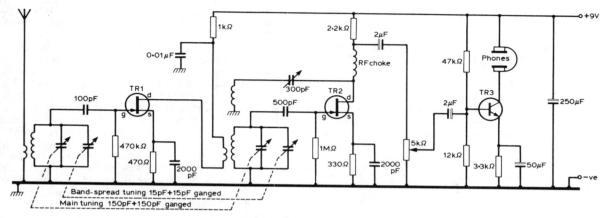

Fig 4.2.   Circuit of trf receiver

the transistor by the link coil coupled to the next stage. TR2 is a fet operating as a detector, and regeneration is provided by the feedback from the drain to the gate of the transistor, this being adjustable by means of the variable capacitor. The regeneration may be peaked for optimum sensitivity and selectivity, and may be advanced into an oscillating condition for the reception of cw. The tuned circuit in the gate of the transistor is tuned to the signal frequency and the tuning capacitor is ganged with that of the rf amplifier tuned circuit. In a practical circuit the coils would use adjustable cores and small trimming capacitors would be included for alignment purposes.

Tuning is by the two ganged 150pF capacitors, one for the rf stage and the other in the detection stage. Across these main tuning capacitors are *bandspread* capacitors of much lower value. These permit a small portion of the tuning range of the main tuning capacitors to be spread over the whole scale of the bandspread capacitors. Thus bandspread tuning makes tuning considerably easier on the short-wave bands.

The superheterodyne receiver

The basic limitations of inadequate selectivity and lack of gain of the straight receiver led to the development of the *supersonic heterodyne* principle in the mid-'twenties. In the supersonic heterodyne (or *superhet* as it is colloquially known) receiver, the frequency of the incoming signals is changed to a fixed fairly-low

frequency at which most of the gain and all the selectivity of the receiver is obtained.

Because this fixed frequency is lower than the signal frequency but higher than the audio frequency, it became known in the early days of the superhet as the *intermediate frequency* (i.f.). As the circuits operating at the intermediate frequency, once adjusted, need no further tuning, high amplification and good stability are possible.

In order to convert the signal frequency to the intermediate frequency, a frequency-mixing process is necessary. In the mixer the signal frequency is mixed with the output of an oscillator, the frequency of which is varied by the receiver tuning control. This oscillator is called the *local oscillator*.

The resulting intermediate frequency is amplified and fed to detector and audio amplifier stages which are similar in function to those used in the straight receiver already discussed. The output of the i.f. amplifier is used to provide a voltage, the amplitude of which is proportional to the amplitude of the input signal. This is used to control the gain of the receiver (*automatic gain control* or *agc*) to compensate for variation of the received signal.

In order to receive telegraphy (cw) signals, it is necessary to provide a signal to beat with the intermediate frequency to produce a beat note which is audible. This signal is generated by the *beat frequency oscillator* (bfo) which operates at the same frequency as the i.f. but is variable about this frequency by about ±3kHz.

Fig 4.3 is a block diagram of the simplest possible

Fig 4.3.   Block diagram of simplest superheterodyne receiver

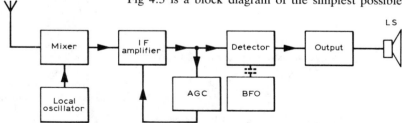

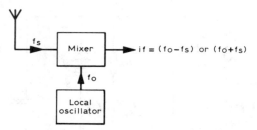

Fig 4.4. The superheterodyne mixing process

superhet receiver. The basic design implications of each stage of a superhet receiver will now be discussed in greater detail.

Mixers

The mixing process of the superhet receiver is shown in Fig 4.4. As is inevitable in the mixing process, two frequencies appear at the mixer output, these being the sum and difference of the signal and local oscillator frequencies. Only one of these is wanted as the intermediate frequency and in fact only one frequency is accepted by the following i.f. amplifier. The reason for this will be seen later.

To take a simple numerical example, assume an i.f. of 500kHz; if the signal frequency is 1,000kHz, the frequency of the local oscillator must be 1,500వkHz: see Fig 4.5(a).

$$i.f. = f_o - f_s$$
$$500\text{kHz} = 1,500\text{kHz} - 1,000\text{kHz}$$

A very strong signal on a frequency of 2,000kHz, should there happen to be one, can also produce an intermediate frequency of 500kHz: see Fig 4.5(b). This is because

$$i.f. = f_s - f_o$$
$$500\text{kHz} = 2,000\text{kHz} - 1,500\text{kHz}$$

Thus two signals, the wanted one on 1,000kHz and an unwanted one on 2,000kHz, can both result in an

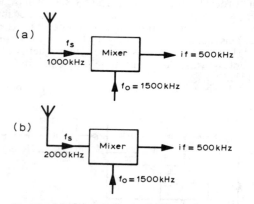

Fig 4.5. (a) Wanted signal. (b) Image frequency

intermediate frequency of 500kHz. The unwanted signal (on 2,000kHz) is called the *second channel* or *image*.

This phenomenon is manifest as the reception of two signals apparently on the same frequency and at the same time. The reception of the unwanted signal is known as *second-channel (or image) interference* and it is a *spurious response* of the receiver in question. It is seen that the second channel is numerically twice the intermediate frequency away from the wanted signal.

Second-channel interference occurs only when there is a signal on the second channel which is strong enough to operate the mixer. The situation is most likely to arise when the mixer circuit is inadequately screened and when the antenna is fed directly to the mixer, ie when there are no rf stages to provide isolation.

The most common example of second-channel interference is the reception of 19m broadcast stations in the 20m amateur band on a simple all-wave receiver having an i.f. of about 465kHz (the frequency separation between the 19m and 20m bands is about twice 465kHz).

As the existence of second-channel interference depends on the response of the signal input circuit of the mixer to a frequency which is separated from the resonant frequency of the input circuit by twice the i.f., it is clear that increasing the i.f. will reduce the incidence of image interference.

Fig 4.6 shows a typical mixer/oscillator arrangement using transistors. Bipolar transistors, FETs and MOSFETs are all suitable for this application and the typical arrangement shown here is a Colpitts oscillator, the collector supply being stabilized by a 6·8V zener diode. The oscillator output is fed to a buffer stage to provide isolation between the oscillator and the mixer. The mixer uses a dual-gate mosfet which is particularly suitable for mixer applications, having two gates. The input (rf) tuned circuit is between gate 1 and earth, and the output (i.f.) tuned circuit is between the drain and the 12V supply. The oscillator voltage from the buffer is applied to gate 2.

The receiver local oscillator has the same requirements of frequency stability etc as the vfo in a transmitter. The discussion of vfo stability in Chapter 5 is therefore equally applicable to receiver local oscillators. The situation is complicated by the necessity for the receiver local oscillator to be switched to cover a number of frequency bands.

Generally the local oscillator frequency is on the high side of the signal frequency. The reason for this is as follows. Assume a receiver tunes to signals in the range 1,500kHz to 4,500kHz and has an i.f. of 1,000kHz. The signal frequency range has ratio of 3 to 1 (4,500 to 1,500) and because $f \propto 1/\sqrt{C}$, the change in capacitance must therefore have a ratio of 9 to 1, say, 20pF to 180pF. The oscillator could tune from 500kHz to 3,500kHz, a frequency range of 7 to 1 which will require a capacitance change of 49 to 1, or it could tune from 2,500kHz to 5,500kHz, a frequency range of 2·2 to 1, this requiring a capacitance change of about 5 to 1. A capacitor which can vary from, say, 20pF to 100pF is more practical than one tuning from 20pF to 980pF.

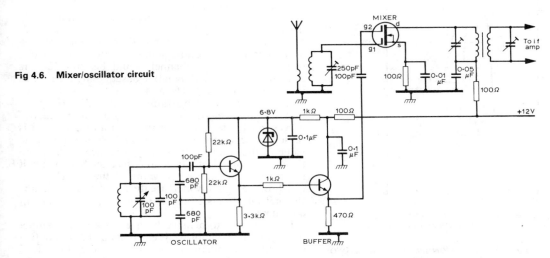

Fig 4.6. Mixer/oscillator circuit

Tracking. The tuned circuit of the local oscillator must maintain throughout its tuning range a constant frequency separation equal to the i.f. from the mixer tuned circuit. This requisite is known as *tracking*.

The need for tracking arises because the oscillator and mixer tuned circuits cannot be identical in inductance and capacitance. For example, for a signal frequency range of 5–10MHz with an i.f. of 500kHz, the mixer tuned circuit must cover 10MHz to 5MHz (ratio 2:1), while if the oscillator is on the high side, its tuned circuit must cover 10·5MHz to 5·5MHz (ratio 1·9:1). Thus the oscillator tuning capacitor often has a smaller capacitance than the mixer capacitor.

The wider the frequency range, the more difficult tracking becomes; in practice the optimum solution generally considered is that tracking should be correct at both ends of the tuning range and also at a point near the middle.

Tracking is generally achieved in the better class of receiver by the careful adjustment of a small trimming capacitor in parallel with the oscillator tuning capacitor at the high-frequency end of each range, and the inductance of the tuning coil (by means of a dust core) at the low-frequency end.

RF amplifiers

RF amplifiers, ie tuned amplifiers operating at the signal frequency, are employed in the majority of high-quality receivers and also in transceivers. The tuning is ganged with the mixer/local oscillator tuning control.

Basically, an rf stage improves the sensitivity of the receiver, ie it increases the signal/noise ratio. The additional selectivity resulting from the extra tuned circuits may be advantageous in a number of ways, ie the chance of second-channel interference is reduced, as is radiation from the local oscillator via the antenna. This additional rf selectivity is always useful.

The older receivers with an i.f. of around 465kHz always employed two rf stages and the second-channel interference then only became unacceptable above about 30MHz. If the i.f. frequency was 1·6MHz, one rf stage could be considered to be adequate.

In modern practice, a high i.f. (9MHz) may be used without any rf amplification before the mixer. However the optimum design of the rf/mixer combination of a superhet receiver is complex, particularly at vhf, and beyond the scope of this manual.

The i.f. amplifier

The output of the mixer is fed to the *i.f. amplifier*. This consists of one, two or sometimes three tuned stages of amplification operating at the intermediate frequency. A typical i.f amplifier stage is shown in Fig 4.7.

The keystone of the i.f. amplifier is the tuned circuit connected to the collector of the transistor. This is normally associated with a similar tuned circuit, the

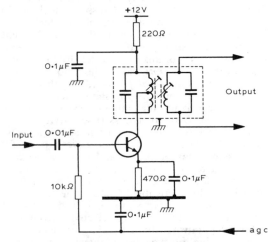

Fig 4.7. I.F. amplifier circuit

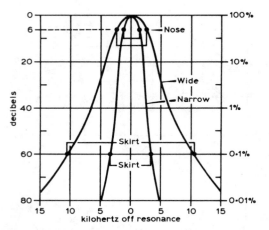

Fig 4.8. Typical overall selectivity of i.f. amplifier based on tuned circuits (from *A Guide to Amateur Radio*)

pair being known as an *i.f. transformer* (ift). These two tuned circuits are designed as a coupled pair (see Chapter 2) and are located together in a screening can. As shown in Fig 4.7 these two circuits are resonated by tuning the inductors. Alternatively the inductors may be fixed and tuning is then by small variable capacitors.

Because the i.f. amplifier is tuned it will respond to one frequency only, the sum *or* the difference frequency of the mixer output, but not to both. In the example quoted earlier the difference frequency (wanted) was 500kHz, while the unwanted (sum) frequency was 2,500kHz. An amplifier tuned to 500kHz will have zero response at 2,500kHz.

The selectivity of an i.f. amplifier is determined entirely by the design of the coupled tuned circuits which make up the i.f. transformers and by the loading of the windings by the preceding or following stages. It is relatively unimportant whether these transformers are coupled together by valves or transistors.

Typical overall i.f. selectivity curves are shown in Fig 4.8. In this diagram, the change in response is shown in two ways; on the left-hand side in decibels, which is the correct way to express changes in level, and on the right as a percentage, maximum response being 100 per cent. There are two widths of this curve which are important, the *nose* width and the *skirt* width. The ratio of these is often referred to as the *shape factor;* ideally this should be close to unity. In practice the shape factor may be about 2·5–6·0 which may mean that the skirt bandwidth can be up to 18kHz or so. The skirt selectivity is normally considered to be more important as it is a measure of the bandwidth over which a very powerful unwanted signal may be received. This is particularly important in a receiver for use in the amateur bands where there is a very large range of signal strengths.

Ideally it should be possible to modify the bandwidth to meet conditions and types of signal. In the simplest case this would mean switching selectivity from 2·5–3kHz for telephony to about 0·4kHz for telegraphy. Ways of achieving this have been indicated in Chapter

2; however, these often present difficult electrical and mechanical design problems.

The value of the intermediate frequency in the early days of the superhet receiver was 100–110kHz; with the increasing number of broadcast stations coming into operation, second-channel interference became serious (the second channel would be 200–220kHz away from the wanted signal). Consequently the i.f. was increased to 455–470kHz, and this value is still in general use for receivers operating at up to 30MHz.

It will be seen from the discussion on resonance curves in Chapter 2 that, as the Q of a tuned circuit is reasonably constant, the bandwidth becomes less as the value of the resonant frequency is reduced. Therefore to improve the selectivity, ie to reduce the bandwidth, it is necessary to reduce the value of the i.f. This step will, however, greatly increase the likelihood of second-channel interference, as has been discussed earlier in this chapter.

It is possible to achieve both good second-channel performance and improved selectivity by the use of two different intermediate frequencies, eg a high first i.f. of commonly 1·6MHz which is then converted to a very-low second i.f. such as 85kHz by means of a second mixer/local oscillator. This arrangement is the *double superhet* and is capable of a very good performance. For example, two i.f. stages at 85kHz, that is three i.f. transformers (six tuned circuits), will give a nose bandwidth of 2·5–3kHz and a skirt bandwidth of not much more than about 6–7kHz when correctly tuned. The high first i.f. of 1·6MHz ensures a perfectly satisfactory second-channel characteristic.

The most commonly used intermediate frequencies are 85kHz, 455–470kHz and 1·6MHz but others, such as 50, 100, 560, 735 and 915kHz, have been used in particular receivers.

A better i.f. selectivity characteristic can be obtained by the use of a *bandpass filter*. One such version is based on the use of quartz crystals; two, three or four pairs of crystals carefully matched in frequency may be used. The older general-purpose receiver invariably used a crystal filter which employed a single crystal in conjunction with a phasing capacitor. This simple arrangement gave a nose bandwidth of less than 0·5kHz and so was very useful for receiving telegraphy. However, the skirt bandwidth, being determined solely by the tuned circuits, was often very wide.

Another form of bandpass filter is the mechanical type. This is a mechanically resonant device which receives electrical energy, converts it into a mechanical vibration which is then converted back into electrical energy at the output. The mechanical vibration is set up in a series of six to nine metal discs by the magnetostrictive effect.

Filters of the bandpass type have a much flatter top to the selectivity curve and shape factors of 1·5–2·5. They are made in various bandwidths from 0·5–10kHz at frequencies of commonly 455kHz and 3–9MHz. They are compact but tend to be expensive. This type of filter has a sufficiently steep characteristic (ie low shape factor) to filter out the unwanted sideband of a

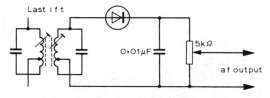

Fig 4.9. Basic circuit of diode detector

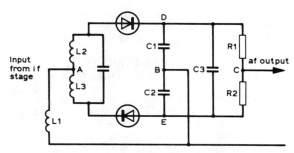

Fig 4.11. Basic circuit of the ratio detector

double-sideband signal and is therefore the basis of the filter method of single-sideband generation. It is also used in the receive function of the ssb transceiver (see Chapter 5).

The detector

The purpose of the detector is to rectify or demodulate the output of the i.f. amplifier, in order that the modulation originally superimposed upon the carrier wave at the transmitter can be recovered as a varying direct voltage, which can be amplified and converted into sound by the loudspeaker.

If the carrier is unmodulated, as in telegraphy, it is necessary to mix with the i.f. amplifier output another signal of a slightly different frequency which is generated by a *beat frequency oscillator* (bfo) in order to produce a difference frequency in the audible range, ie an audible beat note which is then demodulated by the detector.

Diode or envelope detector. The simplest and most commonly used detector is a single diode operating as a half-wave rectifier as shown in Fig 4.9. The output is developed across the resistor (the diode load) and then fed to the following audio amplifier.

This arrangement is also known as an *envelope detector* as its object is to recover the modulation envelope. It is the normally used circuit for the detection of an amplitude-modulated signal and for cw telegraphy when used with a bfo.

Detection of an fm signal. A frequency-modulated (fm) signal can be resolved by the envelope detector by detuning the signal from the peak of the response to a

point about half-way down the curve as shown in Fig 4.10. It will be seen that a frequency variation is converted into a variation of amplitude. This is not a particularly good system as its efficiency depends on the slope of the response curve. This should not be too steep; in other words the selectivity should not be too high, a condition which is directly opposed to the requirements of an effective amateur-bands receiver.

Optimum resolution of an fm signal requires a special form of detector. The most effective circuit is the Foster-Seeley discriminator. This is capable of excellent linearity over a wide band, ie it produces very little distortion. It is however susceptible to amplitude variations and is therefore normally preceded by one or possibly two limiter stages to remove all variations of amplitude.

A simpler arrangement which is widely used in entertainment receivers is the ratio detector shown in Fig 4.11. In the circuit L2 and L3 are made equal in value, as are C1 and C2, and R1 and R2. The circuit between points A and B can be regarded as a form of "bridge", with L2 C1 and L3 C2 forming the arms. The tertiary winding L1 acts as a constant supply, the "bridge" being loaded by the resistors R1 R2.

At resonance the sum (with due regard to phase) of the voltages across L1 plus L2 will be equal to that across L1 plus L3 and no voltage will be present between points B and C. Off resonance, ie as the incoming frequency varies with modulation, the voltage across L1 plus L2 will be different from the voltage across L1 plus L3. The bridge is now unbalanced and a voltage exists between points B and C. The total current flowing between points D and E will not alter with a change of signal frequency, only the ratio of the voltages across C1 and C2 will alter. This voltage in step with the varying signal frequency constitutes the af output.

Because the voltage across C1 plus C2 is normally constant, a capacitor C3 of about $8\mu F$ is connected as shown. Any rapid changes in the amplitude of the incoming signal will be smoothed out by this capacitor; it acts as a limiter to rapid changes of signal amplitude. The ratio detector therefore need not be preceded by a limiter.

Detection of an ssb signal. The detection of a single-sideband (ssb) signal necessitates the insertion of a

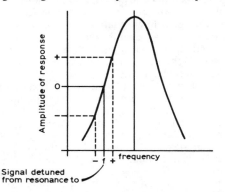

Fig 4.10. Conversion of an fm signal into an amplitude variation by detuning the signal

signal into the detector to simulate the carrier wave which was suppressed in the transmitter. This signal is generated in the receiver by the *carrier insertion oscillator* (cio).

This function can be fulfilled by the bfo of an a.m./cw receiver, and by the use of the usual diode envelope detector reasonably satisfactory results may be obtained. However the diode detector system has directly opposite requirements for optimum cw detection and optimum ssb detection. CW use requires a very small input signal from the bfo whereas ssb detection requires a much larger bfo signal. As the bfo injection voltage is never adjustable, it should be set to suit whichever mode is of most interest. A large bfo voltage is likely to affect the operation of the agc system as discussed later in this chapter.

The *product detector* is the preferred circuit arrangement for the resolution of an ssb signal. This is a frequency mixer circuit, and one of several varieties is shown in Fig 4.12. The frequencies involved in this mixing process are the receiver i.f. and the frequency to which the bfo (or cio) is set. The bfo frequency will have been adjusted to produce an acceptable audible beat frequency. The mixer output frequencies are the audio frequency required (difference) and the sum of the intermediate and bfo frequencies—the following stages will not operate at the sum frequency. The circuit shown uses a fet. The i.f. amplifier output is connected to the gate and the bfo/cio injection voltage is taken to the source.

The product detector is also a very effective demodulator of cw telegraphy signals. A further advantage is that the bfo injection voltage necessary is small and is the same for ssb and cw.

Thus the modern all-mode receiver will include two detectors, ie a diode envelope detector for a.m. and a product detector for ssb/cw. The vhf receiver is most likely to include also a ratio detector for fm.

Beat frequency oscillator
The bfo is a conventional oscillator which operates at the i.f. of the receiver. Its frequency is generally variable ±3–4kHz by means of a front-panel control in order to provide the audible beat note discussed earlier, and to enable this note to be set at a frequency which is acceptable to the operator. The bfo is switched on and off by a front-panel control. Coupling between the bfo and detector is very loose—5pF or so, or even by stray capacitance.

Carrier insertion oscillator
The carrier insertion oscillator generates a signal to simulate the carrier wave which has been suppressed in the transmitter. It also performs the same function as the bfo when receiving telegraphy.

In order to achieve the frequency stability necessary in an ssb system, the cio would be crystal controlled, a separate crystal being used for each sideband. The crystal frequencies are typically ±1·5kHz from the intermediate frequency.

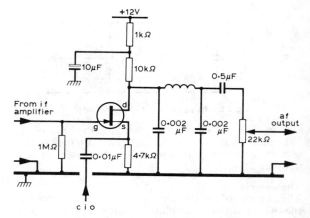

Fig 4.12.   Circuit of product detector

Automatic gain control
Automatic gain control (agc) refers to the control of the gain of the receiver in sympathy with the strength of the received signal. The object is to ensure that the output of the receiver remains constant or nearly so, irrespective of the incoming signal strength which may undergo considerable variation due to propagation conditions (fading) or simply due to the relative signal strengths of the several stations operating in a net.

The basis of the operation of an agc system is as follows. As the received signal strength increases so does the receiver output, and a sample of this is taken from some point in the output stages and fed back in such a way as to reduce the overall gain of the receiver. As the signal fades or a weaker signal is being received the output falls and a lower control voltage results, hence increasing the receiver gain.

The gain of the i.f. amplifier is controlled by feeding the agc voltage to the base of each transistor in order to vary the emitter current and hence the collector voltage. This arises as a result of the voltage drop across a series resistor in the collector supply.

The point in the receiver from which the agc control voltage is taken depends mainly on its complexity, and inevitably it is after the i.f. amplifier. In a simple receiver the agc voltage would be taken from the detector diode circuit. A separate diode to develop the agc voltage, fed via a small capacitor (say, 33pF) from the same point as the detector diode, provides a more flexible arrangement from the design aspect and is generally to be preferred. In a high-grade communication receiver, there may be a separate i.f. amplifier stage which feeds only the agc diode. This enables a much greater degree of control to be obtained.

There is no standard application of the agc voltage to the receiver stages. This depends on the design of the receiver—agc is certainly applied to the i.f. stages, but for reasons which are beyond the scope of this manual, it is often not applied to the first rf amplifier or to the mixer.

The simplest arrangement is shown in Fig 4.13.

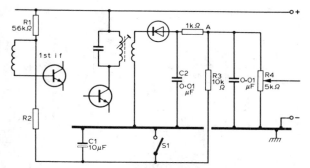

Fig 4.13. Basic configuration of agc system

R1–R4 form a divider which provides the diode with a small forward bias to make it more sensitive to weak signals. Any increase or decrease in voltage at point A due to changing signal strength will be applied to the base of the first i.f. amplifier transistor. Any audio component is filtered out by R2 and C1.

Effective agc for cw reception presents a number of difficulties. The rectified bfo voltage may well reduce the gain even in the absence of a signal. For this reason agc is often switched out of operation (by S1 in Fig 4.13, ganged to the bfo on/off switch) when receiving cw signals.

A receiver intended for cw/ssb reception will invariably employ a product detector. This provides much better isolation between the locally generated bfo/cio voltage and the agc circuit, and hence agc on cw reception is much more effective. The agc voltage in a cw/ssb receiver is sometimes obtained by sampling and rectifying the audio at some point in the audio amplifier since a carrier wave is not transmitted. There is not much to choose between the two methods.

By suitable design, an agc system can provide a characteristic which exhibits little change in output level (less than 4dB) for a very large change in input signal (90–100dB). However, a more significant characteristic, particularly for ssb with the intermittent nature of the signal and its syllabic variations, is the speed of operation of the agc system. The agc must take effect quickly—the *attack time* must be of the order of 2ms but the *release* should be much slower, about 200–300ms. These times are governed by the time constants (ie products of resistance and capacitance) in the agc circuit.

Audio stages
The audio side of the communication receiver is conventional in every way, bearing in mind the restricted audio bandwidth necessary for communication purposes. The audio power output is normally 1–2W peak to a small loudspeaker located within the receiver cabinet. Generally provision is made to plug in a pair of headphones at the input side of the output stage.

The inclusion of some form of additional selectivity or filter in the audio chain is not uncommon in the more complex receiver, particularly in the older general-purpose receiver.

This may take two forms, one being a sharp notch filter, in which the notch can be tuned across the audio band. The gain in the notch is very much reduced and so it can attenuate a particular interfering frequency. Alternatively a sharp peak of amplification at a particular frequency, say 1,000Hz, may be provided, and by careful adjustment of the bfo to give a 1,000Hz beat note the overall selectivity for cw may be improved.

Calibration oscillator
This is a conventional crystal oscillator operating usually at 100kHz. It provides a calibration "pip" every 100kHz throughout the receiver tuning range. Generally provision is made to adjust the tuning scale or the pointer slightly to enable the calibration to be corrected at the 100kHz points. In the better class of equipment there are facilities for checking the accuracy of the crystal frequency against a standard frequency transmission.

Noise limiters
Most electrical interference to reception results from the short pulse of energy, often of large amplitude, which may be radiated every time a spark occurs. A spark may occur intermittently, eg from a faulty switch or thermostat, or regularly, eg from vehicle ignition systems or commutator motors. Thus the amplitude-modulation receiver, and this of course includes ssb systems, is particularly susceptible to this form of interference.

A noise limiter is essentially a shunt circuit employing one or two diodes which act as clippers or limiters to remove the large variations of amplitude which exceed the modulation level. The noise limiter is normally situated after the detector circuits and includes a control to vary the clipping level. Fig 4.14 shows the mode of operation of a noise limiter.

Signal-strength meters
Most commercial receivers now incorporate a signal-strength meter (S-meter). Normally this consists of a low-reading milliammeter, often in a bridge circuit, which is used to monitor the agc control voltage. This of course varies in sympathy with the incoming signal.

The meter is calibrated in S-units up to S9 and

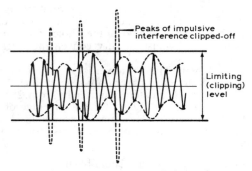

Fig 4.14. Illustration of noise limiter action

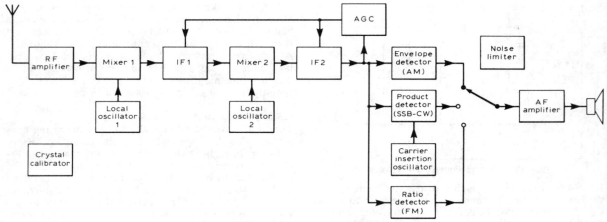

Fig 4.15.   Block diagram of double-superheterodyne receiver

decibels up to 40 or 60 above S9. There is no generally agreed definition of an S-unit (it may be 4 or 6dB) or of the zero point of the meter. Unless an S-meter has been specially calibrated against a signal generator on each band, no great reliance should be placed on its readings.

A complete receiver

A block diagram of a double-superhet receiver incorporating the points discussed so far in this chapter is shown in Fig 4.15. For obvious reasons this is known as a *communication receiver*—it is intended for communication purposes and not entertainment. As a point of interest, many of the early amateur communication receivers were all-wave broadcast receivers to which a bfo was fitted and then installed in a metal cabinet.

Consideration of Fig 4.15 raises the query as to which local oscillator is tuned—in fact either can be tuned as follows:

(a) LO1 tuned and LO2 fixed frequency
(b) LO1 fixed frequency and LO2 tuned.

For stability reasons, the fixed-frequency oscillator should be crystal controlled.

The arrangement (a) allows, by appropriate design of the rf/mixer/local oscillator tuned circuits, each amateur band to be spread over the whole of the tuning scale which is obviously a very convenient arrangement.

In arrangement (b) the rf/mixer/local oscillator tuned circuits are designed to cover only a small range, usually 500kHz. Each amateur band apart from 28MHz can be covered in one range; for full coverage of the 28MHz band four 500kHz segments are required. The switched frequency ranges covered in this arrangement are therefore:

1,500–2,000kHz covering 160m band
3,500–4,000kHz   „   80m   „

7,000–7,500kHz   covering   40m band
14,000–14,500kHz   „   20m   „
21,000–21,500kHz   „   15m   „
28,000–28,500kHz ⎫
28,500–29,000kHz ⎬   „   10m   „
29,000–29,500kHz ⎪
29,500–30,000kHz ⎭

The local oscillator frequency (crystal controlled) is chosen to convert the above rf ranges to the i.f. range required, which may be for example 5,000–5,500kHz. The rest of the receiver is therefore a standard single-superhet having a single tuning range of 5,000–5,500kHz.

This is a very common arrangement—it provides a constant tuning rate on each band which is slow enough for satisfactory tuning of an ssb signal, ie a tuning rate of no more than 25kHz per revolution of the tuning knob. This configuration is now the basis of many amateur communication receivers.

VHF receivers

The principles described above will of course apply to receivers for the vhf and higher frequency ranges. The intermediate frequency will be higher, typically 5MHz to 12MHz and the i.f. bandwidth may well be greater to accommodate the slightly poorer frequency stability of the vhf (uhf) transmitter.

Fig 4.15 illustrates the principle of the conversion of a receiver tuning range to a different range, ie the basic receiver covering 5,000 to 5,500kHz is converted to cover each amateur band in turn.

A converter, which is essentially the rf/mixer/LO1 section of Fig 4.15 with LO1 crystal controlled, is very commonly used to extend the coverage of an hf communication receiver to the vhf/uhf amateur bands. The output of the mixer is taken to the antenna socket of the main receiver by coaxial cable to avoid the pick-up of unwanted signals on this lead.

Direct-conversion receivers

The basis of the superhet is the conversion of all signals to a fixed intermediate frequency followed by demodulation and af amplification to drive a loudspeaker. The incoming signals can however be converted directly to af, and thus a much-simplified type of superhet results. This is known as the *synchrodyne*; it is not a new principle but has become popular recently in amateur radio as the *direct-conversion receiver*.

The local oscillator operates very close to the signal frequency so that the output of the mixer (which is equivalent to a product detector) is in the af range. This is normally followed by a low-pass filter to restrict the audio bandwidth to about 3kHz and a high-gain audio amplifier to drive a loudspeaker.

The mixer is usually preceded by a simple untuned rf stage. Due to the difficulties of making a sufficiently stable oscillator, the direct-conversion receiver is often restricted to the lower-frequency amateur bands where it is capable of surprisingly good performance, although obviously not in the same class as a good-quality communication receiver.

The oscillator followed by a buffer amplifier can also be used to drive a power amplifier, thus creating a low-power transceiver. A number of these are now available commercially.

CHAPTER 5

Transmitters

The harmonic relationships between the previously available hf amateur bands, and between these bands and certain tv channels, have resulted in a fairly standard approach to transmitter design in order to minimize the possibility of causing interference to television (tvi).

These relationships are listed in Tables 5.1 and 5.2 which indicate:

(a) The harmonic relationship of some hf amateur bands. Thus the appropriate portions of the frequency range of an oscillator having a maximum frequency coverage of 1,750–2,000kHz could be multiplied in frequency to cover all these bands.

(b) The harmonic relationship between the amateur bands and some tv frequencies, particularly Channel 1. Hence the avoidance of unwanted harmonic output is very important.

While it may now be reasonably argued that Band 1 tv receivers are obsolescent, frequencies in this band, ie 41–68MHz, will ultimately be used by other services which will probably be susceptible to this form of interference. Consequently it is likely that the design philosophy resulting from the above will be applied, particularly to home-constructed equipment, for many years to come.

An alternative but much more complex approach uses a mixer to combine the outputs of a variable frequency oscillator and a fixed frequency (crystal) oscillator. By switching in other crystals of the appropriate frequency, this arrangement can produce an output in any band required, and so it can deal with bands which are not in harmonic relationship, eg the new 10, 18 and 24MHz bands. For other reasons, this type of circuit must be used in the ssb transmitter and so will be discussed later in this chapter.

Table 5.2
Band 1 tv frequencies and amateur band harmonics likely to create interference

Channel	Sound	Vision	Most likely harmonics	
1	41·5	45	2 × 21	3 × 14
2	48·25	51·75		
3	53·25	56·75	2 × 28	4 × 14
4	58·25	61·75	2 × 28	
5	63·25	66·75	3 × 21	

Typical transmitter

The standard arrangement of an hf bands transmitter is shown in the block diagram of Fig 5.1 and consists of a frequency-determination circuit followed by one or more frequency-multiplication circuits which feed the power amplifier. This amplifier, as its name suggests, amplifies the output of the frequency multiplier and feeds the antenna.

The combination of the vfo and frequency multiplier is known as the *exciter*. The output of each multiplier stage must be switched in turn to the input of the power amplifier as shown in Fig 5.2.

Transmitter design

To permit *netting*, a variable frequency oscillator (vfo) is normally used as the frequency-determining circuit in the hf bands transmitter.

Any of the many different oscillator circuits may be used as the vfo, but the generally used circuits are the Colpitts or the Clapp-Gouriet.

The vfo
The factor of prime importance in the design of the vfo is its frequency stability, because

Table 5.1
Harmonically related hf bands

Limits of hf bands (kHz)	Equivalent to
1,810– 2,000	1,810–2,000 × 1
3,500– 3,800	1,750–1,900 × 2
7,000– 7,100	1,750–1,775 × 4
14,000–14,350	1,750–1,794 × 8
21,000–21,450	1,750–1,787 × 12
28,000–29,700	1,750–1,856 × 16

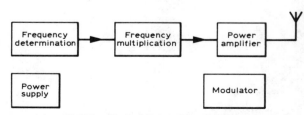

Fig 5.1. Block diagram of transmitter

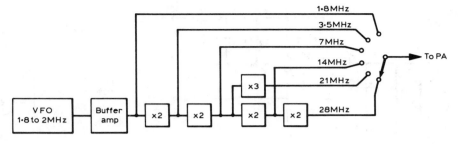

(a) the frequency must not drift outside the permitted band;

(b) the frequency must not drift outside the pass band of the receiver which is tuned to the transmission.

Frequency stability is particularly important in a transmitter intended for single sideband operation.

The frequency of an oscillator is determined by the resonant frequency of its tuned circuit, thus

$$f = \frac{1}{2\pi\sqrt{LC}}$$

Therefore the magnitude of L, the inductance of the coil, and of C, the capacitance necessary to tune L to the required frequency, should not vary under any circumstances.

The factors which may cause L and C to vary are

(a) mechanical shock:

    (i) the coil must be tightly wound (preferably under tension) on a grooved former, preferably ceramic or made from a low-loss material.

    (ii) The variable capacitor should be of good quality, ie mechanically sound;

    (iii) The wiring between the coil and capacitor should be as short and rigid as possible, so that it cannot move.

(b) change in ambient temperature:

The coil and capacitor inevitably have a temperature coefficient, the effects of which are manifest as a mechanical movement, hence (a)(i) and (a)(ii) above are doubly important.

Preferably the coil should be air cored as any form of dust-iron core will cause an additional variation of the inductance of the coil with temperature. The effect of temperature on the tuned circuit may be minimized by locating it as far as possible from any source of heat.

In the Colpitts and similar oscillators, the effect of change in transistor capacitances is minimized by the particular circuit configuration, see Fig 5.3. C1 and C2 are large and swamp the transistor capacitances, but they are part of the frequency-determining capacitance, and so their change in value with temperature is important. These capacitors should be of good quality, preferably having mica as the dielectric. These will have a small positive temperature coefficient which may be compensated for by the experimental addition of a

low-value ceramic dielectric capacitor which has a large negative temperature coefficient (C3 in Fig 5.3).

To summarize, the tuned circuit of a vfo must (a) be soundly made, (b) use best-quality components.

External influences on the vfo

The vfo should be considered as a source of a *small* output voltage at a constant frequency, and the power level must be low to avoid generation of excess heat.

The vfo should be very lightly loaded by the following stage; excess loading may ultimately stop the oscillation, and any change in loading, if heavy (eg during keying) may well cause a change in frequency. The vfo should ideally be followed by an isolating stage such as a Class A buffer amplifier.

Variation of supply voltage can cause a change in transistor parameters and hence in frequency. Thus stabilization of the supply voltage is advisable. This is normally achieved by the use of a zener diode (see Chapter 6).

For frequency stability reasons, it is considered inadvisable to key a vfo; furthermore it should operate at the lowest frequency possible. This is because the effects of the likely sources of frequency drift as discussed above, expressed as a percentage of the frequency, increase numerically as the frequency increases. A vfo at 1·8MHz requires a frequency multiplication of 16 times to reach 28MHz, and any drift in the vfo is therefore also multiplied by 16. If operation at 1·8MHz is not required, a vfo frequency of 3·5MHz is a better compromise between multiplication factor (×8 to 28MHz) and vfo stability.

Due to the large difference in permitted power levels between the 1·8MHz band and the other hf bands it is generally more convenient to provide a small separate 1·8MHz transmitter.

It should be noted that some frequency drift is inevitable during the first few minutes of operation after

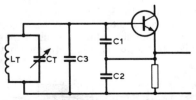

Fig 5.3. Connection between tuned circuit (L_T, C_T) and transistor in Colpitts-type oscillator

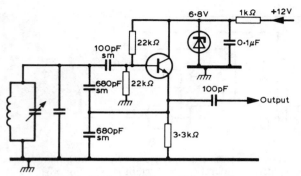

Fig 5.4. Typical Colpitts oscillator circuit

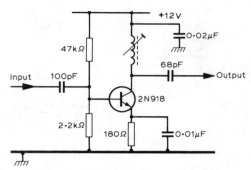

Fig 5.5. Basic circuit of frequency multiplier

switch on from cold; it is the drift after this period which must be reduced to the minimum.

Fig 5.4 is the circuit diagram of a Colpitts vfo.

Frequency multiplication

Frequency multipliers are normally low-power transistors operating in Class C in order to produce a collector current which is rich in harmonics. The circuit of such a stage is shown in Fig 5.5.

The tuned circuit is resonant at $n \times f$, where f is the frequency of the input voltage and n is usually 2 or 3. Higher multiplications may be used but the output is rather low. The tuned circuit may consist of a small coil and variable capacitor or a slug-tuned coil and fixed capacitor. Such a coil may be made to resonate with the stray circuit capacitance (order of 20–25pF) at the higher frequency bands (21 and 28MHz). The output is coupled to the following stage by a capacitor which varies from about 100pF at 1·8MHz to about 22pF at 28MHz.

Exciters for vhf and uhf transmitters

The exciters normally used on the vhf (70MHz and 144MHz) and uhf (432MHz) bands are similar in design to those used on the hf bands, ie a stable frequency source is followed by a series of multipliers. Due to the increased circuit losses at the higher frequencies, a buffer amplifier may be necessary before the output stage.

For stability reasons, crystal oscillators (frequencies in the region of 6MHz, 8MHz or sometimes 12MHz) are most often used, but more complex techniques such as mixer-type vfos and phase-locked loops are now becoming more common. A block diagram of an exciter for 144MHz is shown in Fig 5.6. It should be noted that to prevent tvi, a stage multiplying to 48MHz is avoided.

It will be seen that the addition of a further tripler stage will give an output at 432MHz and that with a slightly different crystal frequency, the first two multiplying stages will provide an output at 70MHz.

Transistor power amplifiers

Transistor rf power amplifiers differ significantly in circuit design from valve amplifiers. This arises mainly because of the much lower input and output impedances of the transistor compared with the thermionic valve. These impedances decrease as the power level increases.

It must be remembered that transistors have very little thermal overload capacity and so the standard precautions for their use are particularly important in high-power amplifiers, ie close attention must be paid to the de-rating factor and heat sinking. Considerable de-rating may be advisable if amplitude modulation is to be used, therefore ssb or nbfm is to be preferred.

Layout and bypassing of the collector supply must be carefully considered to avoid the creation of interference (see Chapter 8). The antenna must be accurately matched to the transmitter output as transistor output stages are more sensitive in this respect than valve stages.

Adjustment and operation are generally more critical.

Power amplifiers at vhf

For low powers, ie less than 25W (output) or so, the transistor is a relatively cheap and very convenient solution, particularly for mobile or portable operation if the power level desired can be obtained from a 12V supply.

The generally preferred output arrangement for a transistor pa at 144MHz is the L-pi circuit. This is a combination of the series-tuned L and the conventional pi circuit.

A typical circuit is shown in Fig 5.7. This uses a Mullard BLY83 and gives an output of 7W for a collector supply voltage of 12V, and 12W at 24V. These powers

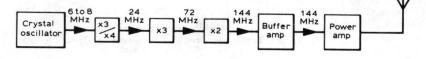

Fig 5.6. Block diagram of 144MHz transmitter

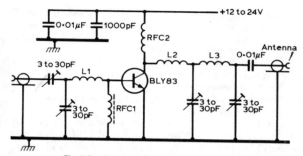

Fig 5.7. Low-power pa for 144MHz

are capable of very good performance at vhf due to the much more effective antennas which are possible at these frequencies. The collector supply is decoupled by $0 \cdot 01\mu F$ and 1,000pF capacitors in parallel. The $0 \cdot 01\mu F$ capacitor next to the output socket is for dc blocking. The relative simplicity of the circuit, which was built on a printed circuit board measuring 127 by 38mm, should be noted.

For operation at medium and high power levels at these frequencies, the use of valves in the pa stage is almost essential. The reader is referred to the RSGB *VHF/UHF Manual* for circuit details.

Power amplifiers at hf

A similar arrangement to that of Fig 5.7 can be used for single-band low-power work on the hf bands, but in general the requirements here tend to be a great deal more severe, ie higher powers are generally called for with operation over several bands (eg 3·5–28MHz).

The lower input and output impedances of transistors which were referred to earlier mean that in a pa having an output of 100W, these impedances will be of the order of 1–10Ω. Conventional pi-network designs at such low impedances lead to impractical values of inductance and capacitance. Thus there is no transistor equivalent of the standard high-power, band-switched pi-output power amplifier using valves.

This situation may well change as high-power field-effect transistors become available.

The solution adopted at high power is to transform the impedance of the rf input to a transistor pa down from 50Ω and then transform the output impedance of the transistor back up to the normal 50Ω. The basic arrangement is shown in Fig 5.8. The transformers used have ratios of about 4:1 and two such transformers may be used in cascade to provide a greater ratio.

These transformers are known as *transmission line* or *broadband* transformers and typically consist of relatively few turns of wire on a toroidal core. The primary and secondary windings are wound together as a pair of wires (a *bifilar winding*) or the two wires may be twisted together.

Because this type of transformer is broadband, it can operate over a wide frequency range, say, from 3–30MHz. If the drive circuits are similarly designed, the whole transmitter becomes broadband, ie apart from the vfo no band switching or re-tuning is required.

This is obviously highly satisfactory from the operational point of view; however, the design of such transformers is complex and the constructional work involved is not for the inexperienced amateur.

The fact that the rf circuits are broadbanded means that any harmonic or spurious frequency which may be generated is also amplified and appears at the output. Consequently the output must be filtered to avoid the radiation of any unwanted frequencies. The low-pass filter and antenna matching unit combination described in Chapter 7 would be adequate.

Modulation

This is the name given to the process of acting upon the rf carrier wave produced by a telegraphy transmitter in order to transmit speech, morse code (or, of course, music!).

The carrier wave is an alternating current of constant amplitude, frequency and, with respect to a fixed point in time, phase. Modulation may be achieved by the periodic variation of

(a) amplitude, hence *amplitude modulation*, or
(b) frequency, hence *frequency modulation*.

The rate of variation of the amplitude or frequency of the carrier wave, ie the *modulating frequency* (f_m) is assumed to be low compared with the carrier frequency (f_c).

Sidebands

In all modulation processes frequencies above and below the carrier wave are produced, these being termed *side frequencies*. The bands of side frequencies are called *sidebands*.

In a.m. the highest side frequency is the sum of the carrier frequency (f_c) and the highest modulating frequency (f_m), eg if f_c is 1,950kHz and f_m is 5kHz the highest and lowest side frequencies are 1,955kHz and 1,945kHz, ie the sidebands extend from 1,955kHz to 1,945kHz as shown in Fig 5.9. The *bandwidth* occupied by this transmission is 10kHz.

For fm this situation is much more complex and theoretically the sidebands in an fm system are infinitely wide. The change, which is both positive and negative, in the frequency of the carrier (known as the *centre frequency*) is called the *deviation*. The deviation

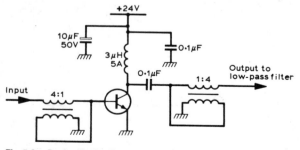

Fig 5.8. Basic circuit diagram of pa suitable for use on the hf bands

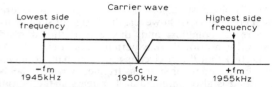

Fig 5.9. Relationship between carrier and sidebands in an a.m. system

is proportional to the amplitude of the modulating signal, so that the limits of the "swing", ie twice the deviation, are determined by the peaks of the modulating voltage. The rate at which the carrier frequency is deviated is equal to the frequency of the modulating signal, eg if a carrier wave of 7,075kHz is modulated by a 3kHz tone of specified amplitude to produce a deviation of 2·5kHz, the carrier frequency will swing between 7,072·5 and 7,077·5kHz (ie the swing is 5kHz) 3,000 times per second. If the amplitude of the 3kHz tone were doubled, the carrier frequency would swing between 7,070 and 7,080kHz but the rate of variation would still be 3kHz.

The ratio of the deviation to the frequency of the modulating signal is the *modulating index*. This ratio is obviously not constant, as the deviation depends on the amplitude of the modulating signal. Its limiting value, or the ratio of the maximum deviation to the highest modulating frequency, is called the *deviation ratio*. In the example quoted earlier, the deviation ratio is 2·5kHz divided by 3kHz or 0·833 for the first given amplitude, and 5·0kHz divided by 3kHz or 1·67 when the amplitude is doubled.

Bandwidth of a modulated wave

For the faithful reproduction of speech and music, it is necessary to transmit frequencies over the whole audible range (ie approximately 20Hz to 16kHz). In a communication system, intelligibility rather than fidelity is of prime importance and in the overcrowded

conditions of the present-day amateur bands it is obviously most important to ensure that no transmission occupies a greater bandwidth than is absolutely necessary for intelligible communication.

Experience shows that the intelligible transmission of speech requires that only frequencies of up to 2·5–3kHz need be transmitted.

Thus the bandwith of an a.m. transmission should not be greater than about 5–6kHz.

This restriction of the audio bandwidth is achieved by the use of a low-pass filter having a cut-off frequency of about 2·5kHz in the low-level stages of the modulating circuits.

In fm, as applied to communication, the deviation should be restricted so that the bandwidth occupied is approximately the same as in an a.m. transmission. This is known as *narrow band frequency modulation* or nbfm and the deviation used is ±2·5kHz or so (as compared with the ±75kHz of the high-fidelity broadcast station).

Modulation depth

The amplitude-modulated wave is shown graphically in Fig 5.10. Here (a) represents the unmodulated carrier wave of constant amplitude and frequency which, when modulated by the audio-frequency wave (b), acquires a varying amplitude, as shown at (c). This is the modulated carrier wave, and the two curved lines touching the crests of the modulated carrier wave constitute the modulation envelope. The modulation amplitude is represented by either *x* or *y* (which in most cases can be assumed to be equal) and the ratio of this to the amplitude of the unmodulated carrier wave is known as the *modulation depth* or *modulation factor*. This ratio may also be expressed as a percentage. When the amplitude of the modulating signal is increased, as at (d), the condition (e) is reached, where the negative peak of the modulating signal has reduced the amplitude of the carrier to zero, while the positive peak increased the carrier amplitude to twice the unmodulated value. This represents 100 per cent modulation, or a modulation factor of 1.

Further increase of the modulating signal amplitude, as indicated by (f), produces the condition (g), where the carrier wave is reduced to zero for an appreciable period by the negative peaks of the modulating signal. This condition is known as *over-modulation*. The breaking up of the carrier in this way causes distortion and the introduction of harmonics of the modulating frequencies, which are radiated as spurious sidebands; this causes the transmission to occupy a much greater bandwidth than necessary, and considerable interference is likely to be experienced in nearby receivers (see Chapter 8). The radiation of such spurious sidebands by over-modulation (sometimes known as *splatter* or *spitch*) must be avoided at all costs.

There is no direct equivalent of overmodulation in an fm system; an increase in the amplitude of the modulating signal will cause an increase in the deviation produced by the transmitter. The recommended deviation would therefore be exceeded and the transmission

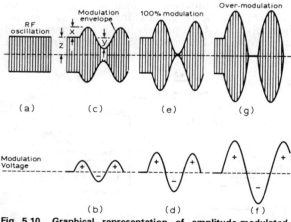

Fig 5.10. Graphical representation of amplitude-modulated wave

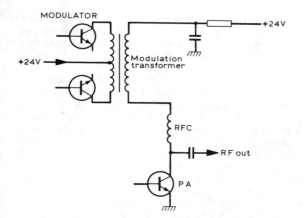

Fig 5.11. Amplitude modulation using transformer coupling to pa stage

would occupy a wider bandwidth, ie it would be fm rather than nbfm.

Ultimately the maximum deviation possible is restricted by the design of the rf circuits in the transmitter and the receiver, and attempts to exceed this will result in a distorted signal. However, this would require gross maladjustment and really excessive audio input to the frequency modulator.

Single sideband operation

Consideration of Fig 5.9 indicates two significant aspects of an amplitude-modulation system.

(a) The carrier wave itself does not contain any intelligence, its frequency being f_c.

(b) Both sidebands are identical as they both result from the modulating frequency f_m and the width of each is equal to the highest modulating frequency. Both sidebands therefore carry the same intelligence.

It follows that the carrier need not be transmitted and, as both sidebands contain the same intelligence, only one of them need be transmitted. This has led to the adoption of the system known as *single sideband suppressed carrier*, generally abbreviated to *ssb*.

Modulation methods

Amplitude modulation

It can be shown that the effective power in a carrier wave modulated to a depth of 100 per cent by a sinusoidal modulating signal (ie a single pure tone) is 1·5 times the unmodulated carrier power. Thus to fully modulate the carrier, the power in it must be increased by 50 per cent.

This extra power which is, in fact, "added" to the ht supply to the transmitter pa stage must be supplied by the *modulator*, which is a fairly high-power audio-frequency amplifier. To fully modulate a transmitter

operating at an input of 150W to the pa stage would require an af power of 75W.

The output of the modulator is coupled into the ht supply to the pa by the modulation transformer as shown in outline in Fig 5.11. The ratio of this transformer is determined by the output impedance of the modulator and the modulating impedance of the pa stage.

This is the most effective method of amplitude modulation as the pa stage operates in Class C, giving the highest efficiency. The disadvantage is that large and expensive modulating equipment is necessary for full-power operation, ie as indicated above the basic power required would be 75W, to which must be added an allowance to cover losses in the modulation transformer, so that the design aim should be 100W or so.

Keying

Keying is the switching on and off (by a morse key) of a transmitter in order to break up the continuous carrier wave into the dots and dashes of the morse code. It is therefore the most elementary form of amplitude modulation. Keying implies the switching of an electric circuit and therefore, in order to minimize sparking at the contacts of the key, it should take place at a point in the circuit where the power or current is at a minimum.

In order to avoid the possibility of causing chirp and small changes in transmitter frequency, it is recommended that the vfo itself should not be keyed. The logical point to key is therefore the stage after the vfo which ideally should be an isolating buffer amplifier, although it may be the first frequency multiplier stage.

The process of keying may cause serious interference. This and the steps to overcome it are discussed in Chapter 8.

Frequency modulation

Frequency modulation requires the variation of the frequency of the oscillator of the transmitter. This can be achieved in several ways, according to the form of the oscillator used.

In the case of a vfo as might be used on the hf bands, the frequency can be varied by a reactance modulator. This is a circuit arranged to present a varying reactance across the tuned circuit of the vfo. Thus variations in the reactance caused by the modulating voltage will alter the vfo frequency. A change in oscillator frequency can also be achieved by the use of a variable-capacitance diode (varactor).

It should be noted that when the fundamental oscillator frequency is multiplied to reach the final frequency, the frequency deviation is also multiplied by the same factor. Thus in an hf bands fm transmitter, deviation of the oscillator must be adjusted for each band to take account of the frequency multiplication used.

Most fm operation is on specific frequencies (channels) on the vhf bands and a crystal-controlled oscillator is generally used for stability reasons. A frequency multiplication of 18 times is commonly used in a 144MHz transmitter, hence for a final deviation of

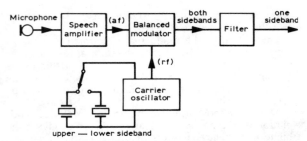

Fig 5.12.   Block diagram of ssb generator

2·5kHz to 3kHz, the fundamental oscillator has to be deviated by less than 200Hz. The pulling of an 8MHz oscillator by this small amount is easily achieved by a varactor.

Single sideband

The single sideband (ssb) transmitter performs two distinct functions. These are (a) suppression of the carrier wave and (b) elimination of one sideband.

The carrier is suppressed by feeding the output of the carrier-frequency oscillator and the modulating voltage into a circuit known as a *balanced modulator*. This is a form of bridge circuit which when correctly balanced will cause the rf input to be suppressed, and so only the two sidebands appear at the output. The unwanted sideband is then removed by means of a filter, the characteristics of which are critical. The bandwidth should be about 2·5kHz and the *shape factor* should ideally be 1·5–2, ie the bandwidth at very low levels where the attenuation is greatest should be less than about 5kHz.

This combination, shown in block form in Fig 5.12, is called the *sideband generator*. The single sideband so produced is in fact a band of frequencies corresponding to one sideband of an a.m. system. It can be produced at a fairly low frequency, typically 455kHz, in which case the frequency band is 455–458kHz. Alternatively the sideband can be generated in the megahertz region, eg at 9MHz, in which case the frequency band would be 9·000–9·003MHz.

From consideration of a typical band of frequencies, it is clear that frequency multiplication cannot be used to cover several bands. For example, suppose the sideband is generated at 3·5MHz. The frequency band is then 3·500–3·503MHz; if this is doubled it becomes 7·000–7·006MHz, ie the width of the sideband is also doubled. This is obviously not permissible and hence frequency translation to different bands must be done by the process of frequency mixing as mentioned in Chapter 2.

Fig 5.13 is a block diagram of a mixer-type exciter in which the outputs of a vfo and a crystal oscillator are mixed to produce an output in the required amateur band.

The vfo will typically cover a range of 500kHz; its actual frequency (order of 3–6MHz) and the crystal frequencies must be chosen so that the wanted and unwanted products in the output of the mixer shall be as far apart in frequency as possible. The mixer is followed by a tuned amplifier having coupled tuned circuits in the output to improve the rejection of the unwanted product.

This exciter, followed by the conventional pa, becomes a very satisfactory (but complex) alternative to the circuit described earlier in this chapter for the following reasons. (a) The absence of internally generated frequencies which could cause tvi, eg frequency multiplication by Class C amplifiers. (b) Frequency stability is improved and is not dependent on the band in use because any drift in the vfo is not increased by the multiplication factors of the circuit of Fig 5.2. However, as explained earlier, this circuit is necessary for any frequency multiplication in an ssb transmitter.

Depending upon the frequency at which the sideband is generated, one or more mixing processes may be required to introduce the output of a vfo and to reach the final frequency.

Fig 5.14 is a block diagram of an ssb transmitter in which the ssb is generated at a high frequency, say 9MHz, hence only one mixing process is needed to translate the ssb generation frequency to the output frequency. This diagram is a combination of Figs 5.12 and 5.13.

The output stage of an ssb transmitter must be a *linear amplifier* in order to amplify what is in effect a modulated rf signal without distortion. Linear amplifiers operate in Class AB or Class B, as opposed to Class C. The efficiency is therefore somewhat lower.

By convention the lower sideband is transmitted at radio frequencies below 10MHz and the upper sideband above 10MHz. The sideband required is selected by switching the crystal in the sideband generator (see Fig 5.12).

An ssb transmitter is therefore inevitably complex and a detailed discussion is beyond the scope of this manual. In particular, frequencies to be used must be carefully chosen to avoid the generation of unwanted or high-order products by the mixers (see Chapter 2). These may create spurious responses in receivers close to the transmitter.

The frequency stability of both the transmitter and receiver is especially important in an ssb communication system. A filter having very good characteristics is required in the sideband generator and also in the

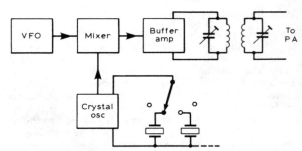

Fig 5.13.   Block diagram of mixer-type vfo

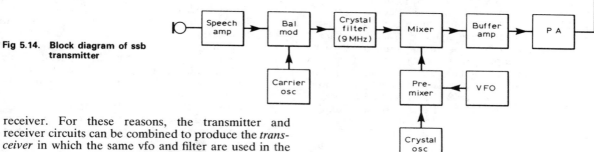

Fig 5.14. Block diagram of ssb transmitter

receiver. For these reasons, the transmitter and receiver circuits can be combined to produce the *transceiver* in which the same vfo and filter are used in the transmit and receive functions. The transceiver is shown in block diagram form in Fig 5.15.

The transceiver has now become the preferred arrangement for ssb operation and is often followed by a separate linear amplifier to boost the power level to the maximum permitted by the licence conditions.

The ssb transceiver and transmitter may also be used for telegraphy. It may be argued that this is an unnecessarily complex approach to telegraphy operation, but the advantages accruing from the use of transceiver circuitry are obviously worth having.

Transmitter power level
The UK amateur licence now defines maximum power on all bands up to 440MHz and for all modes in terms of output rather than input. The actual levels are quoted in "dBW", ie so many decibels above one watt (see Appendix 6).

The powers permitted on the various bands are given on p89 and their equivalents in watts for the various levels are as follows

26dBW = 400W	22dBW = 160W
20dBW = 100W	16dBW = 40W
15dBW = 32W	9dBW = 8W

In the case of a telegraphy, or an amplitude (or

frequency) modulated, transmitter it is considerably easier to measure input power than output power. This is because input power is the product of the direct voltage applied to the output stage and the direct current drawn by the output stage. This current does not vary.

The inputs corresponding to the maximum carrier powers now permitted for modes other than ssb (note that there is no change as regards ssb) are shown in Table 5.3. They assume an output stage efficiency of 66 per cent and 55 per cent for output stages operating in Class C and Class AB respectively.

Table 5.3
Inputs corresponding to maximum permitted carrier powers

Output	Input	
	Class C	Class AB
20dBW (100W)	150W	180W
16dBW (40W)	60W	73W
9dBW (8W)	12W	14W

Derivation of the ssb power level
In an amplitude-modulated transmitter, the maximum output power permitted (in the absence of modulation) is 100W (20dBW).

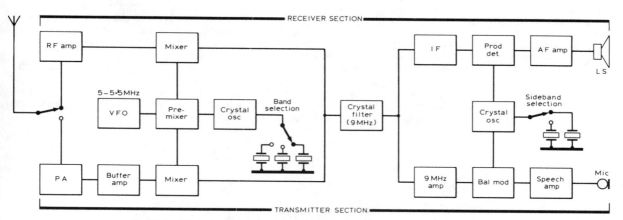

Fig 5.15. Block diagram of ssb transceiver (from *A Guide to Amateur Radio*)

When the transmitter is modulated to a depth of 100 per cent, the amplitude of the peaks of the modulation envelope is twice that of the unmodulated carrier wave (see Fig 5.10). As we are considering a voltage waveform, and since power equals V^2/R (R is the value of the load resistor and V is the unmodulated carrier amplitude), the output power of each cycle of rf energy at the peaks of modulation is $(2V)^2/R$ (because V is the unmodulated carrier amplitude and hence the modulated carrier amplitude is $2V$). This is equal to $4V^2/R$ or four times the unmodulated carrier power. Hence the power at the peak of the modulation envelope or the *peak envelope power* is 4 × 100 or 400W. This is the maximum power permitted by the UK amateur licence.

Comparison of modulation methods

Amplitude modulation of the collector of the output stage of the transmitter is the most efficient form of a.m., since the output stage is most likely to operate in Class C which has the highest efficiency. The disadvantages of a.m. are that in the case of full-power operation large and expensive modulating equipment is necessary; furthermore, because both sidebands are transmitted, the bandwidth needed is correspondingly doubled.

The effectiveness of an fm system depends mainly on the receiver used. Although fm can be resolved by de-tuning an a.m. receiver so that the signal is centred on the slope of the i.f. characteristic, optimum reception requires the use of a *discriminator* for the demodulation of an fm signal (see Chapter 4).

Narrow-band frequency modulation (nbfm) is widely used at vhf due to the ready availability of commercial equipment for mobile and hand-held use. It is capable of good solid coverage of a relatively small area under average propagation conditions. Coverage is increased by the use of repeaters and by exceptional propagation conditions.

Due to the absence of variation in amplitude, the use of nbfm on the hf bands may often eliminate tvi. This modulation method has been slow in being exploited because discriminators are rarely fitted to hf communication receivers.

It can be shown that ssb is the most effective form of speech communication. The circuitry employed, particularly in the case of the transceiver, is complex and therefore expensive, however it is usually very compact. The linear output stage is more critical in adjustment and operation. Ideally, the cathode-ray oscilloscope should be used for setting-up.

The overall advantages of ssb may be summarized as follows:

(a) The rf spectrum required to transmit a given signal by ssb is exactly that of the original signal, thus maximum use can be made of the available spectrum.

(b) Since in an ssb system only the essential signals are transmitted, ie no superfluous carrier or mirror-image sideband, there is a considerable effective power gain.

(c) Most important of all, ssb systems are affected far less adversely by the transmission disturbances inherent in ionospheric propagation than are a.m. and fm etc.

The symbols used to designate the various classes of emission should be noted (see p89). The most common ones are A1A, A3E, J3E and F3E.

Transmitter interference

It will be appreciated that the transmitter is a potential source of interference to television and other services. The design and construction of the transmitter must therefore take account of the need to minimize the production and radiation of unwanted harmonics and spurious oscillations. The implications of transmitter interference are discussed in Chapter 8.

The adjustment and tuning of transmitters

For obvious reasons a transmitter should never be adjusted on a radiating antenna; the transmitter output should be dissipated in a dummy load. Details of such a load are given in Chapter 9. The most critical adjustment is that of the modulation to prevent overmodulation, excessive deviation or non-linearity (distortion), according to which modulation system is used.

The adjustment of commercially made transmitters generally presents no problems if the maker's instructions are followed, as the circuit design is such that the audio level at the place of modulation is not excessive. However, it must be remembered that ultimately the level depends on how loud one speaks into the microphone. This is particularly important in the case of ssb where excessive audio will cause non-linearity in the output stage and hence serious distortion. The use of the oscilloscope in adjustment of an ssb transmitter is described in Chapter 9.

Tuning of the transmitter consists of resonating the various tuned circuits. These are generally preset, apart from those in the output stage which may need adjustment for each band. The measurement procedures are described in Chapter 9.

CHAPTER 6

Power supplies

The direct supplies of up to 12V which are required by solid-state circuits are obtained from batteries of primary or secondary cells (for example, in mobile equipment). Fixed equipment is most conveniently served by a power unit which transforms, rectifies and smooths the public 240V 50Hz supply.

Rectifying circuits

Silicon diodes are used as the rectifying elements. Fig 6.1 shows the half-wave rectifying circuit in which current flows in the transformer secondary circuit (ie load, rectifier and secondary winding) only during the positive half-cycle. Fig 6.2 shows the full-wave rectifier. The diodes conduct on alternate half-cycles, and it may be seen that this is a combination of two half-wave circuits. The load current waveform varies considerably in amplitude but as it does not change polarity it is a direct voltage.

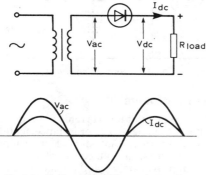

Fig 6.1. Half-wave rectifier and waveforms

The amplitude variation is known as the *ripple*. The frequency of the ripple in the full-wave arrangement is 100Hz, while in the half-wave circuit it is 50Hz. Fig 6.3 shows the bridge rectifier circuit. The output is full-wave, ie 100Hz ripple. At any one instant two of the diodes are in series carrying current. The transformer secondary winding does not have a centre tap and is required to supply a voltage of V_{ac} only (compare the full-wave arrangement of Fig 6.2 where the transformer supplies $2 \times V_{ac}$).

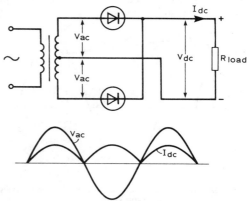

Fig 6.2. Full-wave rectifier and waveforms

Reservoir capacitor

C in Fig 6.4 is called a *reservoir capacitor*. Its purpose is to store energy during the positive half-cycle and to supply the load during the negative half-cycle. The diode only conducts during the time V_{ac} exceeds the voltage across the reservoir capacitor (Fig 6.5). If the value of C is made very large, say $10,000\mu F$, then a large pulse of current will be needed to charge it, because the time during which the diode conducts will be short.

Consider Fig 6.6, in which the load has been disconnected. The capacitor will charge up to have a voltage across it which will be equal to the peak voltage of V_{ac}. If V_{ac} is 12V rms then the peak voltage will be $12 \times \sqrt{2} = 17V$. On the negative half-cycle, the peak voltage

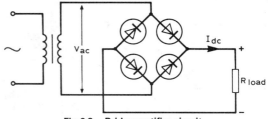

Fig 6.3. Bridge rectifier circuit

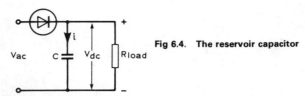

Fig 6.4. The reservoir capacitor

across the input terminals will also be 17V but the polarity will be as shown in Fig 6.6. The reverse voltage across the diode is now 34V. This is called the *peak inverse voltage* (piv). Allowing also for supply mains fluctuation of ±6 per cent, a diode rated at approximately 50V piv could be used.

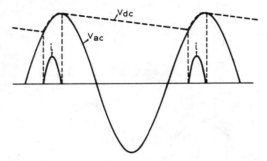

Fig 6.5. Output waveforms of rectifier circuit using a reservoir capacitor

The piv on the diodes in the half-wave and full-wave circuits may be taken as π multiplied by the direct output voltage; in the bridge circuit it is $\pi/2$ multiplied by the output voltage. The mean current in the diode in the full-wave and bridge circuits is numerically equal to one-half of the dc output current. In the half-wave circuit it is equal to the output current.

Smoothing circuits

By adding a choke L_s and a capacitor C_s as in Fig 6.7, the fluctuations in V_{dc} can be greatly reduced or "smoothed". These fluctuations are known as the *ripple* voltage, and in fact the output of the rectifier circuit as shown in Fig 6.5 consists of a direct voltage with an alternating voltage, ie the ripple, superimposed upon it. Thus L_s functions as a smoothing choke by opposing the alternating voltage and C_s provides a low-impedance path to earth for this voltage.

A resistor may sometimes be used in place of the choke but it is not so effective. In the high-current supplies required by some transistor circuits, a smoothing choke is unacceptably large and expensive, and in this case very high values of C_s would be used (eg 30,000μF).

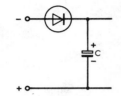

Fig 6.6. Peak inverse voltage across a rectifier

A practical circuit may contain other components as in Fig 6.8. The primary circuit contains the mains switch and a fuse. A metallic screen, placed between the primary and secondary windings, is connected to the earth terminal. This screen helps to reduce mains-borne interference, and to protect the secondary winding from the voltage on the primary, should a short-circuit occur between them. This screen is generally made of very thin copper (0·1mm thick) and of course is *not* continuous, otherwise it would act as a short-circuited winding. C1 may have a value of 1,000μF and C2 4,700μF. R1 will help with smoothing but must have a comparatively low value to avoid excessive voltage drop across it. The light-emitting diode indicates the ON condition. The resistor R2 will be 470Ω ¼ W.

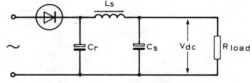

Fig 6.7. Smoothing circuit

Voltage multipliers

When high voltages at low currents are required a voltage multiplier can be used. For instance, a 500V winding on a transformer can be made to supply about 1,400V dc by using a voltage doubler. 500V $\times$ $\sqrt{2}$ doubled is approximately 1,400V when the circuit has a very light load. Such voltages are used in cathode-ray oscilloscopes.

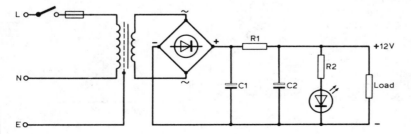

Fig 6.8. Practical power supply circuit (note the symbol for a bridge rectifier)

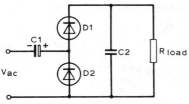

Fig 6.9.   Voltage-doubler circuit

Fig 6.9 shows a voltage-doubler circuit. On the negative half-cycle D2 conducts and charges C1 to $\sqrt{2} \times V_{ac}$. On the following positive half-cycle D2 switches off and D1 conducts. The peak voltage across C2 is now the peak value of V_{ac} plus the voltage across C1.

Due to the availability of electrolytic capacitors of up to $450\mu F$ capacitance at working voltages up to 500V, the voltage-doubler circuit is now used in compact power supplies to provide up to 800V at 300mA.

Properties of silicon diodes

Silicon diodes have a very low internal voltage drop and can deliver large currents. A very rapid increase in voltage, eg a switching transient, may give rise to a large current pulse, especially if the reservoir capacitor has a very large value, and such a *surge* is likely to destroy a silicon diode.

Fig 6.10 shows a means of providing protection of the diode. The capacitor C helps to absorb energy in the pulse, while the resistor R will also tend to limit a surge current, but will also create a voltage drop which may not be desirable.

At this point it might be mentioned that the rms value of large narrow pulses is larger than the dc value. The power rating of resistor R may have to be much larger than would at first appear. If R has a resistance of 12Ω and if I_{dc} is 0·5A, the apparent rating of R would be $0.5 \times 0.5 \times 12 = 3W$, but in practice a 10W resistor may be necessary.

Silicon diodes are commonly available with piv from 50V up to about 1,000V. Mean current capability varies from several amperes at the low piv to an ampere or less at the higher voltage. Several diodes may be connected in series to provide a higher piv capability. If this is done, a surge suppressing capacitor ($0.01\mu F$) and a resistor should be connected in parallel with each diode. The object of the resistor ($330k\Omega$) is to equalize the voltage drop across each diode. Diodes and diode chains used in rectifying circuits should be very conservatively rated, ie five 50V diodes in series should be taken as a 200V diode.

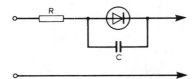

Fig 6.10.   Surge protection of diode

Power supply characteristics

Most electronic circuits require a power supply which is very smooth, ie there is very little ripple voltage superimposed on the direct output voltage. Many circuits (particularly oscillators) require a supply which has an almost constant voltage irrespective of the amount of current being taken from the supply. Such a supply is said to have good *regulation*. Variation of the mains voltage will also cause the output voltage to change.

Variation of the output voltage of a power supply is caused by the fact that the load current also flows through the power supply circuits which inevitably have a certain resistance or impedance. Thus the ideal power supply has a low *source impedance* (cf the internal resistance of a cell). Source impedance can be minimized by careful design, but a more effective solution is the use of a regulated supply which also compensates for input voltage changes.

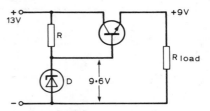

Fig 6.11.   Simple voltage regulator

Regulated power supplies

The simplest voltage regulator uses a zener diode as described in Chapter 3 (Fig 3.18). Reasonably smooth supplies of up to 150V can be obtained in this way, and this circuit is often used for the supply of a vfo. A more effective method is to use a transistor as a regulator in series with the supply to the load as shown in Fig 6.11.

The base of the transistor is kept at a fairly constant forward voltage by the zener diode D. If the load increases, the voltage at the emitter will tend to fall. This in turn allows the transistor to conduct more easily and thus maintain the output voltage.

In order to maintain better control a balancing (bridge) circuit is used, with an extra transistor working as a dc amplifier. Let the voltage in Fig 6.12 divide

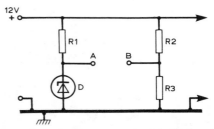

Fig 6.12.   Voltage regulator—basic balancing circuit

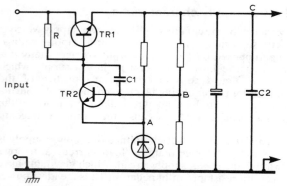

Fig 6.13. Voltage regulator using balancing circuit

emitter voltage of TR1 and so point C returns to its normal voltage.

The small capacitors C1 and C2, about $0.1\mu F$, prevent "hunting" or other instability if the load is constantly varying. There are many refinements in regulated supplies and manufacturers' literature gives much additional information.

The integrated circuit regulator

The modern tendency in regulated power supply design is to use an integrated circuit (ic) regulator. These contain in one small package the series element, reference voltage supply, a high-gain error amplifier and various sensing resistors and transistors. The more complex versions also contain protection circuits against too

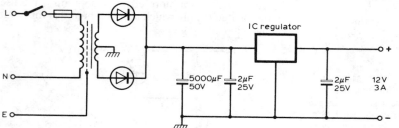

Fig 6.14. Practical power supply unit using ic regulator. The $2\mu F$ capacitors should have short connections to the ic to prevent any unwanted oscillation

equally between R2 and R3. The voltage between point B and chassis will be 6V. If the diode D is rated at 6V then there will be no difference of potential between points A and B. If the line voltage falls then the voltage across R3 will fall, but the voltage across D will remain at 6V. The voltage at A will now be higher than the voltage at B. This change of voltage can be applied to the base of a transistor and so provide a degree of control. Fig 6.13 shows a circuit using such a device.

If the voltage at C increases the voltage at point B will increase. The emitter voltage of TR2 stays constant due to the action of D. Due to the increased base-emitter voltage in TR2, the collector current (and hence the voltage drop in R) will increase. The base-emitter voltage of TR1 is reduced, thus increasing the effective series resistance of TR1. This brings down the

much voltage being applied to them and excess temperature rise. They are relatively cheap and are available up to a maximum regulated current of 10A. They may be connected in parallel for higher currents. The simplicity of this type of power supply may be seen from Fig 6.14.

Safety note

Using a low-voltage but high-current power supply must not be allowed to lull one into a state of false security. The input voltage is 240V, and this can be fatal under some circumstances. The high-current capability may be sufficient to generate molten metal if the supply is accidentally shorted to earth by, say, a ring on one's finger.

CHAPTER 7

Propagation and antennas

Radio communication depends on the radiation of elec-tromagnetic waves from the transmitting antenna. The electromagnetic waves are created by the alternating rf currents in the antenna which arise from the coupling of the output of the transmitter into the antenna system.

The transmitted signal may be regarded as a succes-sion of concentric spheres of ever-increasing radius, each one a unit of one wavelength apart, formed by forces moving outwards from the antenna. These hypothetical spherical surfaces, called *wave-fronts*, approximate to plane surfaces at great distances.

There are two inseparable fields associated with the transmitted signal, an *electric field* (E) due to voltage changes and a *magnetic field* (H) due to current changes, and these always remain at right-angles to one another and to the direction of propagation as the wave proceeds. They always oscillate in phase and the ratio of their amplitudes remains constant. The lines of force in the electric field run in the plane of the transmitting

antenna in the same way as would longitude lines on a globe having the antenna along its axis. The electric field is measured by the change of potential per unit distance, and this value is termed the *field strength*.

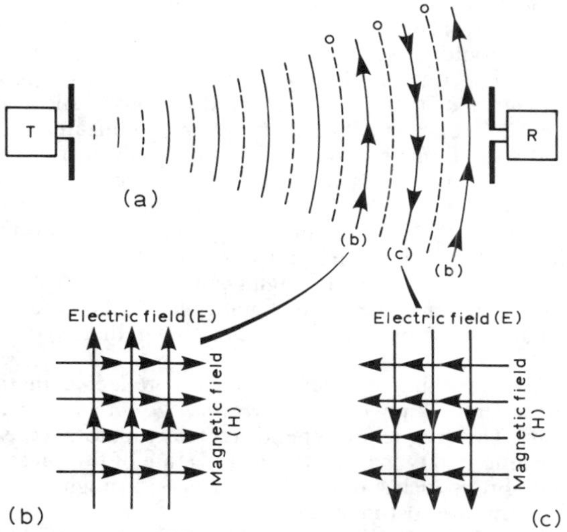

The two fields are constantly changing in magnitude and reverse in direction with every half-cycle of the transmitted carrier. As shown in Fig 7.1, successive wave-fronts passing a suitably-placed second antenna induce in it a received signal which follows all the changes carried by the field and therefore reproduces the character of the transmitted signal. The field strength at the receiving antenna may range from less than $1\mu V/m$ to greater than $100mV/m$.

Waves are said to be *polarized* in the direction of (parallel to) the electric lines of force. Normally the polarization is parallel to the length of the antenna, ie a horizontal antenna produces horizontally-polarized waves. In order to receive maximum signal strength the receiving antenna must be orientated to the same polar-ization. In practice, particularly at vhf, the polarization may be modified by factors such as abnormal weather conditions and reflection from the ionosphere.

The electromagnetic wave is an alternating quantity. Its wavelength (λ) is the distance, in the direction of propagation, between points where the intensity of the field is similar in magnitude and sign, ie the distance travelled in space to complete one cycle. Therefore

$$velocity = frequency \times wavelength$$

$$c = f \times \lambda$$

where c is the velocity of propagation which for elec-tromagnetic waves in space is approximately 300,000,000m/s (186,000 miles/s). Therefore

$$\lambda \text{ (m)} = \frac{300}{f(\text{MHz})}$$

Radio waves are a portion of the spectrum of elec-tromagnetic waves which extends from the longest wavelengths used in communication, about 25,000m, down to X-rays with a wavelength of 10^{-9}m.

The range of frequencies used in radio communica-tion is from about 15kHz to about 14,000MHz, and radar frequencies stretch from about 2,000MHz to about 25,000MHz. Beyond these are infra-red rays, the visible light spectrum, ultra-violet rays and X-rays etc.

Fig 7.1. The fields radiated from a transmitting antenna. (a) The expanding spherical wavefront consists of alternate reversals of electric field, with which are associated simultaneous reversals of the magnetic field at right-angles to it, as shown in (b) and (c). The dotted arcs represent nulls. The lower diagrams should be interpreted as though they have been rotated through 90° of arc, so that the magnetic field lines are perpendicular to the page.

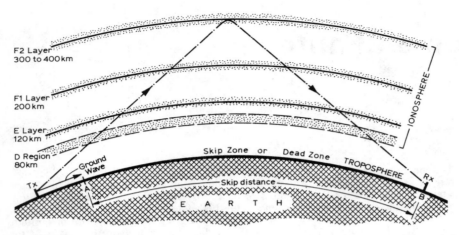

Fig 7.2. Reflection of radio waves by ionized layers

Modes of propagation

The three main modes of propagation of electromagnetic waves are:

(a) Ground (or surface) wave;
(b) Ionospheric wave (or skywave);
(c) Tropospheric wave.

The mode of propagation between two points on the surface of the earth depends on the frequency (wavelength) used, but there is no sharp transition from one mode to another as the frequency increases. This depends on many factors and at some frequencies significant propagation can occur by more than one mode.

Ground-wave propagation

In ground-wave propagation, the radiated wave follows the surface of the earth. It is the major mode of propagation for frequencies up to about 2MHz. Attenuation of the ground wave increases very rapidly above 2MHz and it may extend for only a few kilometres at frequencies of the order of 15–20MHz. At very low frequencies the attenuation decreases to such an extent that reliable world-wide communication is possible at all times. The ground wave is not so affected by atmospheric effects or time of day as other modes.

Ionospheric propagation

Ionospheric propagation is the refraction (ie bending) and hence reflection of radio waves back to earth by layers of ionized gases as shown in Fig 7.2. It is the normal mode of propagation over the frequency range of about 1MHz to 30MHz.

These layers are the F2 layer (height 300–400km); F1 layer (about 200km) and the E layer (about 120km). At night and in mid-winter, the F1 and F2 layers tend to combine into a single layer at a height of about 250km. At about 80km there is a much less distinct layer which is generally known as the D region.

The ionized layers are the result of the ionization of the oxygen, nitrogen and nitric oxide in the rarified atmosphere at these heights by X- and ultra-violet radiation of various wavelengths which comes from the sun. When these gases are ionized the molecules tend to split up into ions and free electrons, and these recombine after sunset. This whole region is therefore known as the *ionosphere.*

The solar radiation which causes the ionization is continually varying; hence the degree of ionization varies considerably according to season and time of day. It has also been found that the degree of ionization depends upon the number of sunspots.

The number of sunspots varies cyclically, with maximum activity occurring at about 11-year intervals. Thus maximum ionization occurs at the same intervals. Sunspot maxima occurred in February 1947, April 1959, May 1968 and December 1980. The next maximum should occur in 1991-2.

As the frequency of the radio wave increases, a greater degree of ionization is needed to cause reflection. The F2 layer normally has the greatest ionization and so it is the F2 layer which reflects the highest frequencies which have passed through the lower layers. It is seen from Fig 7.2 that it is this layer which reflects back to earth at the greatest distance from the transmitter. Therefore it is the characteristics of the F2 layer which are of most interest and significance in long-distance communication. The major significance of the D region is that it absorbs the frequencies under discussion in abnormal circumstances.

The maximum frequency which is reflected in the ionosphere is known as the *maximum usable frequency* (muf). This frequency depends on many factors, ie season, time of day, path, latitude and state of the sunspot cycle. Frequencies above the muf pass through the F2 layer and are lost in space.

Figs 7.3 to 7.6 show the way the muf varies with time of day or night, direction of transmission path, season and sunspot state. These diagrams present the average picture; there is often a quite large variation from day to day. Around the sunspot maximum, the muf may exceed 50MHz for short periods, but at the minimum it rarely exceeds 25MHz.

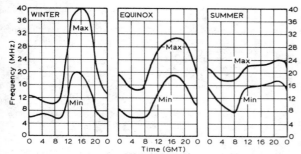

Fig 7.3. MUFs for the London–New York circuit at sunspot maximum and minimum

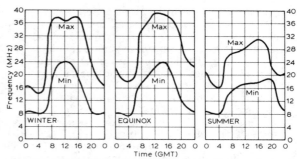

Fig 7.5. MUFs for the London–Cape Town circuit at sunspot maximum and minimum

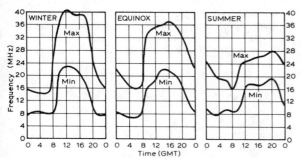

Fig 7.4. MUFs for the London–Buenos Aires circuit at sunspot maximum and minimum

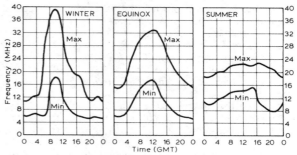

Fig 7.6. MUFs for the London–Chungking circuit at sunspot maximum and minimum

During the summer months, regions of intense ionization can occur in the E layer. This phenomenon results in the reflection of much higher frequencies than normal, eg up to 100MHz or so, and sometimes up to about 150MHz. This is known as *sporadic E* propagation: it may last from an hour or less up to several days and is the cause of exceptionally strong signals on the 28MHz band from stations about 1,500–2,500km away. It also of course affects the 70 and 144MHz bands.

The *critical frequency* is the highest frequency reflected when the radiation is vertical. This frequency is lower than the muf and will be different for each layer. The forecasting of muf from daily measurements of critical frequency made at radio observatories all over the world is of great importance in commercial communications. Forecasts are made for several years ahead and are continually refined as later measurements become available.

There is no simple explanation of the many anomalies in the behaviour of the F2 layer and most of what is known is based on experimental results and deduction. As far as amateur radio is concerned, it is convenient to accept the published variations of muf in particular as of most significance to communication on the amateur bands. The fact that the muf is highest in the early winter months should be noted.

It is clear from Fig 7.2 that there is a region between the transmitter and the point at which the reflected wave returns to earth (B) where no signal is received. This is the *skip zone* or *dead zone*. However, there will be inevitably some ground-wave propagation associated with the transmission and hence, more accurately, the *skip distance (zone)* starts where the ground wave has decayed to zero, ie A in Fig 7.2.

The maximum distance along the surface of the earth which results from a single reflection from the F2 layer is about 4,000km (2,500 miles); thus worldwide communication implies several reflections from the F2 layer to earth, back to the F2 layer, and so on.

Communication by ionospheric propagation may be disturbed or interrupted by abnormal radiations from the sun. The level of ionization in the D region can be suddenly greatly increased by intense bursts of ultraviolet and X- radiation emitted at the time of a solar flare or eruption at the surface of the sun. The increased ionization in the D region results in the absorption of radio waves before they reach the reflecting layers, and thus there can be a complete interruption of communication (*Dellinger fade-out*) over all or part of the hf spectrum which may last for a few minutes to an hour or so. This is known as a *sudden ionospheric disturbance* (sid).

An sid may be followed about two days later by another form of fade-out or black-out, the *ionospheric storm*, and this can last from a few hours to several days. It is thought that ionospheric storms are caused by slower-moving particles, emitted at the same time as the solar flare, which cause increased ionization in the D region but decreased ionization in the F layer. Ionospheric storms are more frequent at sunspot maxima, but more significant at sunspot minima.

Fading of a signal propagated ionospherically, as opposed to the fade-out described earlier, is a common occurrence. The signal received at a given point is rarely constant because of the continually changing conditions in the ionosphere, ie layer height, ionization level and possibly skip distance if the frequency is close to the muf. It is also possible that the signal may arrive by two different paths, ie by one reflection and also by two reflections; in this case, the time delay between the different paths may cause distortion, particularly of music. The effects of fading may be minimized by really effective automatic gain control in the receiver or by using the combined output of two or three antennas spaced over several miles *(diversity reception)*. This is rarely possible in amateur practice.

Tropospheric propagation

This is the major mode of propagation over long distances (ie beyond the line-of-sight range) at frequencies above about 50MHz.

Beyond the optical horizon the radiated wave may, according to weather conditions, be bent or *refracted* round the curvature of the earth. This refraction is caused by gradual changes in the dielectric constant of the atmosphere which occur at heights up to about 2km (6,000ft). This region is known as the *troposphere.*

Changes in dielectric constant are caused by certain combinations of pressure, humidity and temperature. Study of prevailing weather conditions often enables a period of good tropospheric propagation to be forecast.

Miscellaneous modes of propagation

Radio waves at very high frequencies can also be propagated as a result of scattering of the waves from:
(a) the auroral zones round the poles;
(b) the ionized particles which exist in the trails of meteor showers;
(c) within the troposphere itself (troposcatter).

Communication by these modes of propagation requires high power and high-gain antennas.

Waves may be reflected by hills and large buildings; amateur communication by reflection from the moon is now an established but very specialized art.

Antennas

It should be noted that the terms *aerial* and *antenna* mean the same. While "aerial" is possibly more common in the UK, "antenna" is in worldwide use; thus "antenna" is used in this chapter.

The fundamental antenna is a piece of wire which is one half of a wavelength ($\lambda/2$) long, corresponding to the frequency at which radiation is desired. The voltage and current vary over the length of this antenna, as shown in Fig 7.7 (top).

If the piece of wire is made a whole wavelength (1λ)

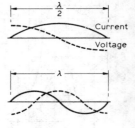

Fig 7.7. Standing waves on resonant antenna showing voltage and current variation. Upper antenna is $\lambda/2$ long (fundamental antenna); lower is 1λ (second-harmonic) antenna

long, the current and voltage variations are as in Fig 7.7 (bottom). This is known as a *full-wave* or *second-harmonic* antenna. Larger multiples of the basic $\lambda/2$ antenna show similar voltage/current variations.

These variations are known as *standing waves,* and this type of antenna is known as a *resonant* antenna.

It is seen that the ratio of voltage and current varies over the length of the antenna, and may be resistive, inductive or capacitive. This ratio is referred to in general terms as the antenna *impedance.*

The *radiation resistance* of an antenna is a fictitious resistance which would dissipate the power radiated by it.

Antenna length

The length of a half-wavelength ($\lambda/2$) in space is

$$\frac{150}{f(\text{MHz})} \text{ metres}$$

The actual length of a $\lambda/2$ antenna is somewhat less than this, owing to:
(a) the velocity of propagation in the wire being different from that in space;
(b) the presence of insulators at the end of the wire and of nearby objects (trees or buildings);
(c) the diameter of the wire or element.

The actual length is normally taken to be 5 per cent less than (or 0·95 of) the electrical length. This constant, 0·95, is sometimes known as the *correction factor,* hence the actual length is

$$\frac{150 \times 0·95}{f(\text{MHz})} = \frac{143}{f(\text{MHz})} \text{ metres}$$

Table 7.1
Approximate lengths of $\lambda/2$ dipoles

Band (MHz)	$\lambda/2$ (m)	$\lambda/2$ (ft)
1·8	75·2	247
3·5	39·2	129
7	20·3	67
14	10·05	33
21	6·7	22
28	4·93	16·2
70	2·02	6·6
144	0·97	38·4in
430	0·32	12·8in

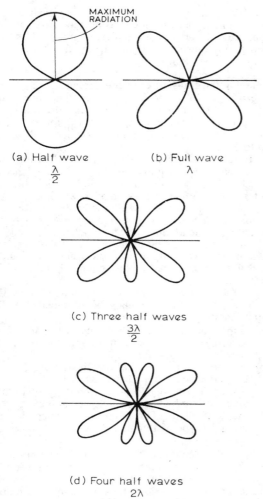

(a) Half wave
$\frac{\lambda}{2}$

(b) Full wave
λ

(c) Three half waves
$\frac{3\lambda}{2}$

(d) Four half waves
2λ

Fig 7.8. Theoretical radiation patterns of resonant antennas

Radiation patterns

If a $\lambda/2$ antenna is assumed to be parallel to and at least a wavelength above perfect ground, and also remote from all other objects, the radiation is concentrated at right angles to its length, as shown in Fig 7.8(a). This is the radiation pattern of a $\lambda/2$ antenna and, as the antenna radiates in directions all round the wire, the radiation pattern in space is the shape formed by imagining the pattern of Fig 7.8(a) to be rotated round the antenna as an axis.

Radiation patterns of antennas working on higher harmonics are shown in Figs 7.8(b), (c) and (d), where it is seen that the effect is to produce more lobes; the four lobes of the full-wave (1λ) case tend to swing towards the ends of the antenna, and subsidiary lobes appear. Thus in the case of an extremely long antenna the radiation tends to be concentrated at the ends.

It should be emphasized that these are theoretical patterns, which in practice are modified by many factors, principally nearness of the earth and large objects. However, they do indicate the trends to be expected.

If one end of the antenna is tilted, the lobes tend to move together and hence radiation tends to become concentrated off the lower end. Consideration of the $\lambda/2$ pattern shows that, when the antenna is vertical, radiation is all round (omni-directional).

Angle of radiation

This is the angle with respect to a tangent at the surface of the earth at which the maximum radiation occurs. Its value depends principally upon the height of the antenna above the ground; the higher the antenna, the lower the angle of radiation. It is seen from Fig 7.2 that long-distance communication requires a low angle of radiation which implies an antenna height of at least $\lambda/2$.

Directional antennas

It is possible to modify the radiation pattern of an antenna in order to concentrate the radiation in a particular direction. Thus a *directional* or a *beam* antenna is created.

This is generally achieved by the addition of parasitic elements known as a *director* and a *reflector* parallel to the antenna, as shown in Fig 7.9(a), which also shows the approximate spacing in terms of the operating wavelength. This arrangement is known as the *Yagi array*. The radiation pattern is shown in Fig 7.9(b). The addition of more directors produces a narrower beam, but more than one director is usually only possible at vhf, where up to eight or nine directors may be used. The H-type antenna used for vhf television reception is the simplest possible Yagi, having only a reflector in addition to the antenna element.

Means must be provided for rotating a beam antenna so that it can be turned to the required direction.

A similar effect may be achieved by the use of two (or more) antennas at the appropriate spacing and fed in the correct phase relationship. Antennas of this type (eg the W8JK beam) were once popular in amateur

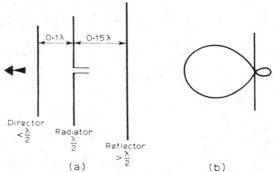

Fig 7.9. (a) Arrangement of Yagi directional (beam) antenna
(b) Radiation pattern of directional antenna

practice but have generally been superseded by the Yagi.

An additional feature of the directional antenna is the fact that when used for reception, signals to the back of the beam are attenuated, ie interfering signals from an unwanted direction may be significantly reduced in strength. The characteristics of a beam antenna are the *forward gain* (compared with a dipole) and *front-to-back ratio*, these terms being self-explanatory.

Transmission lines

For obvious reasons, the antenna should be erected as high and as far away from buildings etc as is possible. In order to transfer the power from the transmitter to the antenna over what may be a significant distance in the most effective manner, a *transmission line* is required. This form of connection, often known as a *feeder*, may be *balanced* or *unbalanced*.

In a balanced line both wires have an equal potential to ground, ie neither can be earthed. In the unbalanced line one side is normally earthed.

RF connections of this type are sub-divided according to a property known as the *characteristic impedance* (Z_o), which is measured in ohms.

The characteristic impedance of a balanced line depends on the diameter of the wire and the spacing between the two wires. Balanced or *twin-feeder* cable is commercially available in impedances of 75Ω and 300Ω (300Ω ribbon), and can be quite easily made with higher impedances by spacing apart two lengths of 14swg (2mm) or 16swg (1·6mm) wire with low-loss spacers tied to the wire every 50cm or so.

The normal unbalanced feeder is the familiar coaxial cable which is made in a range of grades and impedances. The characteristic impedance of a coaxial cable depends on the diameter of the wire (the inner) and the internal diameter of the screen (the outer). The commonly used impedances are 50Ω and 70Ω. The characteristic impedance of both types also depends on the dielectric used.

The velocity of propagation of an electromagnetic wave in a feeder or transmission line is less than in free space. The ratio of the two velocities is known as the *velocity ratio* or *velocity factor*. For most solid polythene coaxial cables, the velocity factor is about 0·66, whereas for 300Ω twin feeder it is about 0·85.

Consideration of the variation of voltage and current along a transmission line shows that, when the line is shorted at the far end, the impedance at those points which are an even multiple of λ/4 (ie a multiple of λ/2) at the operating frequency from the shorted end is very low (theoretically a short-circuit), while at odd multiples of λ/4 the impedance is very high (theoretically it is infinite). If the line is open-circuit at the far end, the opposite holds: the impedance is very high at even multiples of λ/4 and very low at odd multiples of λ/4.

Thus a length of coaxial cable which is λ/4 long at the operating frequency and is open-circuit at one end presents a virtual short-circuit at the other end *at the*

operating frequency only. Such a "stub" can be connected in parallel with the coaxial transmitter-antenna connection to provide a significant amount of attenuation to any unwanted output at, say, the frequency of the local tv station.

Coupling the transmitter to the antenna

The majority of commercial transmitters have output circuits which are designed to "look into" an unbalanced load of approximately 50Ω. Equipment having variable tuning in the output circuits will usually accept up to 75Ω.

For maximum transfer of power from the transmitter to the load, it is a requirement that their impedances be matched. An ideal situation would be one where the antenna (load) feed point was 50Ω, which in turn was coupled by a feeder of 50Ω characteristic impedance to a transmitter whose output circuitry was designed to accept a 50Ω load. Such an antenna/feeder installation would be said to be perfectly matched. This results in maximum power output from the transmitter, and in turn this is transferred to the antenna, where it is all radiated.

In practice, the feed point of an antenna may vary quite widely from its nominal value of impedance. Two typical causes are:

(a) Siting conditions, the proximity of the antenna to local objects and, with hf antennas in particular, height above ground.

(b) Although the antenna may be adjusted to its optimum feed impedance at a particular frequency, excursions to other frequencies within an amateur band will cause a change in impedance at the feed point. The degree of change depends upon the type of antenna, some varying more than others.

When the impedances are matched, all the power delivered to the load (antenna) is dissipated (radiated). However, if the antenna does not present the correct termination there is said to be a *mismatched* condition at the antenna. Now, some of the power is reflected from this mismatch, and opposes the power being delivered by the transmitter.

Forward or incident power travels from the transmitter to the load and returned or reflected power is reflected from the load when it is mismatched. With both waves travelling simultaneously on the feeder, rf voltages and currents now vary along the length of the feeder, instead of being of constant value as they would be under matched conditions. This variation is expressed by the *standing wave ratio* (swr). Thus:

$$\text{swr} = \frac{V_{\max}}{V_{\min}} = \frac{I_{\max}}{I_{\min}} = \frac{Z_o}{R}$$

where Z_o is the characteristic impedance of the feeder and R the load resistance in ohms.

SWR is measured by means of a simple reflectometer (swr meter): see Chapter 9. As it is impossible to obtain a perfect match, ie swr = 1·0:1, in practice, the consequences of swr are:

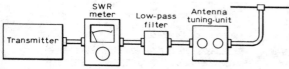

Fig 7.10. Preferred arrangement of transmitter-to-antenna circuit

(a) A reduction in power output from current commercial solid-state transmitters, which incorporate automatic swr shutdown protection circuits.
(b) Greater loss in the feeder. How much greater depends both on feeder type and frequency. In general it can be said to be inconsequential at hf (up to 30MHz), but may be significant at vhf (144MHz) and will be certainly so at uhf (432MHz).
(c) Use of very high power with an excessive swr may cause breakdown of the feeder or units "in line", such as filters or switches. Breakdown can be caused by flashover (due to high voltage) or melting of conductors or dielectric (due to high current).

Note that a high swr, of itself, does not cause a feeder to radiate, nor produce tvi, nor other interference.

If there is a mismatch between the antenna and its feeder, then the feeder will have a vswr present. The transmitter, "looking into" the input end of the feeder, will "see" an impedance; that is, resistance plus reactance. The value of this impedance depends, in part, on the length of the feeder in terms of wavelength. It follows that the impedance can be changed by altering the length of the feeder, which acts as an impedance transformer. Note that it is the input impedance that changes and not the swr, which is constant throughout the length of the feeder.

It is the purpose of an antenna tuning unit (atu) to match the transmitter output to the impedance seen at the input to the feeder. Fig 7.10 shows the preferred arrangement of an atu together with an swr meter and low-pass filter. The arrangement just discussed is the preferred one from every point of view; however, there is some merit in interchanging the position of the filter and the atu, particularly if the atu is a commercial one with a built-in swr meter. It is permissible to connect an end-fed (and hence high-impedance feed) antenna to the output of the atu as explained later, but then the filter and atu must be connected as Fig 7.10 otherwise the filter cannot function.

The name *antenna tuning unit* is applied by common usage, but such a unit does not "tune" the antenna, it matches it to the transmitter, hence "antenna matching unit" is really a more appropriate term.

Practical antennas

Antennas for use in the amateur bands are usually based on the fundamental antenna, ie the λ/2 dipole. Study of the usual textbooks on amateur radio reveals that many different forms of antenna have been developed. Basic information on the more common types only can be given within the scope of this manual; however, this adequately meets the requirements of the RAE.

The dipole

The impedance of a λ/2 antenna at the centre point is approximately 70Ω (resistive). Thus this point could be coupled directly to the output of a transmitter by 70Ω coaxial cable, resulting in a good impedance match (Fig 7.11). This arrangement is known as a *half-wave dipole* or simply as a *dipole*. For example, the length required for operation in the 40m band (7MHz) is approximately 20m (66ft).

However, if this particular antenna were fed with power at, say, 14MHz or 28MHz, there would be a considerable impedance mismatch, as the impedance at the centre would no longer be 70Ω. It would be very much higher than this and moreover would not be resistive. At a frequency of 21MHz (the third harmonic) the impedance at the centre would be about 90Ω and an acceptable match with 70Ω coaxial cable would exist.

The dipole is a satisfactory and commonly-used antenna but, apart from the example quoted above, it is a single-band antenna. (It should be noted that a dipole cut for 14MHz is similarly a good antenna at the third harmonic, ie 42MHz; this fact may make suppression of tvi more difficult.) The common use of coaxial cable (unbalanced) to feed a dipole is convenient as the output of most transmitters is unbalanced, but consideration of the antenna itself shows that a dipole is balanced so that it should not be fed with an unbalanced cable.

Alternative and more correct arrangements are either the use of 75Ω twin cable between the antenna and the atu, or a balance-unbalance transformer between the top end of the coaxial feeder and the antenna.

The balance-unbalance transformer, commonly called a *balun*, enables a balanced circuit to be coupled to an unbalanced circuit and vice versa. In one commercially available version, it consists of three tightly-coupled windings on a small ferrite core. The arrangement is shown in Fig 7.12.

The trap dipole

The trap dipole, sometimes known as the *W3DZZ antenna* after the callsign of its originator, is a dipole

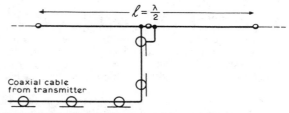

Fig 7.11. λ/2 dipole antenna fed by coaxial cable. Length is approximately equal to 143/*f* metres

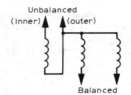

Fig 7.12. Arrangement of windings in balun transformer

having a parallel-tuned circuit or *trap* inserted at a particular point in each leg as shown in Fig 7.13. At resonance, the trap presents high impedance and therefore at the resonant frequency the length beyond the trap is virtually isolated from the centre portion. Below the resonant frequency the trap provides an inductive reactance which reduces the length of antenna required for resonance.

Fig 7.13 gives the dimensions of the trap dipole: the traps are resonant at 7·1MHz. At 7MHz the system operates as a λ/2 dipole, the traps isolating the outer sections. At 3·5MHz it operates as λ/2, the traps electrically lengthening the top. At frequencies above the resonance of the trap, the end sections are not isolated, but the traps do provide series capacitance. This enables the antenna top to resonate at odd harmonics of its fundamental and so at 14MHz, 21MHz and 28MHz the trap dipole functions as a 3λ/2, 5λ/2 and 7λ/2 antenna respectively. A reasonably satisfactory match to a 75Ω feeder is obtained on each band. At 1·8MHz the feeders may be joined together at the transmitter and the system will operate satisfactorily as a top-loaded Marconi antenna against ground or a counterpoise.

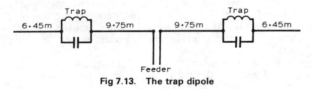

Fig 7.13. The trap dipole

The trap dipole has become very popular as a multi-band antenna in recent years because of the commercial availability of suitable traps. It must be appreciated that, as with all multi-band antennas, it is a compromise arrangement and as such will not give optimum results on every band.

The folded dipole

A dipole arranged as Fig 7.14(a) is said to be *folded*. This is the simplest example of folding, and the impedance at the centre is multiplied by a factor of four; thus it becomes approximately 300Ω. A suitable feeder is therefore 300Ω twin and, in fact, a folded dipole can be made entirely from 300Ω ribbon, as shown in Fig 7.14(b).

The folded dipole is convenient when the feeder is very long, the feeder loss being slightly reduced by the use of 300Ω line.

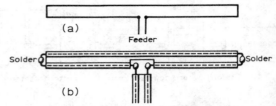

Fig 7.14. (a) Folded dipole. (b) Construction of a folded dipole from 300Ω ribbon feeder

The vertical antenna

A vertical antenna offers the attraction of low-angle, omnidirectional radiation and is popular where space does not allow a long horizontal antenna.

The simplest form is a vertical radiator one quarter of a wavelength (λ/4) long (Fig 7.15); the impedance at the bottom is 30–40Ω and so it can be fed by 50Ω coaxial cable.

The achievement of a satisfactory earth presents the major difficulty. A single earth rod, say 2m long, is unlikely to be satisfactory unless the soil has exceptional conductivity. Two or three such rods bonded together close to the bottom of the radiator may reduce the earth resistance.

Earthing problems with a vertical antenna may be virtually eliminated by erecting it over a perfectly-conducting surface, eg a large sheet of copper. This is known as a *ground plane antenna,* but is only realizable at vhf (eg a λ/4 radiator mounted on a car roof).

In practice a satisfactory ground plane may be made by laying four to six radial wires about λ/4 long on the surface of the ground (they can be buried a few centimetres below the surface if more convenient). Alternatively the radiator may be mounted at the top of a mast which uses the ground-plane radials as guy wires, insulators being introduced at the appropriate points as shown in Fig 7.16. A ground plane erected in this manner does in fact present a better match to 50Ω coaxial cable than does the conventional ground plane.

Traps may be inserted in a vertical antenna to enable it to be used on more than one band.

The end-fed antenna

This is probably the simplest antenna of all as it consists of a length of wire brought from the highest point available direct to the transmitter output. The optimum layout is where the transmitter is at the top of a building. The wire can be straight but good results are often obtained with quite sharp bends in the run of the wire.

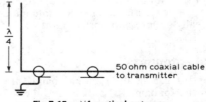

Fig 7.15. λ/4 vertical antenna

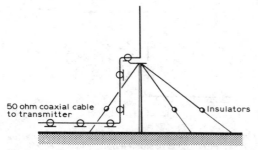

Fig 7.16. Ground-plane antenna mounted on a mast

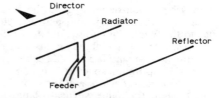

Fig 7.18. Presence of director and reflector lowers impedance of radiator element at central feed point. Correct matching of feeder can be obtained by use of λ/4 stub, open at one end

While the pi-coupler in the output stage of most transmitters tunes satisfactorily with random lengths of wire from about 4m upwards, optimum results are obtained with resonant lengths, ie 20m (66ft), 40m (132ft) etc.

A 40m long end-fed antenna operates on bands from 3·5MHz to 28MHz, while a 80m (264ft) length enables 1·8MHz to be used. The end-fed antenna taken direct to the transmitter output socket as referred to above will almost certainly result in tvi, except in the case of low-power operation on 1·8MHz. The use of an antenna tuning unit as shown in Fig 7.17 is therefore advisable. The atu should be preceded by a low-pass filter and swr meter as shown in Fig 7.10. An end-fed antenna less than λ/2 in length is not particularly effective, although good results are often obtained.

The three-element beam antenna

The Yagi antenna consisting of a radiator and two parasitic elements (a reflector and one director) mounted on a suitable tower with provision for rotating it is known as a *three-element beam*. The radiator is a dipole which must be about 10m (33ft) long for operation at 14MHz; thus physical size normally dictates that 14MHz is the lowest frequency for which the rotating Yagi is used.

The addition of a director and a reflector to the normal dipole has the effect of reducing the centre impedance to the order of 20Ω. Therefore in order to feed it with 70Ω coaxial cable the impedance must be increased. This can be achieved by (a) folding the radiator which increases the impedance to about 80Ω or (b) using some form of impedance-matching transformer between the feeder and the antenna.

A simple form of impedance-matching device is the

quarter-wave stub, open at one end, as shown in Fig 7.18. The point on the stub at which the feeder is attached must be determined experimentally, ie it must be adjusted for minimum swr. Other arrangements are discussed in the *Radio Communication Handbook*.

The actual spacings of the reflector and director relative to the radiator have a significant effect on the characteristics of the system, such as the gain compared with a simple dipole, the front-to-back ratio and the amount by which the impedance is reduced.

Commercial three-element beams are widely used. These use traps for operation on 28MHz, 21MHz and 14MHz. As a result of the different spacing in terms of operating wavelength at these three frequencies, the change in impedance is not excessive, and feeding with 50Ω coaxial cable is an acceptable compromise.

The cubical quad antenna

The cubical quad, generally known simply as the *quad* antenna, is the most popular of the loop antennas. It consists of a square loop of wire as shown in Fig 7.19. The side of the loop is approximately λ/4 in length and it is normally fed with 75Ω coaxial cable at the point shown. The loop can be mounted with a diagonal vertical and fed at the bottom corner; in either case the feed point is a current maximum and the performance is identical. In the configuration shown, the polarization is horizontal.

Parasitic elements may be added to form a beam antenna. The most popular configuration is a radiator plus reflector (the two-element quad), but one or more

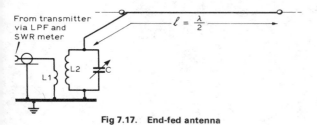

Fig 7.17. End-fed antenna

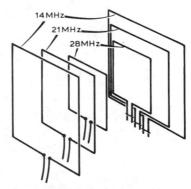

Fig 7.19. A three-band nest of two-element quads (radiator and reflector) maintaining optimum spacing for each band

directors may be added depending on the frequency. Spacings between the radiator and parasitic elements are similar to the Yagi. Commonly, quads for 28MHz, 21MHz and 14MHz are assembled on the same mounting and rotating system and fed by 50Ω cable. In order to maintain the optimum spacing between the elements, the radiators, reflectors and directors for each band cannot be in the same vertical plane (see Fig 7.19).

The quad is made up of wire supported on lightweight spreaders of bamboo or glass fibre.

Front-to-back ratio and swr are optimized on each band by adjustment of the tuning stub on the reflectors, alternatively a reasonable compromise is often obtained by eliminating the stub and making the reflector about 3 per cent greater than the radiator in length.

Commercial data suggest that the quad may give a slightly higher gain than the Yagi and a noticeably better front-to-back ratio. Its smaller turning radius is also often advantageous.

Low-frequency antennas

An effective resonant antenna for the lf bands, particularly 1·8MHz, requires a large space. Shorter lengths are often used tuned against earth in what is known as the *Marconi-type antenna*. A common arrangement is shown in Fig 7.20. The earth should be a short connection to an earth spike and the use of the mains earth or the water-pipe system should be avoided.

Loading of an antenna

Shortness in length of a resonant antenna may be compensated to a certain extent by the addition of a small amount of inductance, for instance as shown in Fig 7.20. Another example is the effect of the trap inductance when the trap dipole (Fig 7.13) is used on the 3·5MHz band. This artifice is commonly used on whip antennas for mobile use and may allow a beam antenna

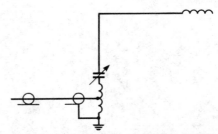

Fig 7.20.   Marconi antenna for use at 1·8MHz; additional loading at outer end is useful if length is less than λ/4

to be made to fit into a smaller than normal space. The process of loading an antenna may degrade its properties to a certain extent.

VHF antennas

Antennas of the general type just described may be used at 70MHz, 144MHz and 432MHz. At higher frequencies, parasitic reflectors and directors are replaced by parabolic-shaped reflectors or "dishes"; however, these are beyond the scope of the RAE. The end-fed and trap antennas have no equivalent at vhf.

Because the physical length of a λ/2 at 144MHz and 432MHz is small, antennas for these bands are very often Yagis employing a large number of directors. Four or more of these Yagis may be stacked with the feeders paralleled in the correct phase relationship to give a very high gain. The quad antenna is also often used at vhf.

Receiving antennas

It is now normal practice for the transmitting antenna to be used for reception. Should a separate receiving antenna be required, 12–18m of wire erected in the clear normally gives good results on all bands. An antenna tuning unit is often advantageous.

CHAPTER 8

Transmitter interference

It is essential that amateurs should know how to design, construct and operate their equipment in a manner which causes the minimum of interference to other users of the rf spectrum. The main problems are likely to be complaints from immediate neighbours (due to interference to domestic tv, radio and audio equipment) and from other radio amateurs (due to transmissions which are unsatisfactory for the crowded amateur bands). Complaints may also come from users of other radio services—particularly those who share amateur bands and also various important vhf services. Depending on circumstances, certain bands and modes of transmission may give rise to a high proportion of interference problems. There is also a greater chance of interference when high transmitter power is used.

Causes of interference

There are many causes of interference, and sometimes several are present at the same time.

Most common are the following:

(a) There is a defect in the transmitting station in that it is of unsatisfactory design or it is operated incorrectly.

(b) The equipment suffering the interference is responding unreasonably to the transmitted signals. The transmitting station is, however, operating correctly within the terms of its licence and is technically not at fault.

(c) Neither the transmitting station nor the affected equipment is at fault. Something nearby is generating the interference (usually harmonics) from the transmitted signal and then radiating it. Probably some rusty guttering or a corroded tv antenna is responsible. However, interference from these *non-linear elements* is very rare, and is not dealt with in this chapter.

The amateur should be capable of determining the category into which his problems fall. This enables him to take appropriate action. Even in cases where the interference is not his fault, he will often be able to help those affected to find a satisfactory cure. However, this chapter is concerned primarily with transmission defects, for which the amateur has direct responsibility.

Transmitting station defects

Interference caused by the transmitting station may be classified broadly into two groups. In one, interference is to users of frequencies immediately adjacent to the wanted transmitter output frequency, such as other radio amateurs and shared-band users. Interference occurs because the transmitted signal occupies an excessive bandwidth. This happens when the signal frequency is unstable (due to drift or chirp) or, when the frequency is stable, the signal is too wide. In the second group, interference is to users of frequencies which are quite remote, and usually affects neighbours' tv and radio reception (but is occasionally more widespread). It is caused by the radiation of harmonics of the transmitter output frequency or of signals generated intentionally inside the transmitter but which are not meant to reach the output. Common to both groups is interference caused by the radiation of unintentional signals, such as parasitics and self-oscillations.

Frequency instability

Drift occurs as a gradual change of frequency, while *chirp* is rapid frequency variations which follow morse keying.

Drift causes interference to users of adjacent frequencies and annoys the amateur trying to receive the transmission. Severe drift may result in a transmission finishing outside the amateur band. It usually occurs when a transmitter is warming up, and the cure is to ensure that oscillator circuits are constructed from components having values which do not change appreciably with temperature, and in some cases to incorporate a compensating device—usually a special capacitor (see Chapter 5). Other causes of drift include variations of the supply voltages to the oscillator (including the heater voltage in valve circuits). Certainly all dc supplies should be stabilized. Mechanical stability of the transmitter chassis and oscillator components is essential if random frequency variations due to chassis movement or vibration are to be avoided.

Chirp can arise in the following way. Each time the key is pressed there is an increase of transmitter power supply current (mainly to the pa stage). This causes the supply voltage to fall and oscillator frequency variations may occur. To avoid this, oscillator dc supplies should be stabilized (as for drift). Chirp may also occur if the transmitter output signal is allowed to feed back into an oscillator circuit—especially if the oscillator is on the same frequency. The frequency of an oscillator circuit can be affected by the load placed on its output. Keying the stage following an oscillator usually causes its load (and hence its frequency) to vary. Such variations are small if the coupling between the oscillator and the keyed stage is minimal. It is better to use a *buffer stage* immediately after the oscillator to ensure that the oscillator load variations are negligible.

Transmissions which are too wide

A single carrier wave which has a stable frequency occupies no bandwidth. It also conveys no information. Information is conveyed by modulating the carrier in amplitude or frequency. This produces sidebands —signals which appear on each side of the carrier. Thus the complete transmission occupies a *band* of frequencies. On the crowded amateur bands an amateur must ensure that he does not make excessive use of the space available by limiting the bandwidth of his transmissions to the minimum necessary for communication. The following techniques are recommended:

Speech. Most transmissions are in the form of *a.m.* (amplitude modulation, mode A3E), *ssb* (single sideband, mode J3E) or *fm* (frequency modulation, mode F3E). All may occupy a considerable bandwidth unless precautions are taken.

Due to the generation of sidebands by the modulation process the bandwidth of an *a.m. transmission* is twice the highest modulating frequency. Any attempt to transmit high-quality speech (containing frequencies up to 15kHz) would occupy an rf bandwidth of 30kHz. As audio frequencies up to 2·5 or 3kHz provide adequate intelligibility for communication purposes, 30kHz is obviously excessive and would cause *splatter* across adjacent transmissions. Accordingly, the transmitter audio stages must be designed to have an overall *low-pass* characteristic, ie to amplify frequencies up to 2·5kHz, but to cut off sharply above this. This gives a transmission bandwidth of 5kHz.

Severe splatter will result when the carrier is *over-modulated*. This occurs when too much audio signal is applied in relation to the carrier, resulting in breaks during modulation troughs (see Chapter 5). Too little modulation makes the transmission appear weak, and to ensure maximum intelligibility the modulation should be kept close to 100 per cent. It is advantageous to use some form of automatic audio compression or limiting circuit which, when adjusted correctly, ensures a high level of modulation but prevents over-modulation. Alternatively an over-modulation indicator may be used (see Chapter 9).

In *ssb transmissions* all the power of the signal is concentrated into one sideband only. Ideally, the transmitted bandwidth is that of the audio modulating signal, ie half that required for a.m. As with a.m., no attempt should be made to transmit high speech frequencies, and the rf bandwidth should be restricted to 2·5 or 3kHz.

Unlike a.m. (where it is common practice to modulate the transmitter output stage) ssb is usually generated at an early stage and amplified in a *linear* amplifier. Ideally, negligible distortion occurs, but this is only true at reasonable power levels. If linear amplifiers are over-driven to obtain more power, serious distortion

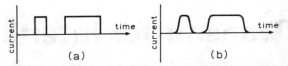

Fig 8.1. Abrupt rise and fall of current in a keyed transmitter as shown in (a) can result in radiation of key clicks. These can be eliminated by reducing the steepness of the rise and fall of current as shown in (b)

occurs, caused by the process of *intermodulation*. New unwanted signals are generated, both inside the transmitted channel (resulting in poor quality) and outside (resulting in splatter across adjacent channels). Over-driving may be prevented by the use of compression or limiting circuits, which can operate either at audio or at radio frequencies.

In *fm transmissions,* information is carried by varying the frequency of the signal either side of a centre frequency. However, the bandwidth occupied may greatly exceed this variation or *deviation* because of the great number of sidebands which fm produces.

The modulating process generates sidebands in a manner somewhat similar to a.m. However, in fm a tone of 2·5kHz creates sidebands not only at 2·5kHz, but also at harmonic frequencies (ie 5kHz, 7·5kHz etc, theoretically stretching to infinity). The level of each additional sideband depends greatly upon the modulating signal level, and is very small if the modulating signal is below a critical level such that the *modulation index* does not exceed about 0·6. The bandwidth is then comparable with that of an A3E transmission. Accordingly, it is essential that the audio bandwidth and amplitude be restricted, and speech clipping or limiting is recommended, even in low-power transmitters. This ensures correct narrow-band frequency modulation (nbfm).

Although the sideband levels are small beyond the highest modulating frequency, they are not entirely negligible. To prevent out-of-band radiation, an fm transmission should be kept well away from band edges.

Morse (cw). Morse is usually sent by the on-off keying of an otherwise continuous wave (cw). Fig 8.1(a) shows a current which is "made" and "broken" by keying to form the morse character "A". The pulses are rectangular and the very rapid rise and fall of current means that this waveform contains a considerable amount of high-frequency energy—even if the keying speed is slow. When such a waveform modulates a transmitter, the high-frequency sidebands may extend over a band several kilohertz wide each side of the carrier. These are audible as clicks on receivers tuned to nearby frequencies and may cause interference at a considerable distance from the transmitter.

Key clicks can be suppressed by slowing down the rise and fall of the waveform, as shown in Fig 8.1(b). A circuit suitable for keying the dc current in a transmitter stage is shown in Fig 8.2. When the key is closed the rise of current is slowed down by the af choke in series with the key. When it is opened the fall of current is slowed down by the charging of the capacitor connected across the key. The resistor is necessary to prevent sparking at the key contacts just as the key is closing (due to the rapid discharge of the capacitor).

The values of L, C and R depend on the circuit which is keyed. Typical values are L, 1 to 10H; C, 0·1 to 1μF; R, 50 to 500Ω. The smallest values consistent with key-click elimination should be chosen.

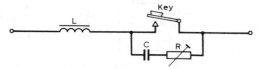

Fig 8.2. Typical key-click filter. L serves to prevent too rapid a rise of current. C, charging through R, serves to continue flow of current momentarily when key contacts open

The suppression of key clicks is easier when keying low-power circuits, or an early stage rather than the pa. Early stage keying may affect an oscillator (see p69) and the following Class C stages may tend to nullify the effect of a key-click filter. However, on the whole it is preferable to key at the lowest power level.

Unwanted transmitter outputs: harmonics, mixer products and spurious oscillations

Harmonics. Harmonics of the wanted output frequency may fall on or near tv and fm radio channels, leading to complaints from neighbours. For example, 5 × 144MHz = 720MHz. This is close to tv Channel 52 in the UK. It should be noted that the hf bands are harmonically related to certain tv channels in Band 1, eg 21MHz ×2 and 14MHz × 3 equals 42MHz (Channel 1). Harmonics from the lower frequency amateur bands may fall *within* a higher band (eg 2 × 3·53MHz = 7·06MHz), thus interfering with other amateurs, or *outside* the hf end (eg 2 × 3·7MHz = 7·4MHz), interfering with other services.

Harmonics occur especially in the high-power stages of a transmitter where Class C amplification is used. This may be very efficient, but it is also very non-linear. Even the relatively linear Class A, Class AB and Class B amplifiers used in ssb transmitters can generate an appreciable level of harmonics. Many hf transmitters employ *pi-networks* for the pa stage tuned circuit. These greatly reduce harmonic levels as they act as low-pass filters.

It is not only the output stages where harmonics occur. Many transmitters use multiplier stages to obtain the final output frequency—especially at vhf and uhf (see Chapter 5). It is possible that radiation from these stages may reach the transmitter output (for example, from the 72MHz stage in a 144MHz transmitter). Furthermore, in this type of transmitter radiation from the 8MHz oscillator (and its harmonics) may modulate the 144MHz output and appear as sidebands at 136 and 152MHz etc. These are close to the resonant frequency of the antenna and will be radiated strongly. They may cause very serious interference to mobile and aircraft communication, and other essential services.

Harmonics may be minimized by adhering to the following principles:

(a) Avoid excessive drive to any stage. Up to a certain point increased drive gives a worthwhile increase of output on the wanted frequency. Beyond this point output may rise only slightly, but unwanted harmonics may increase greatly.

(b) Avoid excessive bias of Class C amplifiers and frequency multipliers as unnecessarily large drive levels will be required. The effect is similar to (a).

(c) Minimize stray capacitive coupling in tuned circuits. Ensure that secondary coupling windings are (where possible) wound at the "earthy" end of the primary winding. Keep the centre point of push-pull tuned circuits at zero rf (earth) potential by the use of split-stator tuning capacitors or by a centre tap on the coil with an rf decoupling (bypass) capacitor.

(d) Arrange the circuit layout to permit very short leads—especially between transistors or valves and their associated tuned circuits. This reduces the chances of parasitic resonances at vhf or uhf.

(e) Arrange for low-impedance earthing and earth-return circuits. Use single-point earthing rather than earth returns via metalwork or printed-circuit tracks.

(f) Screen each stage carefully—especially those where harmonic generation is likely, and in particular the pa stage.

(g) Filter and/or screen internal power-supply leads. Use suitable rf chokes and decoupling capacitors.

(h) Ensure that the *whole transmitter* and each piece of ancillary equipment (swr meter, atu etc) is screened by a metal case. This must be as "rf tight" as possible, being made from a low-resistance material with no large holes or slots. Joints should be free of paint and overlap, with bolts not more than about 5cm apart. "Wrap-around" cases with lift-up lids are usually very poor rf screens.

(j) Filter and/or screen all external leads (microphone, mains, key etc) and all interconnecting leads (from psu, control box etc).

(k) At hf, use a low-pass filter between the transmitter and atu. At vhf and uhf a bandpass filter is more appropriate (and more effective).

(l) Where a selective bandpass filter is not used in the antenna feeder, use an atu which discriminates against harmonics, and preferably also against frequencies below the wanted output frequency. At hf, use an atu even if the antenna feed impedance is nominally suitable for direct connection to the transmitter.

(m) Use good-quality coaxial cable for connections between transmitter, swr meter, atu etc.

(n) Do not rely on the antenna to reject harmonics: ensure that the feed to the antenna is harmonic-free.

Mixer products. Many transmitters use mixing processes to obtain the required output frequency—especially for ssb and vfo-controlled vhf transmissions. Mixers (frequency changers or converters) produce not only the wanted *sum* or *difference* frequencies (see Chapter 2) but also a whole range of undesirable signals. Most significant are harmonics of the local oscillator injection and harmonic mixing products, ie outputs created when the self-generated oscillator harmonics mix with the input signal to produce a large number of sum and difference signals.

For example, an ssb signal generated on 9MHz may be converted for transmission on 14MHz using an oscillator on 5MHz (9MHz + 5MHz = 14MHz). Unfortunately, the mixer may generate a strong signal on 3 × 5MHz = 15MHz, and it is unlikely that succeeding tuned circuits will be sufficiently selective to reject this as it is only 1MHz away from the wanted signal. Balanced and double-balanced mixers greatly reduce this problem because ideally the oscillator, its harmonics and the input signal do not appear at the output.

Unwanted mixer products may be minimized by the following:

(a) Choose signal generation and oscillator frequencies carefully so that unwanted outputs are remote from the wanted output. This simplifies subsequent filtering.
(b) Do not overdrive mixers either with input signal or oscillator injection. This reduces harmonic generation and harmonic mixing.
(c) Use balanced and double-balanced mixers to reduce the number of unwanted outputs.

Spurious oscillations. Unexpected oscillations may occur as *parasitic* oscillations. These are at frequencies quite different from the intended operating frequency of a stage—usually at relatively low frequencies or at vhf. *Self-oscillations* can also occur but these are usually at or close to the intended frequency.

Oscillations at low frequencies may appear as multiple sidebands each side of the transmitter output frequency. They are caused by instability in audio stages and regulated power supplies (often at supersonic frequencies) or by chance resonances of circuit components such as rf chokes and decoupling capacitors. The latter is a particular problem in hf and vhf transistor transmitters where the power transistors have very high current gain at relatively low frequencies. Positive steps must be taken to ensure good lf decoupling. Fig 8.3 shows a tuned stage where Cl, Ll and C2 provide decoupling for the dc supply feed to the parallel-tuned circuit L2 C3. However, there is also a "hidden" parallel-tuned circuit formed by Ll and C2 (the ht end of Ll is earthed at rf via Cl). This resonates at approximately 2MHz. The addition of Rl and C4 completely damps out this resonance and no oscillation at this frequency is possible.

Low-frequency oscillation may also occur where rf chokes are used in both the input and output circuits of an amplifier (particularly if impedances are high). These chokes resonate with the circuit capacitances, and if the output tunes slightly higher than the input, oscillation may occur. This is prevented if the input choke is made much smaller than the output choke so that the input parasitic frequency is kept well above that of the output.

Low-frequency oscillations may be detected as follows:

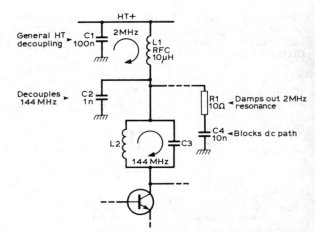

Fig 8.3. Suppression of low-frequency spurious resonance

(a) Check the width of the transmission by monitoring on a receiver. Take care not to overload it. Look for the presence of sidebands when no modulation is applied—these may be several megahertz from the centre frequency, especially on vhf and uhf transmissions.
(b) Remove the input signal from the stage (making temporary adjustments to the bias conditions if this will otherwise cause excessive anode or collector dissipation). Check for the presence of rf oscillations on supposedly decoupled ht feed points. Various equipment may be used, eg a simple rf detector probe, an oscilloscope (up to a few megahertz), a general-coverage receiver etc. In most cases it will not be necessary to make a connection to the circuit, proximity being sufficient. Take care when high voltages are present.

Oscillations at vhf and uhf can occur when in hf transmitters an unfortunate choice of circuit layout results in resonances at these frequencies due to stray capacitances and lead inductances. High-impedance circuits which are physically large are a particular danger, a common example being a valve pa stage where stray circuit capacitance tunes with the lead from the anode cap. Leads to the control and screen grids may also form vhf tuned circuits. It is often impossible to reduce lead lengths, but such resonances may be prevented by the series addition of small vhf chokes or low-value resistors (of about 50Ω) as close as possible to the valve electrodes. Preferably chokes should be "lossy" (ie have a low Q) at vhf, and the use of ferrite beads, or chokes wound using low-value resistors as formers, is recommended.

Oscillations may also occur because at vhf many capacitors are inductive and therefore have poor decoupling properties, particularly if they are of significant physical size. Tubular capacitors should be avoided. Disc ceramic and similar types are preferred, and should be kept as small as the voltage rating permits. Lead lengths must be as short as possible. Feedthrough capacitors are good for vhf and uhf.

The use of multiple (paralleled) decoupling capacitors may be necessary because at the operating frequency of a stage a capacitor of, say, 1,000pF may give optimum effect while at vhf it may be ineffective. The parallel addition of about 50pF should provide good vhf decoupling.

VHF and uhf parasitics may be detected as follows:
(a) Tune a sensitive dip meter or absorption wavemeter over a wide frequency range while holding it close to the stage under suspicion.
(b) Remove the input signal from the stage (making temporary adjustments to the bias conditions if this will otherwise cause excessive collector or anode dissipation). Adjust input and output tuning while monitoring collector or anode current. This should remain completely steady—any change may indicate vhf oscillation. However, a flicker of current reading when tuning is near the normal resonant settings may indicate self-oscillation near the stage operating frequency, and not at vhf.
(c) Touch the transistor input and output leads with a screwdriver with an insulated handle. *Great care* must be exercised when touching high-voltage points. Any change of supply current *may* indicate the presence of oscillation, the frequency and amplitude of which are being altered by the screwdriver capacitance. However, oscillation may occur only when the screwdriver touches, so other tests are necessary.

Self-oscillation can occur when a stage's input and output circuits are both tuned to the same frequency due to poor screening between these circuits. The oscillation frequency will be unstable and will vary if the stage input or output tuning is varied. It may have a rough note. There is a serious risk of strong radiation outside the amateur bands.

The oscillation may not be present all the time, occurring only on modulation peaks or (more likely) when no input drive is applied, ie in the key-up condition on cw or between words on ssb. The result is often a rough cw note with chirps and clicks, or poor-quality "splashy" speech.

Self-oscillations may be dealt with in a manner similar to that for vhf parasitics, using a dip meter or absorption wavemeter. A general-coverage receiver may also be used to listen for and then locate the source of the oscillation.

Mains-borne interference. When end-fed antennas are used the rf earth return from the atu must be considered as part of the antenna system. A good short low-resistance connection is required. The mains earth must *never* be used as an rf earth because it will feed all the antenna current into the mains earth system. As the earth wire is closely coupled to the live and neutral conductors, a large proportion of the transmitter output power may be distributed through the mains wiring into the amateur's own (and neighbouring) property. It is unreasonable to expect domestic tv, radio and audio equipment to be immune to interference in these circumstances. A mains rf earth will also greatly increase the level of mains-borne interference to reception in the amateur station.

For safety reasons the station equipment must be well earthed. The mains earth should be quite suitable. A separate earth should not be connected to equipment already using the mains earth, particularly when the domestic supply uses an earth-leakage trip system.

Transmitting antennas which minimize interference. Some types of antennas increase the risk of interference to neighbours. For example, an inverted-L Marconi antenna has a down-lead and earth lead which are usually close to dwellings. This will induce a strong signal into house wiring and tv coaxial feeders, thus making interference more likely. There is less chance of interference with balanced, horizontal antennas such as centre-fed dipoles, and these should always be fed with balanced feeder, or with coaxial cable via a balun located at the antenna feed point. A dipole *will* function when fed directly from coaxial cable, but there is considerable radiation from the feeder. The system acts somewhat like an inverted-L antenna.

All antennas should be located as far as possible from dwellings, overhead power cables and telephone lines. The use of indoor transmitting antennas is seldom practicable.

Affected equipment defects

Despite all precautions, the amateur may still interfere with those using nearby radio frequencies (usually other amateurs) or with neighbours' tv, radio and audio equipment.

Interference to nearby frequencies
Insufficient receiver selectivity. A receiver with poor overall selectivity will receive signals over a bandwidth greater than that required for communication purposes. The situation is aggravated if the wanted signal is weak and the unwanted signal is strong.
Receiver overload. The selectivity which precedes the first potentially non-linear device (transistor, valve, diode mixer etc) in a receiver or converter is inadequate to remove signals on adjacent frequencies. In consequence, such devices may overload in the presence of strong signals which are many kilohertz (or even megahertz) away. One result is *cross-modulation,* where the modulation of the interfering signal is superimposed on the wanted signal. Another is that the interfering signal seems to splatter over a wide band, due to the generation of intermodulation products.

If the offending frequency is sufficiently remote, it may be rejected by a bandstop filter or rejection trap in the receiver antenna feed. Alternatively a bandpass filter tuned to the wanted frequency may be added. However, if the wanted and interfering frequencies are close, the only cure is to improve the signal-handling performance of the devices which are overloaded.

Television interference (tvi)
The amateur's signal may be picked up on the tv antenna or on the coaxial downlead, and may overload

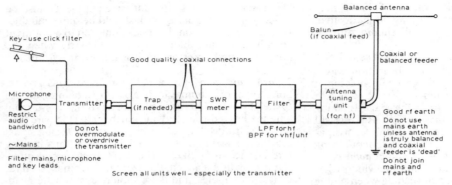

Fig 8.4. Station equipment required for minimum of interference

the tuner, the i.f. amplifier, or indeed any stage in the set (including video and audio stages). Less frequently, it enters via the mains lead or by direct pick-up.

The frequency separation between the amateur and tv bands allows various filters to be inserted in the tv antenna lead. These reject the amateur signal without attenuating the tv signals. For vhf tv reception on Bands 1 and 3 a *high-pass* filter (cutting off below 40MHz) is used to cure tvi from hf transmissions. However, for the 70, 144 and 432MHz amateur bands, *bandstop* filters are more appropriate. For uhf tv on Bands 4 and 5 a high-pass filter (cutting off below 470MHz) is generally suitable, but again, simple bandstop filters (such as notch filters or traps) are useful where only one vhf amateur band causes trouble.

Download pick-up is a problem which affects mainly the lower-frequency amateur bands. There is little pick-up on the antenna itself. Quite large rf currents can flow into the set on both the braid and on the inner conductor. These currents tend to be in-phase, as if the braid and inner were connected together, whereas signals from the tv antenna are in anti-phase. To prevent interference it is necessary to insert between download and set a *braid-breaking* device which blocks in-phase currents, but allows the anti-phase antenna signal to pass without attenuation.

Several techniques are used. A braid-breaking choke may be constructed by winding several turns of thin coaxial cable around a high-permeability ferrite rod or, more effectively, a large ring core. Alternatively, an rf isolation transformer (with separate primary and secondary windings) may be wound on small ferrite beads or a balun core. In some locations it may be possible to divert the interfering current from the set by earthing the braid of the download where it enters the house.

Mains-supply pick-up is often cured by winding the lead of the affected set to form a choke similar to the braid-breaking choke. Direct pick-up in the set itself is difficult to deal with because it probably entails internal modifications.

Interference to radio

Where an external antenna is used, interference to vhf fm radio in Band 2 may be tackled in the same way as interference to vhf tv. Alternatively a bandpass filter for Band 2 may be used.

Medium- and long-wave radios often use internal ferrite-rod antennas. They rarely have external antennas, so filtering is impracticable. Interference may occur due to image or second-channel interference (see Chapter 4), and this causes amateur 1·8MHz band signals to appear when the set is tuned to the medium waveband. Harmonic mixing also occurs where harmonics of the receiver local oscillator beat with an hf amateur signal to give an i.f. output. As a result the signal may be tuned in at several positions on the long or medium wavebands.

Interference to audio equipment

Interference is due entirely to *rectification* of the amateur signal, usually in the early stages of the audio amplifier. Pick-up frequently occurs via the long speaker leads, which often form a dipole "antenna". It may also occur on the mains lead and on the various leads to the tape deck, record turntable etc. Direct pick-up is also possible.

Speaker and mains lead pick-up is often cured by winding the leads to form rf chokes on ferrite rods or rings (as for tvi). RF decoupling capacitors across the amplifier speaker sockets or the use of screened speaker leads may also be effective. However, in difficult cases it is necessary to carry out internal modifications to the audio circuits, usually entailing the addition of rf bypass capacitors and chokes to the offending stages.

Correct station format

Fig 8.4 shows an example of the equipment necessary to ensure the minimum of interference. If interference occurs with this format, it will almost certainly be due to a defect in the affected equipment and not the transmitting station. This avoids the possibility of irritation to a neighbour because of a prolonged (and fruitless) series of tests intended to cure interference by fitting filters to his tv set. In any case, the licensing authorities have every right to expect the amateur to engineer his station in a manner which will minimize official investigations into interference complaints. The function of each component is as follows:

Antenna. Use an antenna which helps to minimize

interference (see p73). Note particularly that end-fed antennas, such as in Fig 7.17, are more likely to produce a high signal level in the house than are dipoles. Keep all antennas as remote as possible from houses.

ATU. This matches the transmitter to the impedance seen at the input to the feeder. Even if the feed impedance is correct, a tuning unit can give a useful rejection of unwanted signals (both on transmit and on receive). When using a balanced antenna feeder, the atu may also function as a balun.

Filter. At vhf and uhf, a single-bandpass filter is best. This removes unwanted transmitter outputs both above and below the required band. For multiband hf operation, it is more convenient to use a low-pass filter which cuts off at about 30MHz. The characteristic impedance of the filter should be 50/75Ω.

SWR meter. This facilitates the tuning of the atu for the correct matching of the impedances. As it usually contains rectifier diodes (see Fig 9.10) it should be located before the filter so that any harmonics which are generated will be removed.

Trap. A trap is a simple stop filter for one particular frequency which may be troublesome (eg 2nd or 3rd harmonics). It usually contains only one tuned circuit and may be added if necessary to supplement the attenuation provided by the filter. A simple trap will create some mismatch (which will be tuned out by the transmitter output tuning) and it must be located before the swr meter to prevent a permanent swr reading.

Transmitter. Filter leads where they leave the case. Use a key-click filter and restrict audio bandwidth to 2·5kHz. Do not overmodulate or overdrive.

Cases. Enclose each piece of equipment in metal cases to prevent leakage of rf signals. The importance of good screening cannot be emphasized sufficiently.

Interconnections. Use good-quality coaxial connections between units.

Earth connection. Do not use the mains earth as an rf earth return. It is also unwise to use the domestic water supply or central heating piping because this too may create a high field strength in the house. For obvious safety reasons no connections of any kind should be made to the gas supply.

Frequency measurement

It is absolutely essential that no transmissions be made outside the amateur bands, and signals should be located sufficiently inside band edges to allow for the spread of sidebands. The Home Office requirements for frequency checking and simple measuring equipment are dealt with in Chapter 9.

An inductively coupled absorption wavemeter is invaluable as a test instrument during the construction of transmitters, but for day-to-day operation of the station it is more convenient to use a tuneable "field-strength" meter (misnamed). This may consist essentially of an absorption wavemeter equipped with a short whip antenna, a detector circuit and a microammeter, and is used to check that the transmission is on the intended band. This avoids the possibility of tuning a transmitter to the wrong band which can happen, for example, if the bandswitch is set for 7MHz but the pa is inadvertently resonated on 14MHz. This error may not be immediately apparent on the station receiver.

It is convenient to have a crystal calibrator as a band-edge marker, permanently connected to (and preferably built into) the station receiver. 100kHz markers identify almost all the amateur band edges, while 25kHz markers give additional points against which to check the receiver dial calibration.

CHAPTER 9

Measurements

Correct operation of amateur radio equipment involves measurements to ensure optimum performance, to comply with the terms of the amateur transmitting licence and to avoid interference to other users. The purpose of these measurements is to give the operator information regarding the conditions under which his equipment is functioning. There are three basic parameters: voltage, current and frequency.

For example, in even the simplest transmitter it is necessary to know the drive to the various stages (current measurements), the input power to the pa (current and voltage measurements) and the frequency of the radiated signal.

DC measurements

The basis of most instruments for the measurement of voltage, current and resistance is the *moving-coil meter*. This comprises a coil of wire, generally wound on a rectangular former, and mounted on pivots in the field of a permanent magnet (Fig 9.1). The coil develops a torque proportional to (i) the current flowing through it and (ii) the strength of the field of the permanent magnet. Current is fed to the coil through two hair springs mounted near to each end of the spindle. These springs also serve to return the pointer to the zero position (on the left-hand side of its travel in standard meters) when the current ceases to flow. Provision for adjusting the position of the pointer is made by a *zero adjuster*, accessible from the front of the instrument.

Since the movement of the coil and its associated pointer is proportional to the field of the magnet and that of the current being measured, the scale is linear. The moving-coil instrument can be used only on dc, but it can be adapted to measure ac.

It is usual to *damp* the coil system (ie prevent it swinging freely after a change of current), a common method being to wind the coil on an aluminium former, which then acts as a short-circuited, single-turn coil in which the eddy currents serve to oppose the movement. The degree of eddy-current damping is also dependent on the external resistance across the terminals of the moving coil and is greatest when the resistance is low. It is a wise precaution to protect sensitive instruments not in use by short circuiting the terminals.

When a moving-coil meter is used for measuring current it is called an *ammeter, milliammeter* or *microammeter*, depending on its *full-scale deflection* (fsd). A *dc voltmeter* is a milliammeter or microammeter equipped with a voltage-dropping resistor in series with it. The accuracy of a meter depends on many factors, eg size, quality, accuracy of shunt or multiplier resistor, the scale deflection (ie full-scale or half-scale reading). Usually, the size of meter most likely to be used in amateur radio would be 60–75mm in diameter and the accuracy would be of the order of 3 per cent to 5 per cent.

Milliammeters

Milliammeters and microammeters are commonly manufactured with basic full-scale deflections of 0–50μA, 0–100μA, 0–500μA, 0–1mA, 0–5mA and 0–10mA. For higher current ranges, a shunt resistor is connected across the meter (Fig 9.2(a)). The value of the shunt may be obtained from the formula

$$R_s = \frac{R_m}{n - 1}$$

where R_s is the resistance of the shunt, R_m is the resistance of the meter, and n is the scale-multiplying factor.

For example, if a milliammeter of 10Ω resistance and an fsd of 1mA is to be used to measure 100mA, a shunt must be provided to carry the excess current, ie $100 - 1mA$ (= 99mA). Thus the required resistance of the shunt is

$$R_s = \frac{10}{100 - 1} = \frac{10}{99} = 0.101\Omega$$

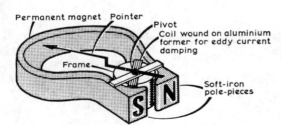

Permanent magnet Pointer
Pivot
Coil wound on aluminium former for eddy current damping
Frame
Soft-iron pole-pieces

Fig 9.1. Construction of moving-coil meter

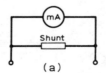

mA

Shunt

(a)

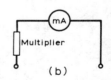

mA

Multiplier

(b)

Fig 9.2 Extending range of mc meter (a) to read higher current with parallel shunt; (b) to measure voltage with series resistor or multiplier

When moving-coil meters are used in circuits where high voltages are present (ie in pa anode circuits), care must be taken to avoid accidental electric shock from the zero adjuster, which may be live. If the instrument is of the flush-mounting type, the front of the meter may be covered with a piece of clear plastic about 1–2mm thick.

Voltmeters

A milliammeter may be used to read dc voltages by connecting a resistor, termed a *multiplier*, in series with it (Fig 9.2(b)). The value of the multiplier depends on the fsd of the meter and may be calculated from Ohm's Law.

For low-voltage ranges, the value of the multiplier can be obtained from

$$R_s = R_M \left(\frac{V}{V_M} - 1 \right)$$

where R_s is the resistance of the multiplier, R_M the resistance of the meter, V the required voltage and V_M the voltage across the meter (this can be determined by applying Ohm's Law to the resistance of the meter and current flowing through it). In practice, however, the resistance of the meter can be ignored and the formula simplified to

$$R_s = \frac{1,000V}{I}$$

where V is the desired range and I is the fsd of the meter in milliamps.

For example, a 0–5mA meter is to be used as the basis of a voltmeter to read 100V. Then

$$R_s = \frac{1,000 \times 100}{5} = 20,000\Omega$$

The dissipation of the voltage multiplier at fsd of the meter must be checked. In the above example, the dissipation is

$$\begin{aligned} W &= I^2R \\ &= 0.005 \times 0.005 \times 20,000 \\ &= 0.5W \end{aligned}$$

To minimize the temperature rise and hence the increase in value of the multiplier resistor, it should be conservatively rated. A 1W resistor would be satisfactory.

It is usual to describe the sensitivity of a voltmeter in *ohms per volt;* in the example considered above, the meter reading 100V for a full-scale deflection of 5mA would be said to have a sensitivity of 200Ω/V.

Whenever a voltage measurement is made on a circuit of appreciable resistance, the current taken by the voltmeter should be considered to ensure that the operating conditions are not significantly altered by connecting the voltmeter.

A sensitivity of 200Ω/V is much too low for use in radio circuits. 1,000Ω/V is barely acceptable in some circumstances but 10,000Ω/V or ideally 20,000Ω/V, corresponding to full-scale deflections of 100μA or 50μA respectively, is the preferred sensitivity.

The accuracy of a voltmeter depends on the accuracy of the multipliers. Precision resistors are the most suitable, but rather costly, and may be replaced in homebuilt equipment by 1 per cent high-stability carbon film resistors of adequate power rating.

AC measurements

The moving-coil meter can be adapted to measure ac by the addition of a small bridge rectifier known as an *instrument rectifier*. Although such a meter indicates the average value, ie 0·636 of the peak value of a sine wave, it is usually calibrated in rms values. Rectifier meters may be used at frequencies of up to about 10kHz, but are only accurate when the waveform is sinusoidal. Multiplier resistors can be added to a rectifier instrument but current measurement requires a special transformer known as a *current transformer*.

Thermocouple meters

In conjunction with a thermocouple, a moving-coil instrument can be used to read alternating currents of up to radio frequencies. The thermocouple is a junction of two dissimilar metals which when heated generates a dc voltage. The junction is heated by the current to be measured passing through a *heater*, to which it is attached. A disadvantage of the arrangement is that low current readings are rather severely compressed. Thermocouple instruments read true rms values irrespective of waveform. Unless specially designed, such instruments become less accurate as frequency increases, owing to the effect of the shunt capacitance.

Thermojunction meters must be used with great care as the thermojunction can be burnt out by a current not much greater than the maximum reading of the meter.

Multi-range meters

Many commercial multi-range meters are available. These consist of a number of voltage multipliers and current shunts, an instrument rectifier and current transformer, all of which are switched to provide a large number of dc and ac voltage and current ranges on a high-sensitivity meter.

Voltage measurement at high frequencies

The rectifier instrument is usable at frequencies in the lower audio range and has a reasonable accuracy (order of 4 per cent) provided that the waveform to be measured is sinusoidal. In the rf range an *electronic voltmeter* is required. This consists of a diode detector which produces a direct voltage proportional to the peak value of the alternating voltage. This is followed by amplifier circuits feeding a meter calibrated in volts. The electronic voltmeter can give accurate readings up to a frequency of several hundreds of megahertz and may have a sensitivity of the order of 10MΩ/V, thus the load it places on the circuit is so small that it can be ignored.

Measurement of voltage and current in a transmitter

Measurement, or at least indication of maximum and minimum current, is essential in the tuning of a transmitter.

Low-power semiconductor multiplier/amplifier chains may be resonated by tuning the input for maximum collector current and then resonating the collector tuned circuit for minimum collector current.

A meter of suitable range should be permanently wired into the pa collector circuit. This circuit may be retuned every time the antenna or wavelength is changed and the pa current must be checked to ensure that the dc input power to the pa does not exceed the maximum permitted value, for of course dc input = voltage × current. It is satisfactory to measure the anode or collector voltage at the dc input terminal of the pa, as application of a voltmeter to the actual anode or collector throws the pa off-tune and gives an erroneous reading.

Dummy loads

A dummy load consists of a non-inductive resistor having a wattage rating equal to the expected output power. Such a dummy load would have a resistance of about 50Ω or 70Ω and may if required consist of a parallel or series/parallel connection of carbon resistors; for example 10 5W 680Ω resistors may be connected in parallel to provide a 50W 68Ω load which would be satisfactory for a 75W input transmitter. The dissipation of the load may be increased by immersing it in oil. A dummy load should be screened.

Frequency measurement

The reasons for frequency measurement are:

(i) the accurate measurement of transmitter frequency to ensure that the transmission is within the licensed band;

(ii) to ensure that the tuned circuits in the transmitter cover the required frequency range.

Assuming that a receiver having a reasonably accurate frequency calibration is available, the calibration can be checked against short-wave broadcast stations of known frequency or against standard frequency transmissions, for example MSF Rugby (2·5, 5 and 10MHz) or WWV (10, 15, 20 and 25MHz).

An accurate calibration may also be made by listening to the beats produced in the receiver from harmonics of a crystal oscillator. When used in conjunction with a general coverage receiver, a 100kHz crystal is usually adequate for checking frequencies up to about 4MHz. For higher frequencies, the spacing between 100kHz marker points may be too small to resolve, and a crystal of 500kHz or preferably 1MHz should be used in addition. If the receiver covers only the amateur bands, the bandspread is normally adequate to resolve the harmonics from the 100kHz crystal.

100kHz crystals for use in frequency standards are available with frequency accuracies of 0·005 per cent.

One of these should be considered as the prime frequency standard, as higher-frequency crystals may be slightly less accurate. A 100kHz crystal can be checked by comparing its second harmonic with the BBC long-wave transmitter at Droitwich, the frequency of which is maintained at 200kHz to an extremely high degree of accuracy.

A calibration graph or table can now be drawn up for each range of the receiver. It must be kept in mind that the accuracy of this depends on the precision of the receiver dial mechanism, its logging arrangement and the presence of bandspread. The frequency of operation of a transmitter may then be measured using the receiver, calibrated as above.

Obviously the receiver cannot be tuned to even a low-power transmitter in the immediate vicinity, but it can "listen to" the output of the vfo, the frequency of which may then be determined and hence the final output frequency of the transmitter. Although the vfo is screened, it will be found necessary to reduce considerably the receiver rf gain. The tuning range of a vfo can be quite easily adjusted to the required value in this manner.

The absorption frequency meter

The absorption frequency meter consists of a coil tuned by a variable capacitor, with a scale calibrated in frequency. It operates by absorbing power from a tuned circuit when tuned to the same frequency as that circuit. The tuned circuit must therefore be activated, and the absorption of power is indicated by a small change or flick in the transistor or valve feed current flowing through the tuned circuit as the resonance point is passed.

Such a frequency meter has the advantages of (a) rugged construction and simplicity; (b) low cost; (c) no power supply required; (d) direct reading calibration with no confusing production of beat notes or harmonics.

The disadvantages are that:

(a) only the *order* of the frequency being checked is indicated, not the actual value. Thus an absorption frequency meter may show whether a transmitter frequency is nearer one end or the other of an amateur band, but it is quite incapable of showing whether the frequency is just inside or just outside the limit of the band;

(b) it lacks sensitivity. To obtain an indication in low-power transmitters, or in receiver tuned circuits, the absorption frequency meter must be held close to the coil being checked. Screening or other components may make difficult, if not impossible, the use of the instrument;

(c) the presence of the frequency meter may cause an appreciable de-tuning of the circuit under test.

The great merit of an absorption frequency meter is in checking that frequency-multiplying stages are tuned to the correct harmonic, for example, in checking whether a particular stage being driven by a 7MHz oscillator is tuned to 21MHz (third harmonic) or to

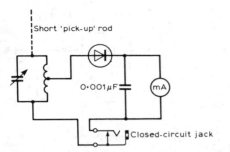

Fig 9.3. **Absorption wavemeter with microammeter as indicator of resonance**

28MHz (fourth harmonic). Such checking of harmonics is especially necessary in the initial tuning up of vhf equipment, which may operate on the 18th harmonic or higher of a given crystal frequency.

A rectifier and a microammeter can be added to the absorption frequency meter so that the meter itself can indicate resonance. This is shown in Fig 9.3. With the addition of a short antenna coupled to the coil, this arrangement becomes the so-called *"field strength meter"* which may also be used for searching for parasitic oscillations in the transmitter. If a close-circuit jack for headphones is connected in series with the meter, the circuit can be used for monitoring an amplitude-modulated transmission.

The dip meter

This is more flexible than the absorption meter in that the tuned circuit under test does not have to be energized.

It consists of an oscillator using a fet or a valve. When the oscillator is tuned to the frequency of the tuned circuit under test, power is absorbed from the oscillator. This is indicated by a dip in the grid current in the case of a valve or the source current when a fet is used (hence the name—*dip oscillator*). The dip oscillator has the same accuracy as the absorption meter but has the disadvantage that a power supply is needed (battery in the case of the fet oscillator).

The heterodyne frequency meter

A *heterodyne frequency meter* consists essentially of an oscillator. The frequency of oscillation may be crystal-controlled or may be made to cover a limited frequency range.

In the latter case, the components of the main tuned circuit must be carefully chosen to minimize the effects of temperature changes and vibration, and the slow-motion drive of the capacitor must permit resetting with precision to any desired point of the tuning scale.

A heterodyne frequency meter may (in addition to the main oscillator valve) use other stages, either for calibration checks or for amplification of harmonics to extend the frequency range.

The advantages are:

(a) Precision readings. A good instrument should

enable frequencies to be measured to better than 1kHz on the hf bands. It will thus readily indicate whether a given transmitter frequency is just inside or just outside a particular amateur band;

(b) Ease of coupling to transmitter or receiver. Generally, a few centimetres of wire as antenna will suffice;

(c) The use of harmonics permits the instrument to be used over a wide frequency range without coil-changing or switching, both of which introduce the possibility of inconsistent readings;

(d) Calibration can generally be checked at intervals against standard frequency transmitters such as MSF or WWV or major broadcasting stations.

The disadvantages are:

(a) Power supply required;

(b) Calibration is affected by voltages applied to the oscillator. Voltage stabilization of the power supply is desirable;

(c) Precision design entails high cost;

(d) The presence of harmonics may give rise to confusing beat notes with the frequency being checked, and the operator must guard against being misled.

Absorption and heterodyne frequency meters are thus complementary to each other. The first gives an initial check of the order of the frequency, the second a much more precise indication of the actual value.

Fig 9.4 gives the circuit of a simple heterodyne frequency meter which is based on a widely used surplus instrument, the Class D wavemeter. Checking of the calibration is achieved by the use of two crystals.

A triode-hexode valve is used. The triode section, with the components to the right-hand side of the diagram, operates as a crystal oscillator. The crystals are connected between grid and anode in a simple Pierce circuit and have frequencies of 100 and 1,000kHz

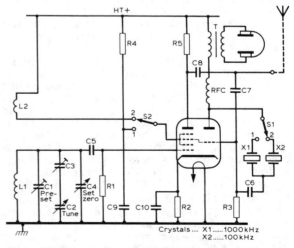

Fig 9.4. **Circuit of an accurate frequency meter. Left-hand electrodes of valve and associated components form oscillator tunable over a range of 100kHz and modulated by harmonics of 100kHz crystal. The 1,000kHz crystal provides check points over a wide frequency coverage**

respectively. Either can be selected by switch S1. Headphones are connected in the anode circuit of the triode through the matching transformer T.

(a) *Production of 1,000kHz check points.* With switches S1 and S2 in position 1 (they may operate from the same shaft), and ht and lt applied to the valve, oscillation occurs at 1,000kHz. This frequency, and its attendant harmonics, varies the electron flow in the hexode portion of the valve, which acts as an amplifier. The output in the anode circuit is taken via the small coupling capacitor C8 to the output terminal of the frequency meter, to which a short length of wire may be connected as an antenna. The harmonic output is sufficient to give check points at 1MHz spacing throughout the spectrum of the hf bands.

(b) *Production of 100kHz check points and intermediate measurement of frequencies.* With S1 in position 2, similar oscillation and amplification is obtained at 100kHz, and harmonics of this frequency, the action being as above. As the high-order harmonics required for use in the hf bands tend to be weak, it is better to use the hexode section of the valve as an oscillator, working more in the region of the hf bands, and to modulate the output of this oscillator at a frequency of 100kHz and harmonics. The hexode and the components to the left hand of the diagram form this oscillator.

A reaction (or feedback) coil L2 is inductively coupled to the grid coil L1 and is brought into circuit when switch S2 is set to position 2, with switch S1 also in position 2. If this oscillator were set to, say, 7,000kHz, modulation at 100kHz would give, in addition to this fundamental frequency, sideband frequencies of 6,900 and 7,100kHz. The second harmonic (200kHz) of the modulation would give frequencies of 6,800 and 7,200kHz, and so on. Shifting the oscillator to, say, 7,001kHz, the corresponding figures would be 6,901 and 7,101kHz, 6,801 and 7,201kHz etc.

By making the oscillation of the hexode section cover a range of 100kHz, a complete coverage of generated frequencies is obtained.

In the circuit of Fig 9.4, L1 is pre-tuned to 7,000kHz by the capacitor C1, C2 being set to maximum value (vanes full meshed). The value of C2 is chosen so that when this capacitor is at minimum setting, the frequency has risen to 7,100kHz, eg a coverage of 100kHz. Preset series capacitor C3 enables the tuning range of C2 to be adjusted accurately to 100kHz. Thus C2 is the tuning capacitor, which should be of first-class construction, with vanes cut to provide a linear change of frequency with rotation. The tuning dial of this capacitor should be marked from 0 to 100kHz and be similarly of high quality.

(c) *To measure a frequency.* With ht and lt switched on, and S1, S2 in position 2, the instrument is allowed to warm up to operating temperature. Calibration is first checked as follows: the operator listens in the headphones and sets the tuning capacitor approximately to the dial reading of 0kHz. A beat note is heard, the hexode oscillator beating with the harmonic of the

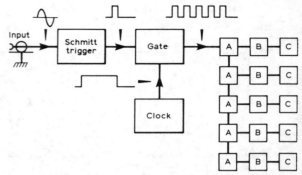

Fig 9.5. Simple block diagram of digital frequency meter

100kHz oscillator, and this beat note should fall to zero at a dial reading of 0kHz exactly. Similarly at the 100kHz end of the dial. Any slight shift due to temperature change can be corrected by adjustment of the panel control C4 which is a variable capacitor of a few picofarads only, set normally at mid-scale.

The operator next tunes C2 until a beat note is heard through the oscillator beating with the frequency of the transmitter being checked. This beat note is brought to zero by careful tuning of C2, and the dial is then read. Suppose the reading is 32kHz, then the last two figures of the frequency being measured are 32. Thus, if the transmitter has been set to between 7,000 and 7,100kHz, the indicated frequency is 7,032kHz.

Note that the operator must know to within 100kHz the frequency being measured; normally he will know this from earlier calibration of the transmitter tuning, or from earlier calibration of the receiver if an incoming signal is being checked for frequency.

Digital frequency meter

The fourth type of frequency meter utilizes digital integrated circuits to count the number of complete sine waves in a given period. This method provides the simplest and most accurate means of measuring frequency. Furthermore with the ever-decreasing cost of integrated circuits, digital frequency meters (DFMs) are rapidly becoming the cheapest form of accurate frequency measurement.

The principle of operation of a dfm is quite simple although the integrated circuits which perform the various operations are themselves very complex.

Consider the block diagram shown in Fig 9.5.

The signal whose frequency is to be measured is applied to the input of a Schmitt trigger. This circuit produces one pulse for every complete sine wave applied to its input. It is necessary to convert the sine waves into pulses as the digital circuits in the rest of the instrument will not work efficiently on sine waves. The pulses from the Schmitt trigger are then applied to an AND gate. This circuit will only let the pulses through when there is a pulse applied to its other input port. This second pulse is generated by the *clock* (see Fig 9.6).

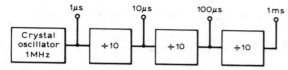

Fig 9.6. Simple block diagram of crystal-controlled clock used in dfm

The clock is a group of circuits which produce pulses with a very accurate duration. The accuracy of the pulse duration is determined by a crystal-controlled oscillator, usually at 1 or 5MHz. Thus if the clock pulse duration is 1ms and out of the gate by some means five pulses are counted, it can be seen that frequency has been measured because five pulses have occurred in that millisecond. Each pulse represents one complete sine wave cycle so this represents five cycles per millisecond or 5,000 cycles in one second, that is 5kHz.

To illustrate some of the pitfalls that can be encountered with dfm measurements, it is necessary to define two terms, "resolution" and "accuracy". *Resolution* is the smallest division to which a reading can be made, while *accuracy* is the closeness to the true value.

Knowing these definitions and looking again at the dfm measurement it can rapidly be seen that the resolution can be increased by increasing the period of the clock pulse.

This leads to a simple rule: *the resolution of a dfm is determined by the reciprocal of the clock period*, ie to measure to 1kHz it is necessary to use a clock pulse of 1ms. To measure to 1MHz 1μs is required and so on. One might think therefore that if the clock pulses can be made longer and longer more and more accurate results could be obtained. This is however not correct. The accuracy of the instrument as a whole is limited by the accuracy of the clock pulse. This in turn is determined by the crystal oscillator—which of course has errors in the crystal frequency and also drifts with temperature.

Amateur DFMs are accurate to about ±5Hz, and this is more than adequate for most applications.

Having discussed "accuracy" and "resolution", it can now be described how the string of pulses is converted into a number that can be displayed. To do this consider again the block diagram (Fig 9.5).

The pulses from the gate are fed to a series of integrated circuits (A) whose function can best be described by thinking of them as "buckets". When the first "bucket" is full of pulses it empties its entire contents into the next "bucket" which is 10 times the size of the first. When the second "bucket" is full it too empties its contents into the third which is again 10 times the size of the second "bucket" and so the process continues. It can be easily seen from this that the first "bucket" represents units, the second tens, the third hundreds and so forth. Thus, if for instance 5,761 pulses are received from the gate, the first "bucket", ie "units" will contain one pulse, the second will contain six, the third seven and the fourth five. The string of pulses has therefore been sorted into "buckets"

containing units, tens, hundreds and thousands of hertz. The next job is to display the number contained in each "bucket". This is done by section B. This group of integrated circuits looks at the number of pulses in each "bucket" and converts it from logic signals into a form that can operate the display devices (C). Section B also contains circuits to memorize the number in the "buckets" between measurements. This avoids the display flickering.

Many different types of integrated circuits can be used to make DFMs. The most common type will operate up to 20MHz but the latest integrated circuits can extend this range to 1,000MHz.

To conclude, the dfm is the most accurate way of making frequency measurements, having an accuracy of about ±5Hz in amateur equipment. It is also becoming the cheapest form of accurate frequency measurement and is much simpler to use than the heterodyne frequency meter.

The cathode-ray oscilloscope

The cathode-ray oscilloscope is probably the most valuable tool used in electronics. The heart of the oscilloscope is the cathode-ray tube. In this device, electrons emitted from an indirectly heated cathode are focused into a beam of small diameter which, when it strikes the front of the tube or screen, causes a special coating on the internal surface of the screen to fluoresce, creating a spot of light which may be blue or green according to the coating material used. On its way to the screen, the electron beam passes between one pair of parallel plates and then another pair at right angles to the first. These are called the *X* and *Y deflector plates*. If a voltage is applied between the deflection plates, the beam is deflected one way or the other according to the polarity of the voltage applied, and so the spot on the screen moves. Thus, if a voltage proportional to time is applied to one pair of plates, the horizontal deflection (X) plates, and an alternating voltage is applied to the vertical deflection (Y) plates, the spot traces out the waveform of the alternating voltage.

Timebase
The voltage applied to the X plates (ie horizontal motion) is generated inside the oscilloscope itself by what is usually referred to as the *timebase*. The speed of the timebase can be varied over a large range to accommodate signals of widely differing frequencies.

For the less-expensive oscilloscope as used by the amateur, the range of the timebase is from 1μs/cm to 1s/cm. Thus frequencies of up to 1MHz can be displayed.

Y amplifiers
The signals to be observed are usually very small. If they are applied directly to the Y plates little, if any, movement in the vertical direction would be observed. It is necessary, therefore, to amplify the signals before applying them to the Y plates. This amplifier is called the *Y amplifier* and is built into the oscilloscope.

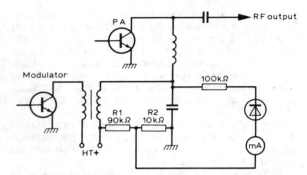

Fig 9.7. Over-modulation indicator biased to show when modulation depth exceeds 90 per cent. Critical percentage can be altered by varying R1 and R2

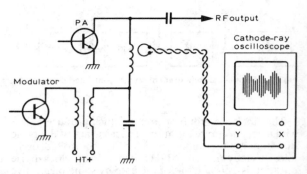

Fig 9.8. Arrangement for measuring modulation depth in which waveform of modulated carrier is displayed. Linear oscilloscope timebase is necessary

Several ranges of amplification are available, and each is calibrated so that a known voltage applied to the input causes a pre-determined deflection in the vertical direction. For amateur equipment the range of the Y amplifiers is from 5mV/cm to 100V/cm.

It should also be noted that the Y amplifiers have a limited bandwidth. Outside this bandwidth the calibration is not valid.

Trigger

To get a stationary display on the oscilloscope it is necessary to start the timebase at the same point on the waveform for every sweep. This is accomplished by the *trigger* circuits, the TRIGGER LEVEL control performing this function. On some older oscilloscopes stabilization is accomplished by altering the frequency of the timebase until it synchronizes with the input waveform—such oscilloscopes have a SYNC control.

Measurements of modulation

It is imperative to ensure that, when amplitude modulation is used, the modulation depth on peaks does not exceed 100 per cent as over-modulation creates serious interference (see Chapter 8).

A simple circuit which gives an indication when the modulation peaks exceed, say, 90 per cent is shown in Fig 9.7. The critical percentage can be adjusted by varying the potential divider R1 and R2.

The circuit functions because the diode cannot conduct as long as the negative peak of the modulating voltage is less than the dc voltage on the pa or whatever percentage of it is set by R1 and R2. If the negative peak is greater, it cancels the dc supply voltage, the diode conducts and the milliammeter shows a flick of current. If R1 and R2 are eliminated and the negative terminal of the milliammeter is connected to chassis, the diode will then conduct at 100 per cent modulation. The peak inverse voltage of the diode should be at least three times the dc supply voltage.

The actual depth of modulation may be measured by displaying the waveform of the modulated output of the transmitter on an oscilloscope.

The circuit arrangement is shown in Fig 9.8 which is largely self-explanatory. Typical patterns produced are shown in Fig 9.9. By measuring the height R corresponding to a modulation peak, and the heights of the unmodulated carrier, the depth of modulation can be calculated directly.

$$M = \frac{R - S}{S} \times 100 \text{ per cent}$$

VSWR measurement

As mentioned in Chapter 7, rf currents do not travel in wires in a similar manner to direct currents. This means that normal milliammeters and voltmeters cannot be used to measure currents and voltages, as these can vary depending on where along the wire they are measured. Obviously a different parameter is needed to define the performance of an rf circuit. This is called the *voltage standing wave ratio* (vswr).

VSWR is measured using a reflectometer bridge of the type shown in Fig 9.10. This works on the principle that when an rf transmission line is terminated in an impedance other than the characteristic impedance, ie the line is not properly matched, part of the signal is reflected back along the line. The ratio of the power reflected to the power incident on the termination is directly related to vswr and is independent of where in the line the reflectometer bridge is connected.

The simplest practical reflectometer bridge is shown in Fig 9.10. An insulated wire is threaded down between the outer shield and the insulation of a coaxial

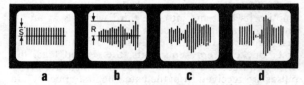

a   b   c   d

Fig 9.9. Typical patterns obtained by method shown in Fig 9.8. (a) Unmodulated carrier; (b) modulation depth is 50 per cent; (c) depth is 100 per cent; (d) over-modulation. Break-up of carrier shows that over-modulation is occurring

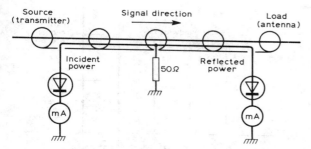

Fig 9.10. **Simple reflectometer for indication of vswr**

cable. When an rf signal passes down the coaxial cable part of it is coupled into the wire. This rf signal is rectified and the resulting dc is displayed on a milliammeter. This is an indication of the "forward" power. A reflected signal that is travelling from termination to source will also be coupled into the wire. However, it will do so in such a way that it is rectified by the other diode and displayed by the other milliammeter. This is the "reflected" power. From the ratio of these two readings it is possible to calculate the vswr. More sophisticated reflectometer bridges have a SENSITIVITY control such that the forward power can be set to a calibration point, usually fsd on the meter. The vswr can then be read directly from the reflected power meter. Often a single meter is switched to read forward or reflected power.

Measurement of the power of an ssb transmitter

The output power and hence the current drawn by the output stage of an ssb transmitter varies at a syllabic rate, ie in accordance with the speech waveform.

Measurement of input power is therefore not possible because the conventional meter is much too slow in operation to follow the rapid variation of the input current.

The power rating of an ssb transmitter is therefore expressed as peak envelope power (p.e.p.) as derived on p53. This is the power which exists at the peaks of the speech waveform. The maximum permitted p.e.p. is 400W (26dBW).

The recommended method of measuring p.e.p. is to monitor the output of the transmitter on a dummy load, by means of a cathode-ray oscilloscope, when the transmitter is modulated by the output of a *two-tone generator* as shown in Fig 9.11. This device contains two af oscillators which produce two non-harmonically related sinusoidal tones of equal amplitude which are combined.

The transmitter operating level is set to produce a mean power output in the dummy load of 200W as measured by the voltage across the load or the current flowing through it. The pattern produced on the oscilloscope will be as in Fig 9.11, and the limits of the deflection V should now be marked by two thin lines drawn by a Chinagraph pencil. The mean power as just measured (200W) is equivalent to a p.e.p. of twice this value, ie 400W. Thus the two lines on the 'scope face represent the deflection which corresponds to an output of 400W p.e.p. It is not essential to set the transmitter output to 200W mean, any power will do, but 200W is a convenient level because it causes a deflection which corresponds to the maximum p.e.p. permitted.

When the two-tone generator is replaced by the microphone, the oscilloscope now shows the extremely peaky speech waveform (Fig 9.12). The maximum deflection must not be allowed to exceed that deflection which corresponds to 400W p.e.p.

Other power levels may be determined as follows. Suppose the deflection corresponding to 400W p.e.p. is

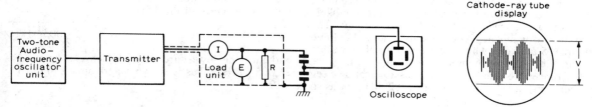

Fig 9.11. **Method of measuring p.e.p. output in relation to mean output with two-tone source.** Mean power output = I^2R or E^2/R; peak envelope power = 2 × mean power represented by V

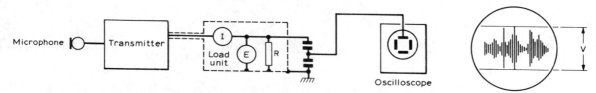

Fig 9.12. **Speech peaks should not exceed p.e.p. level determined by V in two-tone test**

5cm and the deflection resulting from peaks of speech is 2·5cm. The p.e.p. is then

$$400W \times \frac{2 \cdot 5^2}{5^2} = 400W \times \left(\frac{2 \cdot 5}{5}\right)^2$$
$$= 400W \times (\tfrac{1}{2})^2$$
$$= 100W$$

Note that the deflections are squared. This is because the deflection on the oscilloscope is proportional to the voltage which causes it, whereas power is proportional to the square of the voltage.

It will be appreciated that the majority of ssb transmitters and transceivers have outputs of 200W or less. The necessity for p.e.p. measurement only really arises when a high-power transmitter is in use or where a transceiver is followed by a linear amplifier, many of which are rated at power levels greater than permitted by the UK licence.

The procedure described above and illustrated in Fig 9.11 can be used to measure the power output of a transmitter operating in any mode. A single tone of a convenient frequency (say 1,000Hz) should be used to modulate an a.m. transmitter. The modulation depth should be adjusted to 100 per cent by variation of the tone input to the modulator when the transmitter is operating at the input intended. If cw or fm is in use, the transmitter should be in the "key down" or "transmit" state respectively.

Errors in measurement

When taking any measurements, the effect of inaccuracies in the meter used, ie the tolerances, which may be positive or negative, on the meter readings must be taken into account.

To take a simple case, suppose the input to a pa is measured as 15V at 10A, ie 150W. If both meters are reading low by say 5 per cent, the actual input is (15V + 5%) = 15·75V at (10A + 5%) = 10·5A. This is 165W which incidentally is above the UK licence limit. This can be considered as a worst case as it is unlikely that both meters will read low by this amount. The error in reasonably new good-quality meters should be less than 5 per cent, while old meters of unknown history may be in error by more than 10 per cent.

Tolerances are usually expressed as a percentage (eg ±2 per cent), a value (eg ±0·3V or ±200Hz) or as so

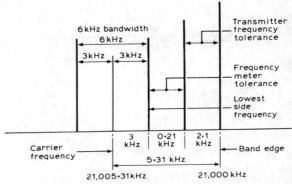

Fig 9.13. Diagrammatic solution of frequency tolerance problem

many "parts per million" (eg ±100ppm). A number of tolerances affecting a reading may be added together, although this is likely to give a pessimistic total. As an example, consider the following sample examination question.

A transmitter operating in the band 21MHz to 21·450MHz has a frequency tolerance of 100 parts in one million and a radiated bandwidth of 6kHz when using emissions of Type A3E. If the frequency checking equipment at the station has a frequency tolerance of 10 parts in one million what is the lowest frequency a licensee can use that ensures no emission below 21MHz?
    (a) 21,005·1kHz
    (b) 21,053·1kHz
    (c) 21,008·31kHz
    (d) 21,005·31kHz.

The tolerances build up as follows:

Band edge	21,000·0kHz
Frequency tolerance is 100ppm, ie 100Hz per megahertz	2·1kHz
Frequency meter tolerance 10ppm	0·21kHz
A3E bandwidth is 6kHz, ie carrier must be in centre of this band	3·0kHz
	21,005·31kHz

and thus the lowest frequency which can be used is 21,005·31kHz. This is shown diagrammatically in Fig 9.13.

CHAPTER 10

Licence conditions

This chapter contains the conditions of the Amateur Licence A, current at press time (May 1982); however, the latest issue of *How to Become a Radio Amateur* should be consulted in case changes have occurred. These conditions are straightforward and unambiguous and must be fully understood in order to answer questions in Paper 1 of the RAE, and of course to operate an amateur radio station in accordance with the requirements of the Secretary of State for the Home Office. It is recommended that the phonetic alphabet given in Note (m) be memorized.

The conditions of the Amateur Licence A

The following extract from the Amateur Licence A gives the conditions under which an amateur may operate his station:

1.
(1) *Licence* ....
of ....
(hereinafter called "the Licensee") is hereby licensed, subject to the terms, provisions and limitations herein contained:

(a) to establish in the United Kingdom an amateur sending and receiving station for wireless telegraphy (hereinafter called "the Station").

(i) At ....
(hereinafter called "the main address") or
(ii) At any premises (hereinafter called "the temporary premises") or any location (hereinafter called "the temporary location") for separate periods none of which shall exceed four consecutive weeks; or
(iii) At any premises (hereinafter called "the alternative premises") provided that at least seven days before the Station is established at the alternative premises notice in writing of the postal address of the alternative premises is given to the General Manager of the Post Office Telephone Area in which the alternative premises are situated or, in the case of the Channel Islands to the Director of the Telecommunications Board of the appropriate Bailiwick. The said General Manager or Director shall also be notified in writing when the Station is no longer established at the alternative premises; or
(iv) In any vehicle or vessel but not on the sea or within any estuary, dock or harbour;
(v) As a pedestrian;

(b) to use the Station for the purpose of sending to, and receiving from, other licensed amateur stations as part of the self-training of the Licensee in communication by wireless telegraphy;

(i) Messages in plain language which are remarks about matters of a personal nature in which the Licensee, or the person with whom he is in communication, has been directly concerned;
(ii) Facsimile signals;
(iii) Radio teleprinter signals;
(iv) Visual images;
(v) Signals (not being in secret code or cypher) which form part of, or relate to, the transmission of such messages, signals or images.

(c) To use the Station, as part of the self-training of the Licensee in communication by wireless telegraphy, during disaster relief operations conducted by the British Red Cross Society, the St John Ambulance Brigade, the Emergency County Planning Officer or any police force in the United Kingdom, or during any exercise relating to such operations, for the purpose of sending to other licensed amateur stations such messages as the Licensee may be requested by the said Society, Brigade, County Planning Officer or police force to send, and of receiving from any other licensed amateur station such messages as the person licensed to use such other licensed amateur station may be requested by the said Society, Brigade, County Planning Officer or such police force to send;

(d) To use the Station for the purpose of receiving transmissions in the Standard Frequency Service.

(2) *Limitations*. The foregoing Licence to establish and use the Station is subject to the following limitations:

(a) The Station shall not be established or used in an aircraft or a public transport vehicle.

(b) The Station shall be used only with emissions which are of the classes specified in the Schedule hereto and are within the frequency bands specified in the Schedule hereto in relation to those respective classes of emission, and with a power not exceeding that specified in the Schedule hereto in relation to the class of emission and frequency band in use at the time.

(c) The Station shall be operated only (i) by the Licensee personally, or (ii) in the presence of and under the direct supervision of the Licensee, by any other person who holds a current wireless telegraphy licence issued by the Secretary of State to use another amateur station or who holds an Amateur Radio Certificate issued by the Secretary of State.

(d) Messages other than initial calls shall not be broadcast to amateur stations in general, but shall be sent only to (i) amateur stations with which communication is established separately and singly, or (ii) groups of particular amateur stations provided that communication is first established separately and singly with each station in any such group.

(e) When the Station is used for the purpose of sending messages by the type of transmission known as radio teleprinter (rtty) it shall be used only with International Telegraph Code No 2 (5—Unit Start—Stop) and with speeds of transmission of 45·5 or 50 bauds.

(f) No message which is grossly offensive or of an indecent or obscene character shall be sent.

2. International requirement

The Licensee shall observe and comply with the relevant provisions of the Telecommunication Convention.

3. Frequency control and measurement

(1) A satisfactory method of frequency stabilization shall be employed in the sending apparatus comprised in the Station.

(2) Equipment shall be provided capable of verifying that the sending apparatus comprised in the Station is operating with emissions within the authorized frequency bands.

4. Non-interference

(1) The apparatus comprised in the Station shall be so designed, constructed, maintained and used that the use of the Station does not cause any undue interference with any wireless telegraphy.

(2) When telegraphy (as distinct from telephony) is being used, arrangements shall be made to ensure that the risk of interference due to key clicks being caused to other wireless telegraphy is eliminated. At all times, every precaution shall be taken to avoid over-modulation, and to keep the radiated energy within the narrowest possible frequency bands having regard to the class of emission in use. In particular, the radiation of harmonics and other spurious emissions shall be suppressed to such a level that they cause no undue interference with any wireless telegraphy. To ensure that the requirements of this subclause are met, tests shall be made from time to time and details of those tests shall be recorded in the Log as required in clause 6 hereof.

5. Operators and access to apparatus

The Licensee shall not permit or suffer any unauthorized person to operate the Station or to have access to the apparatus comprised therein. The Licensee shall ensure that persons operating the Station shall observe the terms, provisions and limitations of this Licence at all times.

6. Log

(1) An indelible record shall be kept in one book (not loose-leaf) (in this Licence called "the Log") showing the following:

Fixed Station

(a) Date.

(b) Time of commencement of period of operation of the Station.

(c) Callsigns of the stations from which messages addressed to the Station are received or to which messages are sent, times of establishing and ending communication with each such station, frequency band(s) and class or classes of emission in each case (including the tests referred to in clause 4(2) hereof; and CQ calls).

(d) Time of closing down the Station.

(e) The address of the temporary premises or the alternative premises or particulars of the temporary location when the Station is established other than as provided in clause 1(1)(a)(i) hereof.

(f) No gaps shall be left between entries and all entries shall be made at the time of sending and receiving.

Mobile Station or as a pedestrian

(g) Entries made in respect of calls made when operating from a vehicle or vessel, or as a pedestrian should be made as soon as practicable after the end of a journey and must consist of date, geographical area of operation, frequency band(s) used and times of commencement and end of journey. A separate log book may be maintained for mobile or pedestrian use.

(2) If the Station is at any time operated by a person other than the Licensee (see clause 1(2)(c)(ii) hereof) the Licensee shall ensure that the Log is signed by that person with his full name, and that the callsign of the station which he is licensed to use, or (if there is no such station) the number of his Amateur Radio Certificate, is shown in the Log.

(3) All times shall be stated in gmt.

7. Receiver

The Station shall be equipped for the reception of messages sent on the frequency or frequencies, and by means of the class or classes of emission, which are in current use at the Station for the purpose of sending.

8. Recorded messages

(1) Messages addressed to the Station from any licensed amateur station with which the Licensee is in communication may be recorded and retransmitted in accordance with this Licence, provided that the retransmission is intended for reception by the originating station only, and that the callsign of that station is not included in the retransmission.

(2) Modulation is prohibited by means of recordings of any kind other than special recordings of sinusoidal tone or tones within the audio frequency spectrum which may be either constant or steadily changing in frequency.

(3) Gramophone or tape recordings of the type intended for entertainment purposes may not be transmitted for any purpose.

9. Callsign and notification of location

(1) Whenever the Station is used the callsign

mentioned on the first page of this Licence shall be transmitted: provided that when the Station is used:

(a) at an address other than the main address the Licensee shall, in order to indicate the country or place of use, vary the prefix letter to the callsign by using the prefix letter(s) appropriate to that country or place, being G for England, GM for Scotland, GW for Wales, GI for Northern Ireland, GJ for Jersey, GU for Guernsey and GD for the Isle of Man;

(b) at the temporary premises the suffix "/A" shall be added to the callsign;

(c) at the temporary location or as a pedestrian the suffix "/P" shall be added to the callsign;

(d) in or on a vehicle or vessel the suffix "/M" shall be added to the callsign.

(2) The callsign, which may be sent either by morse telegraphy at a speed not greater than 20 words per minute or by telephony, shall be sent for identification purposes at the beginning and at the end of each period of sending, and whenever the frequency is changed. When the period of use exceeds 15 minutes the callsign shall be repeated (in the same manner) at the commencement of each succeeding period of 15 minutes.

(3) When telephony is used, the letters of the callsign may be confirmed by the pronouncement of well-known words of which the initial letters are the same as those in the callsign; but words used in this manner shall not be of a facetious or objectionable character.

(4) When the Station is used at the temporary premises or location, the address of the temporary premises or location shall be sent at the beginning and end of the establishment of communication with each separate amateur station, or at intervals of 15 minutes, whichever is the more frequent.

(5) When sending high definition television signals, the callsign sent for identification purposes must be adjusted to the centre of the video channel.

10. Inspection

The Station, this Licence and the Log shall be available for inspection at all reasonable times by a person acting under the authority of the Secretary of State.

11. Station to close down

The Station shall be closed down at any time on the demand of a person acting under the authority of the Secretary of State.

12. Period of Licence, renewal, revocation and variation

This Licence shall continue in force for one year from the date of issue, and thereafter so long as the Licensee pays to the Secretary of State in advance in each year on or before the anniversary of the date of issue the renewal fee prescribed by or under the regulations for the time being in force under section 2(1) of the Wireless Telegraphy Act, 1949; provided that the Secretary of State may at any time after the date of issue (i) revoke this Licence or vary the terms, provisions or limitations thereof by a notice in writing served on the Licensee, or by a general notice published in the

London, Edinburgh and Belfast Gazettes, or in a newspaper published in London, a newspaper published in Edinburgh and a newspaper published in Belfast addressed to all holders of Amateur Licences A, (ii) revoke this Licence by a general notice published by being broadcast by the British Broadcasting Corporation addressed to all holders of Amateur Licences A. Any notice given under this clause may take effect either forthwith or on such subsequent date as may be specified in the notice.

13. This Licence is not transferable

14. Return of Licence

This Licence shall be returned to the Secretary of State when it has expired or been revoked.

15. Previous Licences revoked

Any licence, however described, which the Secretary of State has previously granted to the Licensee in respect of the Station is hereby revoked.

16. Interpretation

(1) In this Licence:

(a) The expressions:

(i) "the Secretary of State" shall mean the Secretary of State for the Home Department;

(ii) "messages" and "signals" shall include visual images sent by television and facsimile transmission;

(iii) "remarks about matters of a personal nature" shall not include messages about business affairs;

(iv) "Standard Frequency Service" shall have the same meaning as in the Radio Regulations and Additional Radio Regulations in force under the International Telecommunication Convention signed at Malaga—Torremolinos on the 25th day of October 1973, where it is defined as "A radio communication service for scientific, technical and other purposes, providing the transmission of specific frequencies of stated high precision, intended for general reception".

(v) "the Telecommunication Convention" shall mean the International Telecommunication Convention signed at Malaga—Torremolinos on the 25th day of October 1973, and the Radio Regulations and Additional Radio Regulations in force thereunder and includes any convention and Regulations which may from time to time be in force in substitution for or in amendment of the said Convention or the said Regulations;

(vi) "the United Kingdom" shall mean the United Kingdom of Great Britain and Northern Ireland, the Isle of Man and the Channel Islands.

(b) References to the operation of the Station shall include references to the speaking into the microphone comprised in the Station;

(c) References to a certificate issued or granted by the Secretary of State shall include references to a certificate issued or granted by the Postmaster General or Minister of Posts and Telecommunications.

(d) Except where the context otherwise requires other words and expressions shall have the same meaning as they have in the Wireless Telegraphy Act 1949 or in the Regulations made under Part 1 thereof.

(2) Section 19(5) of the Wireless Telegraphy Act 1949, shall apply for the purposes of this Licence as it applies for the purpose of the Act.

(3) Nothing in this Licence shall be deemed to authorize the use of the Station for business, advertisement or propaganda purposes or (except as provided by clause 1(1)(c) hereof) for the sending or receiving of news or messages of or on behalf of, or for the benefit or information of any social, political, religious or commercial organization, or anyone other than the Licensee or the person with whom he is in communication.

The following notes are appended to the Amateur Licence for the guidance and information of Licensees:

Notes

(a) The Secretary of State should be notified promptly of any change in the correspondence address of the Licensee. Except as provided in (b) below, correspondence should be sent to the Home Office, Radio Regulatory Department, Radio Regulatory Division, Waterloo Bridge House, Waterloo Road, London SE1 8UA.

(b) Remittances and correspondence about payments to the Secretary of State required under this Licence should be sent to The Cashier, Accounts Branch, Tolworth Tower, Ewell Road, Surbiton, Surrey KT6 7DS. It is unnecessary to send the Licence when making remittances.

(c) Clause 4(1) of the Licence requires that the apparatus comprised in the Station shall be so designed, constructed, maintained and used that the use of the Station does not cause any undue interference with any wireless telegraphy. In order to prevent interference due to close coupling of aerials, the aerial to be used for the Station should be sited as far as possible from any existing television or other receiving aerials in the vicinity. This is particularly important if it is proposed to install an indoor transmitting aerial, eg in the loft, where interference may be conducted through the electricity supply wiring. In some circumstances it might not be possible to use an indoor aerial.

(d) If the Station is situated within half a mile of the boundary of any aerodrome, the height of the aerial or any mast supporting it must not exceed 50 feet above the ground level. An aerial which crosses above or is liable to fall or to be blown on to any overhead power wire (including electric lighting and tramway wires) or power apparatus must be guarded to the reasonable satisfaction of the owner of the power apparatus concerned.

(e) Demands for closing down (see clause 11) can be expected to be received in connection with national emergencies or when interference is being caused to a Government wireless station or other important services. An oral demand by a person acting under the authority of the Secretary of State to close down the Station will be confirmed in writing.

(f) Under Section 1 of the Wireless Telegraphy Act, 1949, it is an offence to use any station or apparatus for wireless telegraphy except under and in accordance with a licence granted by the Secretary of State. Breach of this provision may result in this Licence being revoked and the offender being prosecuted.

(g) If any message, the receipt of which is not authorized by this Licence, is received by means of the Station, neither the Licensee nor any person operating the Station should make known the contents of any such message, its origin or destination, its existence or the fact of its receipt to any persons except a duly authorized officer of Her Majesty's Government, a person acting under the authority of the Secretary of State, or a competent legal tribunal, and should not retain any copy or make any use of any message, or allow it to be reproduced in writing, copied or made use of. It is an offence under section 5 of the Wireless Telegraphy Act, 1949, deliberately to receive messages the receipt of which is unauthorized or (except in the special circumstances mentioned in that section of the Act) to disclose any information as to the contents, sender or addressee of any such message.

(h) It is an offence under Section 5 of the Wireless Telegraphy Act, 1949, to send by wireless telegraphy certain misleading messages.

(i) This Licence does not authorize the Licensee to do any act which is an infringement of any copyright which may exist in the matter sent or received.

(j) This Licence does not absolve the Licensee from obtaining any necessary consent before entering on private or public property with any apparatus.

(k) The Secretary of State regards himself as free to publish the Licensee's name and address at his discretion unless within one month of the date of issue of this Licence the Licensee specifically asks that this should not be done.

(l) The expression "wireless telegraphy" used in this Licence has the meaning assigned to it in the Wireless Telegraphy Act, 1949, and includes radiotelephony.

(m) With reference to clause 9(3) of this Licence it is recommended that for uniformity the phonetic alphabet contained in Appendix 16 of the Radio Regulations, Geneva, 1976, reproduced below should be used when the letters of the callsign are transmitted phonetically.

A Alfa	J Juliett	S Sierra
B Bravo	K Kilo	T Tango
C Charlie	L Lima	U Uniform
D Delta	M Mike	V Victor
E Echo	N November	W Whiskey
F Foxtrot	O Oscar	X X-ray
G Golf	P Papa	Y Yankee
H Hotel	Q Quebec	Z Zulu
I India	R Romeo	

The UK Class A licence schedule

Frequency bands (MHz)	Footnote No.	Power limitations		Classes of emission (see C and D)
		Carrier power supplied to the antenna	Peak envelope power supplied to antenna for ssb operation	
1·81–1·85	2	9dBW	15dBW	A1A
1·85–2·0	2, 4			
3·5–3·8	2, 9, 11, 16			A1B
7·0–7·1	9, 11, 12, 16	20dBW	26dBW	
10·1–10·15	1, 16			A2A
14·0–14·25	9, 11, 12, 16			
14·25–14·35	9, 11, 16			A2B
21·0–21·45	9, 11, 12, 16			
28·0–29·7	9, 11, 12			A3E
70·025–70·5	1, 3	16dBW	22dBW	
144–146	9, 11, 12, 16, 18	20dBW	26dBW	R3E
430–432	1, 6, 7, 18	See note 7	See note 7	
432–435	1, 10, 18			H3E
435–438	1, 10, 14, 18	20dBW	26dBW	
438–440	1, 10, 18			J3E
Frequency bands (MHz)	Footnote No.	Maximum dc input power (see A and B)	SSB operation	F1A
1,240–1,260	1, 10, 17, 18			F1B
1,260–1,270	1, 14, 15, 17, 18			
1,270–1,325	1, 10, 17, 18			F2A
2,300–2,400	1, 10, 17, 18			
2,400–2,450	1, 10, 13, 14, 17, 18			F2B
3,400–3,475	1, 17, 18			F3E
5,650–5,670	1, 10, 13, 14, 15, 17, 18	150W	26dBW	G1A
5,670–5,680	1, 10, 17, 18			G1B
5,755–5,765	1, 10, 17, 18			
5,820–5,830	1, 10, 17, 18			G2A
5,830–5,850	1, 10, 13, 14, 15, 17, 18			G2B
10,000–10,450	1, 10, 17, 18			
10,450–10,500	1, 10, 13, 14, 17, 18			G3E
24,000–24,050	8, 10, 12, 17, 18			
24,050–24,250	1, 8, 10, 17, 18			
2,350–2,400	1, 5, 13, 17, 18	25W mean power and 2·5kW peak power		K1A L2A K2A L3E K3E M2A Q2A V2A
10,050–10,450	1, 5, 17, 18			
5,755–5,765 5,820–5,850	1, 5, 13, 17, 18			

Footnotes
1. This band is allocated to stations in the amateur service on a secondary basis on condition that they shall not cause interference to other services.
2. This band is shared with other services.
3. This band is available to amateurs until further notice provided that use by

the Licensee of any frequency in the band shall cease immediately on the demand of a Government official.
4. The type of transmission known as "radio teleprinter" (rtty) may not be used in this band.
5. Use by the Licensee of any frequency in this band shall be only with the prior written consent of the Secretary of State.
6. This band is not available for use within the area bounded by 53°N 02°E, 55°N 02°E, 53°N 03°W and 55°N 03°W.
7. In this band the power must not exceed 10dBW erp (effective radiated power).
8. Use by the Licensee of any frequency in this band shall only be with written consent of the Secretary of State and such consent shall indicate the power which may be used, taking into consideration the characteristics of the Licensee's station.
9. Slow-scan television may be used in this band.
10. High-definition television (A3F, C3F, F3F, G3F) may be used in this band.
11. Facsimile transmission (A3C, F3C, G3C) may be used in this band, with a bandwidth not greater than 6kHz.
12. The amateur-satellite service also has an allocation in this band.
13. This band is allocated to stations in the amateur-satellite service on a secondary basis, on condition that they shall not cause interference to other services.
14. The amateur-satellite service may operate in this band in accordance with International Radio Regulation 2741, viz:
Space stations in the amateur-satellite service operating in bands shared with other services shall be fitted with appropriate devices for controlling emissions in the event that harmful interference is reported in accordance with the procedure laid down in Article 22 of the Radio Regulations. (Administrations authorizing such space stations shall inform the IFRB and shall ensure that sufficient earth command stations are established before launch to guarantee that any harmful interference which might be reported can be terminated by the authorizing administration (see RR 2612).)
15. The use of the amateur-satellite service in the following bands shall be limited to the direction stated below:
1,260–1,270MHz earth to space
5,650–5,670MHz earth to space
5,830–5,850MHz space to earth
16. The bands allocated to the amateur service at 3·5, 7·0, 10·1, 14·0, 21·0, and 144MHz may, in the event of natural disasters, be used by non-amateur stations to meet the needs of international emergency communications in the disaster area in accordance with regulations of the Radio Regulatory Department.
17. Since high intensities of rf radiation may be harmful, the following safety precaution must be taken: in locations to which people have access, the power density on transmit must not exceed the limits recommended by the competent authorities. Currently this limit is 10mW/cm².
18. Data transmission may be used within the frequency bands 144MHz and above provided (a) the Station callsign is announced in morse or telephony at least once every 15min and (b) emission is contained within the bandwidth normally used for telephony.
A. DC input power is the total direct current power input to (i) the anode circuit of the valve(s) or (ii) any other device energizing the antenna.
B. As an alternative for R3E and J3E single sideband types of emission, the power shall be determined by the peak envelope power (p.e.p.) under linear operation.
C. Double-sideband suppressed-carrier emissions are permitted within the terms of this licence.
D. The symbols used to designate the classes of emission have the meaning assigned to them in the Telecommunication Convention. They are:

Amplitude modulation
A1A   Telegraphy by on-off keying without the use of a modulating audio frequency.
A1B   Automatic telegraphy by on-off keying, without the use of a modulating audio frequency.
A2A   Telegraphy by on-off keying of an amplitude-modulating audio frequency or frequencies, or by on-off keying of the modulated emission.
A2B   Automatic telegraphy by on-off keying of an amplitude-modulating audio frequency or frequencies, or by on-off keying of the modulated emission.
A3E   Telephony, double sideband.
A3C   Facsimile transmission.
H3E   Telephony using single-sideband full-carrier, amplitude modulation.
R3E   Telephony, single sideband, reduced carrier.
J3E   Telephony, single sideband, suppressed carrier.
A3F/C3F Slow-scan television and high-definition television.

Frequency modulation
F1A   Telegraphy by frequency-shift keying without the use of a modulating audio frequency: one of two frequencies being emitted at any instant.

(continued on p120)

CHAPTER 11

Operating practices and procedures, repeaters and satellites

Telegraphy

Effective communication by telegraphy implies the use of internationally-agreed symbols and abbreviations so that difficulties arising from language differences are eliminated to a fairly large extent.

The symbols and abbreviations used in amateur radio are based on the international Q-code and the procedures used in marine and commercial radio telegraphy. Many other abbreviations are based on phonetic English.

The international Q-code is a series of questions and answers and the Q-signals shown in Table 11.1, which are taken from the official list, are commonly used in the amateur service. Amateurs tend to use many of the Q-signals as nouns as well as in question-and-answer form (see Table 11.2).

The most common procedure and punctuation signals are shown in Table 11.3.

Reports on readability and signal strength (and tone in the case of telegraphic signals) are given in terms of the RST code (see Table 11.4).

Speed of sending

The golden rule is "never send at a greater speed than you are able to receive". The speed of sending should depend to a large extent on circumstances; when conditions are poor with low signal strengths or in heavy interference it is sensible to send more slowly. It is a good principle to send at the same speed as the operator at the other end.

In general the good cw operator is the one whose copy is easy to read and who does not send faster than he is capable of doing properly. An indifferently sent 25 words per minute may well be almost unreadable but a properly sent 25wpm is considerably easier to read than a badly sent 20wpm.

The licence conditions require that the callsign be sent at a speed not greater than 20wpm. It should not be assumed from this that high-speed operation is normal. It is probably true to say that the majority of telegraphy on the amateur bands is at a speed of somewhat less than 20wpm.

Table 11.1
The international Q-code (extract)

QRG	Will you tell me my exact frequency? Your exact frequency is ....kHz.
QRH	Does my frequency vary? Your frequency varies.
QRI	What is the tone of my transmission? The tone of your transmission is ....(amateur T1–T9).
QRK	What is the readability of my signals? The readability of your signals is ....(amateur R1–R5).
QRL	Are you busy? I am busy. Please do not interfere.
QRM	Are you being interfered with? I am being interfered with.
QRN	Are you troubled by static? I am troubled by static.
QRO	Shall I increase power? Increase power.
QRP	Shall I decrease power? Decrease power.
QRQ	Shall I send faster? Send faster.
QRS	Shall I send more slowly? Send more slowly.
QRT	Shall I stop sending? Stop sending.
QRU	Have you anything for me? I have nothing for you.
QRV	Are you ready? I am ready.
QRX	When will you call me again? I will call you again at .... hours.
QRZ	Who is calling me? You are being called by ....(on kHz).
QSA	What is the strength of my signals? The strength of your signals is ....(amateur S1–S9).
QSB	Are my signals fading? Your signals are fading.
QSD	Is my keying defective? Your keying is defective.
QSL	Can you give me acknowledgement of receipt? I give you acknowledgement of receipt.
QSO	Can you communicate with ....direct or by relay? I can communicate with ....direct (or by relay through ....).
QSP	Will you relay to? I will relay to ....
QSV	Shall I send a series of VVVs? Send a series of VVVs.
QSY	Shall I change to another frequency? Change to transmission on another frequency (or on .... kHz).
QSZ	Shall I send each word more than once? Send each word twice.
QTH	What is your location? My location is ....
QTR	What is the correct time? The correct time is .... hours.

Table 11.2
Use of Q-signals as nouns

QRA	Address	QRP	Low power
QRG	Frequency	QRT	Close down
QRI	Bad note	QRX	Stand by
QRK	Signal strength	QSB	Fading
QRM	Interference from other stations	QSD	Bad sending
		QSL	Verification card
QRN	Interference from atmospherics or local electrical apparatus	QSO	Radio contact
		QSP	Relay message
		QSY	Change of frequency
QRO	High power	QTH	Location

Table 11.3
Punctuation and procedure signals

Punctuation

Question mark	di-di-dah-dah-di-dit
Full stop	di-dah-di-dah-di-dah
Comma*	dah-dah-di-di-dah-dah

*Sometimes used to indicate exclamation mark.

Procedure Signals

Stroke	dah-di-di-dah-dit
Break sign (=)	dah-di-di-di-dah
End of message ($\overline{AR}$)	di-dah-di-dah-dit
End of work ($\overline{VA}$)	di-di-di-dah-di-dah
Wait ($\overline{AS}$)	di-dah-di-di-dit
Error	di-di-di-di-di-di-di-dit
Invitation to transmit (general) (K)	dah-di-dah
Invitation to transmit (specific station) ($\overline{KN}$)	dah-di-dah-dah-dit

Establishing communication

The first step is to spend a short time listening on the band it is proposed to use in order to check

(a) if conditions are good or bad
(b) who is working who and what signal reports are being exchanged.

The propagation forecasts published in *Radio Communication* are invaluable as an indication of the part of the world likely to be heard at a particular time.

There are two ways of establishing communication:

(a) by calling a specific station.
(b) by transmitting a "CQ" ("general invitation to reply") call.

On most bands there are always many stations to be heard calling "CQ" so it is generally preferable to answer such a call rather than to initiate another. However, a CQ call made when a band appears "dead", particularly on 21 or 28MHz, sometimes results in an unexpected contact.

Calling procedures

Calling a specific station. First of all, "net" on to the frequency of the station it is proposed to call, ie adjust transmitter frequency onto the signal being received. The basic call is:

G7AA G7AA G7AA DE G7ZZ G7ZZ G7ZZ $\overline{KN}$

Note that "$\overline{KN}$" is an invitation to a specific station, G7AA, and no other, to reply.

This basic call may be varied, ie in poor conditions or heavy interference it would be advisable to send the station call (G7ZZ) five or six times.

Initiating a CQ call. The first step is to choose a frequency where no other station is operating—this is often very difficult and it has to be accepted that virtually every signal is likely to cause some interference to another station somewhere.

The basic call is:

CQ CQ CQ DE G7ZZ G7ZZ G7ZZ K

Note here that "K" is a general invitation to *any* station to reply.

Basic calls may be repeated up to five or six times—this depends on conditions and activity on the band. *Never* send a long series of CQ signals without interspersing the station call.

A CQ call may be made specific, eg

CQ DX CQ DX CQ DX DE G7ZZ G7ZZ G7ZZ K

or directional, eg

CQ VK CQ VK CQ VK DE G7ZZ G7ZZ G7ZZ K

Prolonged CQ calls or calls to a specific station should be avoided. These cause unnecessary interference, particularly to stations in the immediate vicinity who generally accept interference from a local station in contact but who will not take too kindly to continuous CQ calls. An unanswered CQ is therefore best followed by a short period of listening.

If a station replying cannot be positively identified due to low signal strength or interference, the signal "QRZ?" ("who is calling me?") may be used, eg

QRZ? QRZ? DE G7ZZ G7ZZ G7ZZ $\overline{KN}$

Note that $\overline{KN}$ and not K is now used.

A "QRZ?" call should be brief and not extended as an additional CQ call. "QRZ?" is *not* an alternative to "CQ".

Having established communication a cw contact (QSO) is likely to follow the general form shown overleaf.

Table 11.4
The RST code

Readability

R1	Unreadable.
R2	Barely readable, occasional words distinguishable.
R3	Readable with considerable difficulty.
R4	Readable with practically no difficulty.
R5	Perfectly readable.

Signal strength

S1	Faint, signals barely perceptible.
S2	Very weak signals.
S3	Weak signals.
S4	Fair signals.
S5	Fairly good signals.
S6	Good signals.
S7	Moderately strong signals.
S8	Strong signals.
S9	Extremely strong signals.

Tone

T1	Extremely rough hissing note.
T2	Very rough ac note, no trace of musicality.
T3	Rough, low-pitched ac note, slightly musical.
T4	Rather rough ac note, moderately musical.
T5	Musically modulated note.
T6	Modulated note, slight trace of whistle.
T7	Near dc note, smooth ripple.
T8	Good dc note, just a trace of ripple.
T9	Purest dc note.

If the note appears to be crystal-controlled add X after the appropriate number. Where there is chirp add C, drift add D, clicks add K.

G9AA G9AA DE G7AA G7AA = GA OM ES MNI TNX
FER CALL = AM VY PSED TO QSO U = UR SIGS R̲S̲T̲
579 = QTH IS LON̲DON̲ = NAME IS GEO = HW? AR
G9AA DE G7AA K̅N̅

The following should be noted:
1. Report, QTH and name are generally sent twice
   (but not more than three times).
2. Each sentence is separated by the break sign
   (dah-di-di-di-dah).
3. Each callsign sent twice at the beginning is generally adequate but may be sent once only or three
   times depending on signal strength and interference etc.
4. Each callsign is sent *once only* at the end—there is
   no point in sending them more than once.
5. Names may just as well be abbreviated.
6. "HW̲?" means "how do you receive me?"
7. "A̅R̅" signifies "end of message"
8. "K̅N̅" means specific station (G9AA) to reply.

The contact may then continue:

G7AA G7AA DE G9AA G9AA = R ES VY GA GEO =
GLD TO QSO AGN = THINK WE QSO LAST YEAR
ON 3R5? = MNI TNX FER RPRT = UR RST 569 QSB
QRM = QTH IS BIRMINGHAM = NAME IS MAC =
RIG IS FT101 AT 150 WATTS INPUT = A̲N̲T̲ IS TRAP
DIPOLE = W̲X̲ IS COLD ES DULL = OK? AR G7AA
DE G9AA K̅N̅

The following should be noted:
1. "R" signifies "received all sent", obviously preferable to such phrases as "solid cpy hr" etc.
2. "3R5"—here "R" indicates a decimal point, ie
   3·5.
The contact then goes on:

G9AA G9AA DE G7AA G7AA = MOST OK MAC BD
QRM AT END = TNX FER RPRT ES INFO ON RIG =
HR HOME MADE TX ES INPUT IS 120 WATTS = RX
IS AR88D = ANT IS 132 FT END FED = YES WE DID
QSO LAST YEAR = COND̲X̲ FB FER DX BUT̲ E̲U̲
STNS VY STRONG = QRU? AR G9AA DE G7AA KN

G7AA G7AA DE G9AA G9AA = R ES TNX ALL =
MNI TNX QSO ES HPE CUAGN SN = P̲S̲E̲ QSL VIA
BURO = VY 73 ES DX = GB OM ES GL A̅R̅ G7AA DE
G9AA K̅N̅.

Note that this is G9AA's last transmission but the con-
tact has not finished because he is about to receive
G7A̲A̲'s final re̲marks. G9AA therefore finishes with
"K̅N̅" and not "V̅A̅".

G9AA G9AA DE G7AA G7AA = R FB SIGS NW OM =
QRT = MNI TNX QSO ES HPE CUAGN = QSL OK
VIA RSGB = 73 ES DX = CHEE̲R̲IO MAC ES ALL
THE BEST A̅R̅ G9AA DE G7AA V̅A̅ CL.

This is the last transmi̲ssion of the contact and G7AA
therefore uses "V̅A̅", meaning "I have finished". "CL"
indicates that G7AA is closing down.
   The above describes a fairly basic contact but in

practice cw contacts range from just an exchange of
RST/QTH/name to a chat lasting an hour or more.
   "K", "K̅N̅" and "V̅A̅" are probably the most mis-
used symbols in amateur radio; remember
   "K" is an invitation to *any* station to reply.
   "K̅N̅" is an invitation to a specific station to reply.
   "V̅A̅" means "I have finished".
   When tuning across a band, if only "G9AA K" is
heard, one is entitled to call G9AA. If "G9AA K̅N̅" is
heard, it means that G9AA is in contact with someone
else or has just called someone, and one should there̲-
fore not call G9AA. On the other hand if "G9AA V̅A̅"
is heard it should indicate that G9AA has just finished
a contact and therefore one is entitled to call him.
   It follows that if these symbols are not used correctly
a considerable amount of annoyance can be created.
   At the conclusion of a contact always listen for a few
seconds—someone may be calling you̲! Do not
immediately send "QRZ?" after sending "V̅A̅" unless
you suspect someone may be waiting for you. A very
short CQ call, ie just "CQ DE G9AA K" will indicate
that you are now ready to accept a call.
   The procedure of "tail-ending" means a very short
call, ie "DE G9AA K̅N̅", to a station immediately he
has finished his last transmission. It is most effective
when both sides o̲f the contact have been heard but it
does require that "V̅A̅" is correctly used. It is accepted
by some good operators but is open to abuse and likely
to cause irritation if used carelessly. It should be
avoided until a fair amount of operating skill has been
acquired.
   Do not "send double" unless specifically asked to do
so or your signals have been reported as, say, RST 339.
   Abbreviations used in amateur telegraphy are understood throughout the world. Many of these are given in
Appendix 6.

Telephony

Whereas a poor or inconsiderate cw operator is a nuis-
ance only to his fellow amateurs, bad telephony operation discredits amateur radio generally. Our hobby can
be too easily judged by the quality of our telephony
transmissions, the subjects discussed and the procedures used.
   The major portion of amateur radio traffic is now
carried out using telephony, especially on vhf and
above. Though this mode does not require the knowledge of codes and abbreviations, correct operation is
more difficult than it may appear at first sight, as is only
too apparent after a listen to any amateur band.
   Part of the problem is that many operators will have
acquired some bad habits in their pronunciation, into-
nation and phraseology even before entering amateur
radio. To these are then added a whole new set of
clichés and mannerisms derived from listening to bad
operators. Some of these can be extremely difficult to
remove once learnt, even if a conscious effort is made.

Conversation
It is important to speak clearly and not too quickly, not
just when talking to someone who does not fully

Table 11.5
Recommended phonetic alphabet

A	Alfa	J	Juliett	S	Sierra
B	Bravo	K	Kilo	T	Tango
C	Charlie	L	Lima	U	Uniform
D	Delta	M	Mike	V	Victor
E	Echo	N	November	W	Whiskey
F	Foxtrot	O	Oscar	X	X-ray
G	Golf	P	Papa	Y	Yankee
H	Hotel	Q	Quebec	Z	Zulu
I	India	R	Romeo		

understand the language, but at all times as this is excellent practice.

The use of cw abbreviations (including "HI") and the Q-code should normally be avoided. The Q-code should only be used on telephony when there is a language difficulty.

Plain language should be used, and clichés and jargon should be kept to a minimum. In particular, avoid the use of "we" when "I" is meant and "handle" when "name" is meant. Other silly habits include saying "that's a roger" instead of "that's correct", and "affirmative" instead of "yes". The reader will no doubt have heard many more. Taken individually each is almost harmless, but when combined together give a false-sounding "radioese" which is actually less effective than plain language in most cases.

Phonetic alphabets should only be employed when they are necessary to clarify the spelling of a word or callsign. The phonetic alphabet recommended in the amateur licence is shown in Table 11.5. Note that words which are facetious or objectionable are forbidden for this purpose by the UK licence conditions.

Unlike cw operation, it is very easy to forget that the conversation is not taking place down a telephone line. Unless duplex operation is actually in use the listening station cannot interject a query if something is not understood, and cannot give an answer until the transmitting station has finished. The result is often a long monologue, in which the listening station has to take notes of all the points raised and questions asked if a useful reply is to be given. This should not be necessary if these points are dealt with one at a time.

Procedure

As noted earlier, when calling a specific station it is good practice to keep calls short and to use the callsign of the station called once or twice only, followed by one's own callsign pronounced carefully and clearly at least twice using the phonetic alphabet, for example:

"WD9ZZZ. This is Golf Four Zulu Zulu Zulu calling, and Golf Four Zulu Zulu Zulu standing by."

Emphasis should be placed on the caller's own callsign, and not on that of the station called. If there is no response, the caller's callsign may be repeated once more after a brief listen.

As in cw operation CQ calls should also be kept short and repeated as often as desired. An example would be:

"CQ, CQ, CQ, CQ. This is Golf Four Zulu Zulu Zulu calling, Golf Four Zulu Zulu Zulu calling CQ and standing by."

There is no need to say which band is being used, and certainly no need to add "for any possible calls, dah-di-dah!" or "K someone please" etc!

When replying to a call both callsigns should be given clearly, so that the calling station can check its callsign has been received correctly. From then on it is not necessary to use the phonetic alphabet for callsigns until the final transmissions. An example would be:

"Whiskey Delta Nine Zulu Zulu Zulu. This is Golf Four Zulu Zulu Zulu."

Once contact is established it is only necessary to give one's callsign at the intervals required by the licensing authority. A normal two-way conversation can thus be enjoyed, without the need for continual identification. If necessary the words "break" or "over" may be added at the end of a transmission to signal a reply from the other station. In good conditions this will not normally be found necessary. When fm is in use it is self-evident when the other station has stopped transmitting and is listening, because the carrier drops.

The situation is more complex where three or more stations are involved, and it is a good idea to give one's own callsign briefly before each transmission, for example:

"From G4ZZZ . . ."

At the end of the transmission the callsign should again be given, together with an indication of whose turn to speak it is next, for example:

". . . WD9ZZZ to transmit. G4ZZZ in the group".

It is not necessary to run through a list of who is in the group, who has just signed off (and who may possibly be listening) after each transmission, although it may be useful to do this occasionally.

Signal reports on telephony are usually given as a single two-digit number, in a similar fashion to the three-digit cw RST code.

It is recommended that both callsigns be given in the final transmission using the phonetic alphabet so that listening stations can check that they have them correct before calling, for example:

". . . This is Golf Four Zulu Zulu Zulu signing clear with Whiskey Delta Nine Zulu Zulu Zulu and Golf Four Zulu Zulu Zulu is now standing by for a call."

Note that some indication to listening stations is useful to indicate what is planned next. Such an indication is also appropriate if an immediate change to another frequency is intended, for example:

". . . This is Golf Four Zulu Zulu Zulu signing clear with Golf Two X-Ray Yankee Zulu Mobile. Golf Four Zulu Zulu Zulu now monitoring S20 for a call."

The restrictions imposed by the UK licence conditions [eg paragraphs 1(b)(i), 16(1)(iii) and 16(3)] are particularly relevant in telephony operation. It should be made a golden rule never to discuss politics, religion or any other matter which may offend the person to whom one is talking or anyone who may be listening.

General

The following comments are equally applicable to both telegraphic and telephonic operation.

Honest reports, particularly on tone, should always be given. Do not give a report of RS(T) 59(9) to a station merely because he has just given you 59(9) or because you want his QSL card! S-meter readings should be treated with reserve, ie RST 519 is almost meaningless. (Awards or certificates of operating proficiency require a minimum signal report of RST 339/RS 33—these represent just about the minimum usable signals).

On some bands there are recommended sections set aside for use by each mode. In some parts of the world (eg the USA) observance of these band divisions is mandatory and their use also depends on the class of licence held by the operator. Band plans do not form part of the RAE syllabus. They are given for reference only in Appendix 6. These are not mandatory for British amateurs but they should be observed at all times.

Directional CQ calls should always be respected—G9AA would be considered a poor operator if he is heard calling an Australian station which has just transmitted a "CQ USA" call.

It is courteous to move off a frequency at the end of a contact if the station contacted was originally operating there.

The long-distance (dx) bands, particularly 14, 21 and 28MHz, should not be used for purely local contacts when these bands are open for long-distance working.

Do not call a station while its operator is in contact with someone else. Similarly, it is considered very poor operating to try to break in to a contact which is already taking place.

The various conditions of the amateur licence should be kept in mind as some of these have a bearing on operation.

Logkeeping

Apart from the fact that a log of all transmissions is required by law, a well-kept log provides a record of contacts and friendships made, reports, conditions and other information on which applications for operating awards can be made.

The requirements of the Home Office with regard to logkeeping are defined in the licence conditions as follows:

1. An indelible record must be kept in one book (not looseleaf).
2. The following data must be recorded:

Date.
Time of commencement of operation (in gmt).
Class(es) of emission.
Frequency band(s).
CQ calls.
Callsigns of stations called and with whom communication is established.
Time of establishing and ending communication with each station.
Tests carried out (eg tvi).
Time of closing the station.
When appropriate, addresses of the temporary/alternative premises or particulars of the temporary location.
All entries must be made at the time of sending/receiving and there should be no gaps between entries.

Entries in respect of operation from a vehicle or vessel or as a pedestrian should be made as soon as practicable after the end of the journey and must consist of date, geographical area of operation, frequency band(s), time of start and end of journey. A separate log may be maintained for mobile or pedestrian use.

The log must be signed by any operator of the station who is not the licensee. The callsign (or Amateur Radio Certificate number) of this operator must be shown.

No particular method of recording the date is specified but it should be noted that "10/1/79" means "10 January 1979" in the UK and most of the world but "1 October 1979" in the USA.

Fig 11.1 illustrates a number of typical log entries which satisfy the licence requirements.

Repeaters and satellites

The past few years have seen the introduction of two new aspects of the amateur service, these being repeaters and satellites. Both of these help the vhf or uhf operator to increase his or her range, although by entirely different means.

The following notes give brief information on typical operation using these devices at the time of going to press. It should however be noted that both repeaters and satellites are experimental devices and therefore subject to change. New and improved satellites may be launched, while existing repeaters may be modified in the light of technical developments.

Repeaters

As the name suggests, these are intended to receive (on the *input channel*) vhf or uhf signals from portable and mobile stations, and re-transmit (relay) them on a different frequency (the *output channel*) within the same amateur band.

Repeaters are unmanned and entirely automatic in operation. They are situated at the top of a hill or where the antenna can be positioned as high as possible. Thus the rather limited range of portable and mobile equipment may be increased from 5–10 miles to

AMATEUR RADIO STATION LOG

DATE	TIME (GMT) start	TIME (GMT) finish	FREQUENCY (MHz)	MODE	STATION called/worked	REPORT sent	REPORT received	QSL sent	QSL rcvd	REMARKS
3 April '82	09.00	09.02	3·6	J3E	CQ					No reply
"	09.09	09.18	3·6	J3E	G7AA	58	57			
"	10.00	10.12	14	A1A	WD1ZZZ	579	579			Bill, Mass.
"	10.13	10.15	14	A1A	CQ					
"	10.15	10.28	14	A1A	VK2ZZZ	569	459			
"	10.30		Station closed down							
4 April '82	17.30	17.33	21	J3E	Test					Tests for TVI
6 April '82	14.00	/A at Room 14, County Hall, Hamington								Demonstration to local guild meeting
"	14.01	14.02	1·8	A3E	CQ					
"	14.02	14.10	1·8	A3E	G4ZZZ	59	59			
"	14.18	14.30	1·8	A3E	G4YYY	57	58			
"	15.00	15.02	14	J3E	CQ					
"	15.02	15.20	14	J3E	KN9XYZ	55	54			
"	15.30	15.40	14	J3E	KN8XYZ	58	57			
"	16.00		Station removed and closed down							
7 April '82	10.00	10.01	14	J3E	CQ					S. PERKS, G2ZZZ Operator
"	10.02	10.15	14	J3E	WD2ZZZ	55	56			S. Perks
"	10.15	10.26	14	J3E	WD3ZZZ	57	57			
"	10.30	10.33	144	F3E	CQ					
"	10.33	10.45	144	F3E	G7ZZZ	59	59			
"	10.47	10.48	144	F3E	G4UUU	57				Did not reply
"	10.53		Station closed down							

Fig 11.1. Typical log entries

something like 30 miles. This is indicated in Fig 11.2. This increase in range is at no cost to the amateur in respect of extra power or improved antennas.

Continuous operation of the repeater transmitter is undesirable and therefore means of remotely turning the repeater on and off is included; this is generally known as *accessing* the repeater. In the case of some repeaters (but not all) accessing is achieved by transmitting a 1,750 ± 5Hz tone (the *toneburst*), which is approximately 0·5s long, at the beginning of each period of use of the repeater. (Some repeaters do not require a toneburst, being carrier operated, ie they are activated by the presence of a user's carrier on the input channel).

The tone switches on the transmitter and starts an internal clock which will turn the repeater transmitter off after typically 1min. This is known as *time-out* and is intended to keep user transmissions short.

Repeaters operate only with frequency modulated signals which must be of the correct frequency and deviation. The frequency and deviation are monitored continuously and if these parameters fall at any time below the standard required for valid access the repeater transmitter may be shut down.

When an "over" is finished and the incoming signal disappears, the repeater will, after a short delay, indicate its readiness for another input transmission by transmitting either a "K" or "T" in morse code.

Satellites

A number of satellites specifically designed for amateur radio have been launched since 1961. These have been called Oscar 1, Oscar 2 etc (from *O*rbiting *S*atellite *C*arrying *A*mateur *R*adio).

The satellites are *transponders*—they will accept cw, ssb or rtty signals over a band of frequencies and retransmit them in another amateur band. Current satellites have 432 to 144MHz, 144 to 432MHz and 144 to 28MHz transponders.

Accessing a satellite does not require an access tone as the satellite monitors incoming signals continuously and its transmitter is permanently operational.

Obviously the satellite will only receive sufficient signal when it is in direct line-of-sight to the transmitter. This happens periodically when the satellite, which is rotating round the earth, appears over the horizon.

The power required to use the Oscar series transponders is 80–100W erp. This power level is usually

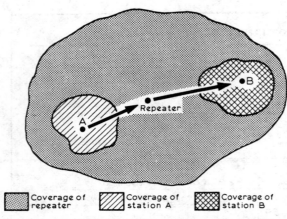

Coverage of repeater   Coverage of station A   Coverage of station B

Fig 11.2. The improved range of communication between mobile stations when using a repeater. The simplex coverage areas of stations A and B shown are constantly changing shape as the two vehicles pass through different terrain, and thus station B would have to be quite close to station A before reliable communication was possible.

achieved with a low-power transmitter (10–15W output) followed by an antenna with a gain of 10dB. The antenna must be pointed in the direction of the satellite to achieve this gain and so it must move in both azimuth and elevation in order to track the satellite properly. This can lead to complex antenna systems if best results are desired, although simple fixed antennas are capable of satisfactory operation if correctly designed.

A brief comparison of the modes of operation of repeaters and satellites may be useful. A repeater accepts fm signals at a single frequency and retransmits them in the same band (the frequency shift is 600kHz in the 144MHz amateur band). An access tone (1,750Hz) is often required (sometimes only for the initial transmission of a contact) and the input signal must be of the correct frequency and deviation.

A satellite transponds a band of frequencies from one amateur band to another and will accept any form of modulation (cw, ssb and rtty are preferred).

A repeater extends the user's range by a relatively small factor and the final range is still essentially local under most conditions. However a satellite permits coverage of very large distances on vhf and uhf.

Safety precautions in the amateur station

The RSGB Safety Recommendations for the Amateur Radio Station given in Appendix 2 should be studied carefully.

It is not possible to define a voltage which is "safe to touch"—no voltage source should ever be touched deliberately. The effects of an electric shock of a particular voltage depend on so many factors, from the source of the voltage to the state of health of the unfortunate person involved.

It is therefore best to consider any voltage about 50V as dangerous and to act accordingly. Probably the three most important precautions are:

(a) Ensure that all equipment is satisfactorily earthed—the integrity of the earthing system should be checked periodically.

(b) Switch off and disconnect from the mains supply before attempting the investigation or repair of any equipment.

(c) Capacitors of high value, particularly if the dielectric is paper, will hold their charge for long periods (days/weeks). Bleed resistor chains should therefore be connected across high-voltage smoothing capacitors in order to dissipate this charge in a few seconds. Bleed resistor chains should be conservatively rated as regards dissipation and ideally should consist of two separate chains in parallel. In spite of the presence of bleed resistor chains, high-voltage smoothing capacitors should be shorted as recommended in paragraph 5 of the safety recommendations before any servicing of a power supply is carried out.

CHAPTER 12

Tackling the RAE

Many candidates study for the examination at a local technical college or evening institute, but a large number prepare themselves privately either with or without the assistance of a correspondence course. Colleges and institutions offering RAE courses are listed in *Radio Communication* and other radio journals, usually during July, August and September each year. Early application is advised so that colleges are aware that there will be sufficient students to warrant the course being organized.

If it appears after enquiry that no course is proposed in the reader's locality, it is suggested that the local radio club or RSGB Group be contacted if this has not already been done. Many clubs are affiliated to the Society and their addresses are listed in the RSGB *Amateur Radio Call Book*. Clubs often run a series of talks helpful to prospective amateurs. If, however, enough prospective candidates for the RAE can be found, then an approach to the principal of the nearest college or institute should be made. Normally 12 candidates will warrant a course being started provided an instructor, preferably a teacher/amateur, and accommodation are available at the college. Courses, one or two evenings each week, usually start in September so make this approach some months beforehand—it might even be possible to find and suggest a suitable instructor as well if the college has not got one!

If no college course is available, do not give up. Many private students are successful every year. A correspondence course can be of immense help. Some college students, too, have found a correspondence course in addition to be a help. Whichever method of preparation is followed, the prospective candidate is strongly urged to contact his or her local club, where practical and willing help is sure to be found. If there appears to be no such club within reach, do not hesitate to contact amateurs in the area (again see the *Call Book*). Most of them will be only too willing to show their radio equipment and give useful help and advice to assist in becoming a radio amateur.

Examination requirements

Because the questions are now multiple choice, do not neglect study of diagrams and calculations (study those in Chapter 2). Remember that fixed capacitors have a tolerance of at least ±1 per cent, so that if a calculator (the use of calculators is allowed) reads 159·376 in answer to a question on capacitive reactance, then settle for the value of 160. Learn to manipulate formulae. During studies note the values of the components in different parts of circuits used for dealing with different frequencies. All diagrams and symbols used in the examination are to British Standard No 3939 (see Appendix 1).

In the examination room

Find out in good time where the examination room is and take a pocket calculator if desired. Nearly all the questions can be answered using simple arithmetic.

After being given the paper sit back, take a deep breath and read the instructions carefully. To indicate which of the choices is considered to be correct, fill in the appropriate box, a, b, c or d on the answer sheet with an HB pencil (the computer then reads this to give a mark). Any calculation or rough work can be done in the question book, which must be handed in with the answer sheet. Do not forget to fill in your candidate number (in pencil) in the appropriate box on the answer sheet.

The multiple-choice questions are not designed to "trick" the candidate. One, or perhaps two, of the distractors (ie the wrong answers) may be unfamiliar and possibly not even in this manual, but they will be plausible. The following example illustrates this point.

> A triangle having all its sides of the same length is called
> (a) a right-angle triangle.
> (b) an isosceles triangle.
> (c) the eternal triangle.
> (d) an equilateral triangle.

Distractor (c) contains the word triangle but hardly in a geometrical sense. You will not find such an extreme example of a question in the examination!

Conclusion

The examination questions cover all the objectives. During studies the whole of the syllabus content should be covered. Do not on the one hand imagine that it is so easy that one can hardly fail, or on the other hand feel that the questions are bound to be beyond one's capabilities. Candidates are not competing against others but are trying to reach a certain standard.

If a question is found to be too difficult, leave it and pass on to the next. One can return to it later and make an intelligent guess. The computer will only record the correct answer. The computer cannot be fooled by filling in all the spaces provided for the answer!

Provided the required standard is reached a pass will be obtained. A great many candidates of all ages and from all walks of life are successful in passing this examination. Good luck!

Radio circuit symbols

* Indicates preferred symbol

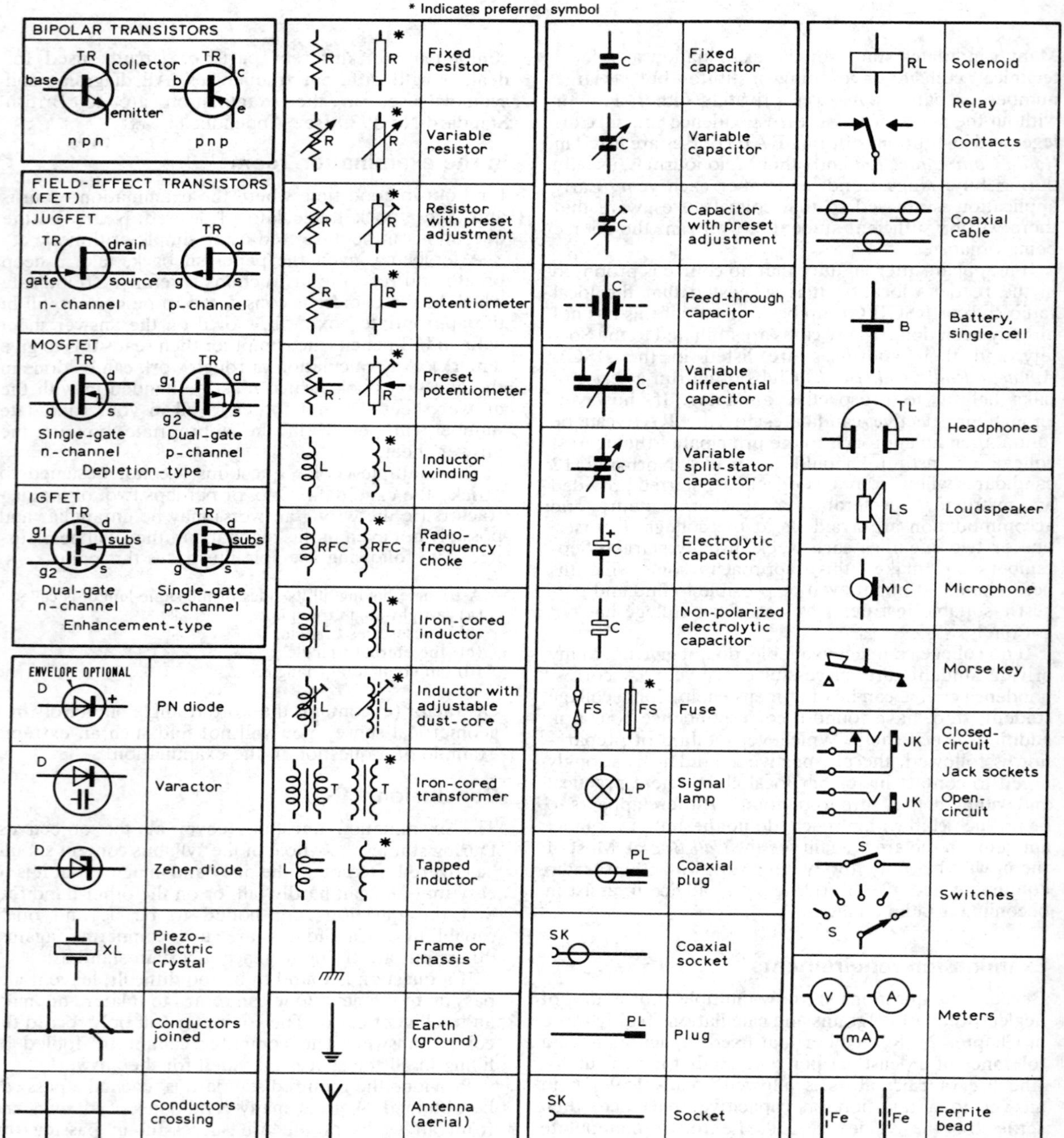

BIPOLAR TRANSISTORS

npn | pnp
base, collector, emitter (TR) | b, c, e (TR)

FIELD-EFFECT TRANSISTORS (FET)

JUGFET

n-channel | p-channel
gate, drain, source (TR) | g, d, s (TR)

MOSFET

Single-gate n-channel | Dual-gate p-channel
g, d, s (TR) | g1, g2, d, s (TR)
Depletion-type

IGFET

Dual-gate n-channel | Single-gate p-channel
g1, g2, d, s, subs (TR) | g, d, s, subs (TR)
Enhancement-type

ENVELOPE OPTIONAL

D (+)	PN diode
D	Varactor
D	Zener diode
XL	Piezo-electric crystal
	Conductors joined
	Conductors crossing

R	Fixed resistor *
R	Variable resistor *
R	Resistor with preset adjustment *
R	Potentiometer *
R	Preset potentiometer
L	Inductor winding *
RFC	Radio-frequency choke *
L	Iron-cored inductor *
L	Inductor with adjustable dust-core *
T	Iron-cored transformer *
L	Tapped inductor *
	Frame or chassis
	Earth (ground)
	Antenna (aerial)

C	Fixed capacitor
C	Variable capacitor
C	Capacitor with preset adjustment
C	Feed-through capacitor
C	Variable differential capacitor
C	Variable split-stator capacitor
C	Electrolytic capacitor
C	Non-polarized electrolytic capacitor
FS	Fuse *
LP	Signal lamp
PL	Coaxial plug
SK	Coaxial socket
PL	Plug
SK	Socket

RL	Solenoid
	Relay
	Contacts
	Coaxial cable
B	Battery, single-cell
TL	Headphones
LS	Loudspeaker
MIC	Microphone
	Morse key
JK	Closed-circuit Jack sockets
JK	Open-circuit
S	Switches
V, A, mA	Meters
Fe, Fe	Ferrite bead

Safety recommendations for the amateur radio station

1. All equipment should be controlled by one master switch, the position of which should be well known to others in the house or club.

2. All equipment should be properly connected to a good and permanent earth. *(Note A)*

3. Wiring should be adequately insulated, especially where voltages greater than 500V are used. Terminals should be suitably protected.

4. Transformers operating at more than 100V rms should be fitted with an earthed screen between the primary and secondary windings.

5. Capacitors of more than $0.01\mu F$ capacitance operating in power packs, modulators, etc (other than for rf bypass or coupling) should have a bleeder resistor connected directly across their terminals. The value of the bleeder resistor should be low enough to ensure rapid discharge. A value of $1/C$ megohms (where C is in microfarads) is recommended. The use of earthed probe leads for discharging capacitors in case the bleeder resistor is defective is also recommended. *(Note B)*. Low-leakage capacitors, such as paper and oil-filled types, should be stored with their terminals short-circuited to prevent static charging.

6. Indicator lamps should be installed showing that the equipment is live. These should be clearly visible at the operating and test position. Faulty indicator lamps should be replaced immediately. Gas-filled (neon) lamps are more reliable than filament types.

7. Double-pole switches should be used for breaking mains circuits on equipment. Fuses of correct rating should be connected to the equipment side of each switch. *(Note C)* Always switch off before changing a fuse. The use of ac/dc equipment should be avoided.

8. In metal-enclosed equipment install primary circuit breakers, such as micro-switches, which operate when the door or lid is opened. Check their operation frequently.

9. Test prods and test lamps should be of the insulated pattern.

10. A rubber mat should be used when the equipment is installed on a floor that is likely to become damp.

11. Switch off before making any adjustments. If adjustments must be made while the equipment is live, use one hand only and keep the other in your pocket. Never attempt two-handed work without switching off first. Use good-quality insulated tools for adjustments.

12. Do not wear headphones while making internal adjustments on live equipment.

13. Ensure that the metal cases of microphones, morse keys etc are properly connected to the chassis.

14. Do not use meters with metal zero-adjusting screws in high-voltage circuits. Beware of live shafts projecting through panels, particularly when metal grub screws are used in control knobs.

15. Antennas should not, under any circumstances, be connected to the mains or other ht source. Where feeders are connected through a capacitor, which may have ht on the other side, a low-resistance dc path to earth should be provided (rf choke).

Note A.—Owing to the common use of plastic water main and sections of plastic pipe in effecting repairs, it is no longer safe to assume that a mains water pipe is effectively connected to earth. Steps must be taken, therefore, to ensure that the earth connection is of sufficiently low resistance to provide safety in the event of a fault. Checks should be made whenever repairs are made to the mains water system in the building.

Note B.—A "wandering earth lead" or an "insulated earthed probe lead" is an insulated lead permanently connected at one end to the chassis of the equipment; at the other end a suitable length of bare wire is provided for touch contacting the high potential terminals to be discharged.

Note C.—Where necessary, surge-proof fuses can be used.

Radio Amateurs' Examination syllabus and objectives

The examination objectives describe in general terms the nature of the examination questions, while the syllabus states the subject matter to which they relate.

PAPER 1: LICENSING CONDITIONS AND TRANSMITTER INTERFERENCE

1. Licensing conditions

Examination objectives
(a) Name the types and state the purposes of Amateur Licences available.
(b) State the qualifications required of their holders.
(c) State accurately the conditions of the Amateur Licence A, and the notes appended to it, with regard to
  (i) period of validity, renewal, revocation, variation and return
  (ii) places in which the station may be established and used
  (iii) purposes for which the station may be used and persons who may use it
  (iv) frequency bands, powers and classes of emission which may be used
  (v) requirements relating to avoidance of interference, restriction of bandwidth, limitation of harmonic and spurious emissions and checking transmitter performance
  (vi) requirements for logkeeping, use of callsigns and recorded messages, inspection and closing down of the station
  (vii) limitations and prohibitions in connection with the use of the station.

Syllabus
1. Types of licence available and the qualifications necessary.
2. Conditions (terms, provisions and limitations) laid down by the Home Office in the Amateur Licence A, including the notes appended and the schedules of classes of emission and frequency bands.

2. Transmitter interference

Examination objectives
(a) Describe the consequences of poor frequency stability.

(b) For spurious emissions
  (i) describe in non-mathematical terms their causes
  (ii) describe methods, appropriate to the Amateur Service, of detecting and recognizing their presence
  (iii) describe in practical terms the measures which should be taken in both the design and construction of transmitters and the use of filters to minimize them.
(c) Describe the simple means of limiting the audio bandwidth of emissions and explain why this is necessary.
(d) State the causes of mains-borne interference and describe methods of suppression.
(e) Demonstrate knowledge of the Home Office guidelines relating to frequency checking equipment.

Syllabus
1. Frequency stability; consequences of poor frequency stability: risks of interference, out-of-band radiation.
2. Spurious emissions, causes and methods of prevention; harmonics of the radiated frequency, direct radiation from frequency-determining and frequency-changing stages of a transmitter, parasitic oscillations, key clicks, excessive sidebands due to over-modulation. Excessive deviation of fm transmitters.
3. Restriction of audio bandwidth, typical methods used and their limitations.
4. Mains-borne interference, causes and methods of suppression.
5. Home Office requirements for frequency checking equipment: Appendix F to *How to Become a Radio Amateur*.

PAPER 2: OPERATING PRACTICES, PROCEDURES AND THEORY

1. Operating practices and procedures

Examination objectives
(a) Describe calling procedures in telegraphy and telephony.
(b) Demonstrate knowledge of maintaining a log.
(c) For satellites and repeaters
  (i) explain why they are used in the Amateur Service
  (ii) describe the method of accessing a repeater.

(d) Explain the reasons for using Q-codes and other abbreviations.

(e) Demonstrate knowledge of the phonetic alphabet and explain why it is used.

(f) For safety in operating
(i) state the precautions recommended
(ii) explain why capacitors should be discharged
(iii) explain why equipment to be repaired should be disconnected from the mains supply.

Syllabus

1. Calling procedures in telegraphy and telephony: general calls to all stations and calls to specific stations.
2. Logkeeping: Clause 6 of the Amateur Licence A.
3. Use of satellites and repeaters; accessing a repeater.
4. Use of Q-codes and other abbreviations appropriate to the Amateur Service.
5. The phonetic alphabet: reasons for its use; recommendations in *How to Become a Radio Amateur*.
6. Safety in the amateur station: recommendations of the Radio Society of Great Britain.

2. Electrical theory

Examination objectives

(a) For basic terms and units
(i) define the terms
(ii) state the SI units for given measurements and define their relationship to each other.

(b) For current, power and resistance
(i) state Ohm's Law and use it to solve simple problems
(ii) calculate total current in series and parallel circuits
(iii) calculate power in a dc circuit
(iv) calculate the effective resistance of resistors in series and parallel circuits
(v) describe the function of resistors in electronic circuits: name types for given applications: give practical values
(vi) state the magnetic and heating effects of currents and their applications.

(c) For inductance and capacitance
(i) define the units
(ii) state the factors which affect the value of the capacitance of a capacitor
(iii) state the factors which affect the value of the inductance of an inductor
(iv) explain what is meant by the time constant of circuits containing resistance and capacitance, and resistance and inductance
(v) calculate total capacitance in series and parallel circuits
(vi) calculate total inductance in series circuits
(vii) explain what is meant by inductive and capacitive reactance
(viii) explain their effects in ac circuits
(ix) solve simple problems on given ac series circuits.

(d) Define the terms describing the sine wave.

(e) Explain simply the terms relating to power, reactance, impedance and resonance.

(f) For transformers and tuned circuits
(i) explain the function and describe the operation of a transformer
(ii) identify series and parallel ac circuits and calculate resonant frequency from given data
(iii) explain voltage amplification and current amplification effects
(iv) state the conditions under which oscillations may be maintained.

(g) For radio and electrical components give typical tolerances and limits on the nominal values.

Syllabus

1. (a) Basic electrical terms, their meaning and use: emf, current, conductor, resistance, insulator, power, series circuit, parallel circuit.
(b) SI units, their use and relationship to each other: volt, coulomb, ampere, ohm, watt, hertz.
2. Current, power and resistance: Ohm's Law. Total current and effective resistance in series and parallel circuits. Power in a dc circuit. Magnetic and heating effects of currents: applications.
3. Inductance and capacitance; appropriate units; effects in ac circuits. Effective inductance and capacitance in circuits. Meaning of inductive and capacitive reactance. Factors affecting capacitance and inductance value. Time constant.
4. Sine wave. Definition of terms: amplitude, period and frequency; instantaneous, peak, peak-to-peak, rms values.
5. Power, reactance, impedance and resonance in ac circuits; simple explanation of terms: phase angle, phase difference, phase lead and lag, reactance, impedance, series resonance, parallel resonance, resonant frequency and Q (magnification) factor.
6. (a) Transformers: function and operation.
(b) Tuned circuits: series and parallel ac circuits, resonant frequency data and calculations; voltage amplification and current amplification effects. Maintenance of oscillations in tuned circuits. Dynamic impedance.
7. Types of components used and their applications in electronic equipment; tolerances and preferred values.

3. Solid state devices

Examination objectives

(a) Explain in simple terms the principles of
(i) operation of npn and pnp transistors
(ii) diode rectification
(iii) biasing and protection of transistors in amplifier circuits
(iv) operation of simple integrated circuits.

(b) Describe the operation of given devices in radio equipment.

(c) Describe and explain the principles of operation of typical power supply circuits with smoothing and voltage stabilization systems.

Syllabus

1. Characteristics and principles of operation of npn

and pnp transistors; principles of diode rectification; control of output current and voltage when transistors are used as audio-frequency and radio-frequency amplifiers. Simple integrated circuits.

2. Use of solid state devices in radio equipment as
   (a) oscillators (crystal and variable frequency types)
   (b) amplifiers (audio-frequency and radio-frequency types)
   (c) frequency changers
   (d) frequency multipliers
   (e) demodulators

3. Typical power-supply circuits; power rectification; smoothing and voltage stabilization systems.

4. Radio receivers

Examination objectives
(a) Explain the principles of reception of given signals.
(b) Describe the operation of simple receiver circuits.
(c) State the advantages and disadvantages of high and low intermediate frequencies.
(d) Explain adjacent channel and image frequency interference and the methods of minimizing them.
(e) Explain the general principles of the demodulation of frequency-modulated signals.
(f) Describe the use of a beat-frequency oscillator for the reception of type A1 signals.
(g) Explain the principles of reception of single-sideband signals.
(h) Describe the purpose of a carrier insertion oscillator.

Syllabus
1. Principles of reception of continuous wave, double-sideband, single-sideband and frequency-modulated signals in terms of radio-frequency amplification, frequency changing (where appropriate), demodulation or detection and automatic gain control, audio amplification. The superheterodyne principle of reception.
2. Advantages and disadvantages of high and low intermediate frequencies; adjacent channel and image frequency interference and its control.
3. Typical receivers; use of a beat-frequency oscillator. Characteristics of a single-sideband signal and the purpose of a carrier insertion oscillator.

5. Transmitters

Examination objectives
(a) For oscillators
   (i) describe their construction
   (ii) state the factors affecting their stability.
(b) Describe the operation of given stages in transmitters. Explain the procedure for the adjustment and tuning of transmitters.
(c) For methods of keying
   (i) describe and explain the methods
   (ii) state the advantages and disadvantages of each.
(d) For modulation and types of emission
   (i) describe and explain the principles of modulation of radio-frequency emissions in given modes

(ii) state the relative advantages of given modes.
(iii) describe the procedure for adjusting the level of modulation.

Syllabus
1. Oscillators used in transmitters; stable variable frequency and crystal controlled oscillators; their construction and factors affecting stability.
2. Transmitter stages: operation of frequency changers, frequency multipliers, high and low power amplifiers (including linear types). Procedure for transmitter adjustment.
3. Methods of keying transmitters for telegraphy; advantages and disadvantages.
4. Methods of modulation and types of emission in current use including single-sideband and frequency modulation; emissions in the A2, A3, A3J, F2 and F3 modes; relative advantages. Adjustment of level of modulation.

6. Propagation and aerials

Examination objectives
(a) Explain given basic terms.
(b) For electromagnetic waves
   (i) explain their production
   (ii) state the relationship between electric and magnetic components.
(c) For the ionosphere, troposphere and upper atmosphere
   (i) describe in simple terms the structure of the ionosphere
   (ii) explain in simple non-mathematical terms the refracting and reflecting properties of the ionosphere and the troposphere
   (iii) explain how given factors affect the ionization of the upper atmosphere
   (iv) state the effect of varying degrees of ionization of the upper atmosphere on the propagation of electromagnetic waves.
(d) Describe in simple terms given forms of propagation.
(e) Explain fade outs and given forms of fading.
(f) For radio waves
   (i) state their velocity in free space
   (ii) state the relationship between velocity, frequency and wavelength
   (iii) calculate frequency and wavelength from given data.
(g) For aerials and transmission lines
   (i) describe and explain their operation and construction
   (ii) describe balanced and unbalanced feeders and explain the principles of propagation of radio waves along transmission lines; describe the effects of standing waves
   (iii) explain the principles of coupling and matching aerials to transmitters and receivers
   (iv) identify from diagrams typical coupling and matching arrangements.

Syllabus

1. Explanation of basic terms: ionosphere, troposphere, atmosphere, field strength, polarization, maximum usable frequency, critical frequency, skip distance.
2. Generation of electromagnetic waves; relationship between electric and magnetic components.
3. Structure of the ionosphere. Refracting and reflecting properties of the ionosphere and troposphere. Effect of sunspot cycle, winter and summer seasons and day and night on the ionization of upper atmosphere; effect of varying degrees of ionization on the propagation of electromagnetic waves.
4. Ground wave, ionospheric and tropospheric propagation.
5. Fade-out and types of fading: selective, interference, polarization, absorption and skip.
6. Velocity of radio waves in free space; relationship between velocity of propagation, frequency and wavelength; calculation of frequency and wavelength.
7. Receiving and transmitting aerials; operation and construction of typical aerials including multiband and directional types; their directional properties. Coupling and matching.
8. Transmission lines, balanced and unbalanced feeders; elementary principles of propagation of radio waves along transmission lines; velocity ratio, standing waves.

7. Measurement

Examination objectives

(a) For the measurement of ac, dc and radio-frequency voltages and currents
  (i) state the types of instruments in common use
  (ii) explain how errors can be caused by the effect of the instrument on the circuit.
(b) For power input and output measurement

(i) explain in detail how dc power input to the final amplifier of a transmitter is measured
(ii) describe the incorporation of metering arrangements in an amateur transmitter
(iii) explain the method of measurement of radio-frequency power output of power amplifiers (including linear types).
(c) For given frequency measuring instruments
  (i) state the purpose for which they are used
  (ii) state the relative accuracy
  (iii) describe in detail their use at an amateur transmitting station.
(d) Describe the construction of dummy loads and explain their use.
(e) Explain the purpose and method of using a standing-wave ratio meter.
(f) Describe in detail the method of setting up an oscilloscope.

Syllabus

1. Types of instruments used in radio work for the measurement of ac, dc and radio-frequency voltages and currents: errors in measurement.
2. Measurement of
(a) dc power input to the final amplifier of a transmitter
(b) radio-frequency power output of power amplifiers (including linear types)
(c) current at radio frequencies.
(Reference to *How to Become a Radio Amateur*.)
3. Purposes, operation and use of absorption wavemeters, heterodyne wavemeters and frequency counters; relative accuracies.
4. Dummy loads; their construction and use in tuning transmitters.
5. Use of standing-wave ratio meters.
6. Setting up and use of a cathode-ray oscilloscope to examine and measure waveform and monitor the depth of modulation.

Practice multiple-choice RAE questions

This appendix contains two sample question papers in the multiple-choice format as defined in Chapter 1. These sample items illustrate the kinds of question included in the examination. They should not however be considered representative of the entire scope of the examination in either content or difficulty.

Part 1 should be completed in 1h. After a break of ¼h, Part 2 should be completed in 1¾h. Answers will be found on p131.

FIRST SAMPLE TEST PAPER

Part 1. Licence conditions and transmitter interference

1. The callsign prefix of the island of Jersey is
   (a) GM.
   (b) GW.
   (c) GJ.
   (d) GD.

2. An Amateur Licence B allows operation in amateur bands
   (a) above 30MHz.
   (b) above 144MHz.
   (c) above 146MHz.
   (d) up to 146MHz.

3. To qualify for a licence an applicant must, among other things, meet an age requirement which is to be
   (a) over 18 years of age.
   (b) between 15 and 70 years of age.
   (c) not under 21 years of age.
   (d) over 14 years of age.

4. The maximum dc input power permitted on the 1·8–2·0MHz band is
   (a) 400W.
   (b) 10W.
   (c) 150W.
   (d) 50W.

5. In the PO Morse Test an amateur has to send and receive messages at a nominal 12wpm consisting of
   (a) mixed plain language and numbers.
   (b) five-letter code groups only.
   (c) ten-number code groups only.
   (d) separate five-figure number groups and plain language.

6. When using his station at a temporary premises or location for a period of less than four weeks an amateur should, in writing, inform
   (a) the local police.
   (b) nobody.
   (c) the nearest town hall.
   (d) the local Telephone Manager at the end of the first week.

7. The holder of an Amateur Licence A may only send signals which
   (a) are listed in the ITU Radio Regulations.
   (b) form part of, or relate to, the transmission of messages to and from other amateur stations.
   (c) are in Home Office approved codes and cyphers.
   (d) when in morse code are sent at speeds not exceeding 12wpm.

8. Recorded messages from other stations may be retransmitted providing they
   (a) do not contain obscene language.
   (b) are intended for reception by the originating station only.
   (c) do not include the callsign of the originating station.
   (d) both (b) and (c) together.

9. The station, licence and log shall be available for inspection at all reasonable times by
   (a) a member of the Radio Society of Great Britain.
   (b) any member of the armed forces.
   (c) a person acting under the authority of the Secretary of State.
   (d) a person nominated by the local council.

10. Entries in the log book need *not* include the
    (a) date.
    (b) time of commencement of operation.
    (c) signature of licensee.
    (d) time of closing down of the station.

11. The receiver used in the station shall be capable of covering
    (a) all amateur bands for which the station is licensed.
    (b) the frequency used for transmission and that used by the local BBC4 programme.
    (c) the frequency being used for transmission.
    (d) (c) together with the second and third harmonics of that transmission.

12. The holder of an Amateur Licence A with callsign G4ZZZ, when working from temporary premises in Wales, should use the callsign
    (a) GW4ZZZ/A.
    (b) GW8ZZZ/A.
    (c) GW4ZZZ.
    (d) G4ZZZ/A.

13. The callsign of the station shall be sent for identification purposes at the beginning and end of each sending period. If the latter exceeds 15 minutes the callsign shall be repeated
    (a) at intervals of five minutes.
    (b) 15 minutes from the start of the period.
    (c) at intervals of 10 minutes.
    (d) at the commencement of each succeeding period of 15 minutes.

14. The apparatus comprised in the station shall be designed, constructed, maintained and used
    (a) so as not to cause any undue interference with any wireless telegraphy.
    (b) to IEE regulations.
    (c) within 20 per cent of the authorized maximum power.
    (d) to the satisfaction of any member of the Post Office staff.

15. The word "shot" should be spelt phonetically, using the phonetic alphabet contained in Appendix 16 of the Radio Regulations, Geneva, 1976, as follows
    (a) Spain Hotel Oscar Toc.
    (b) Sierra Harry Oscar Tango.
    (c) Sugar Hotel Orange Texas.
    (d) Sierra Hotel Oscar Tango.

16. The licensee shall test his transmissions for radiation of harmonics and other spurious emissions, and record such tests in the log
    (a) from time to time.
    (b) once a week.
    (c) yearly.
    (d) at the request of a Home Office official.

17. Which one of the bands listed below is allocated to the amateur service on a secondary basis on condition that it shall cause no interference to other services?
    (a) 1·8 to 2·0MHz.
    (b) 3·5 to 3·8MHz.
    (c) 14·0 to 14·35MHz.
    (d) 144 to 146MHz.

18. Under the licence conditions the frequency control of the station's emissions shall be by
    (a) quartz crystal.
    (b) a frequency synthesizer.
    (c) a satisfactory method of frequency control.
    (d) reference to an accurate wavemeter.

19. The log of the station shall be entered in and kept in
    (a) a special book provided by the Post Office.
    (b) a book (not looseleaf).
    (c) a specially printed book approved by the Home Office.
    (d) a looseleaf note-book.

20. The station may *not* be used for
    (a) broadcasting messages generally.
    (b) reception of signals in the standard frequency service.
    (c) contact with stations outside the United Kingdom.
    (d) working in the 1,215 to 1,290MHz band without special permission from the Home Office.

21. Under the direct supervision of the licensee, in addition to himself, the station may be operated by
    (a) members of the police force.
    (b) visiting foreign amateurs.
    (c) members of the licensee's immediate family.
    (d) a person holding a current wireless telegraphy licence issued by the Secretary of State.

22. The amateur licence continues in force
    (a) for a year from the date of issue.
    (b) until the death of the holder.
    (c) for a year from the date of issue and thereafter subject to payment in advance of the annual renewal fee.
    (d) for a period of five years from the date of issue.

23. The station shall be closed down
    (a) in the event of a general strike.
    (b) when asked to by the local Telephone Manager.
    (c) on demand by a person acting under the authority of the Secretary of State.
    (d) on the outbreak of war.

24. Poor frequency stability in an amateur transmitter can result in
    (a) generation of parasitic oscillations.
    (b) operation outside the amateur bands.
    (c) a reduction in power output.
    (d) instability in the power amplifier.

25. A licensee must be able to verify that his emission is
    (a) within the authorized frequency band.
    (b) accurate to one part in a million.
    (c) within no closer than one per cent of band edge.
    (d) with a total harmonic output power of less than one per cent of the carrier power.

26. In an amateur telephony transmitter the audio bandwidth should be restricted to 2 or 3kHz to
    (a) increase the transmitter output.
    (b) minimize the radio frequency bandwidth required for the signal.
    (c) improve speech quality.
    (d) reduce fading.

27. If an amateur transmitter is operating on a frequency of 14·1MHz the second harmonic will be on a frequency of
    (a) 7·05MHz.
    (b) 28·2MHz.
    (c) 21·15MHz.
    (d) 42·3MHz.

28. What is an important use of the circuit shown below?

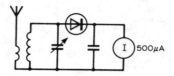

(a) To detect the presence of harmonic radiation.
(b) To measure the bandwidth of an amplitude modulated signal.
(c) To measure the transmitter input power.
(d) To measure the degree of modulation.

29. The circuit shown below is commonly used in amateur stations to reduce harmonic radiation.

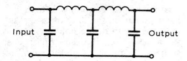

It is called a
(a) high-pass filter.
(b) band-pass filter.
(c) frequency multiplier.
(d) low-pass filter.

30. The waveform shown below is that of an amplitude modulated rf signal.

It can be said to be
(a) 100 per cent modulated.
(b) unstable.
(c) under-modulated.
(d) over-modulated.

31. Spurious emissions from an amateur transmitter may be caused by
(a) oscillation of the power amplifier stage.
(b) insufficient power supply smoothing.
(c) under-modulation.
(d) the antenna too near the ground.

32. Small ferrite beads are sometimes threaded over transmitter input leads in an amplifier to
(a) improve tonal quality.
(b) suppress parasitic oscillation.
(c) tune the amplifier.
(d) reduce the noise level.

33. A single sideband transmitter power amplifier stage would be expected to cause interference with neighbouring stations if
(a) it had shorted turns in the tank circuit.
(b) the power supply was not well smoothed.
(c) it was overdriven.
(d) there was leakage of rf into the power supply cable.

34. Key clicks in a cw transmitter can be prevented by
(a) using a key click filter.
(b) cleaning the key contacts.
(c) using a twisted pair lead to the key.
(d) sending the morse slowly.

35. You are transmitting in the 1·8MHz band with a carrier frequency of 1,839kHz and your neighbour reports interference with his broadcast receiver which is tuned to 909kHz and has an i.f. of 465kHz. Which is the most probable cause of the interference?
(a) A sub-harmonic of the carrier.
(b) Your signal is beating with the third harmonic of the local oscillator of the broadcast receiver.
(c) Second channel interference.
(d) Adjacent channel interference.

Part 2. Operating practices and procedures, and technical part of syllabus

36. "QRP?" is the Q-code for
(a) "have you a power amplifier?"
(b) "shall I reduce my transmitting power?"
(c) "have you a message for me?"
(d) "what time is it?"

37. Before beginning a transmission a good operator should
(a) listen on the transmitting frequency to be used.
(b) sharpen his pencil.
(c) measure his transmitter input power.
(d) open his log book.

38. An extremely strong signal with no interference and a pure note from a telegraphy transmitter would be reported in the RST code as
(a) 559
(b) 555
(c) 469
(d) 599

39. A commonly used method of accessing a 144MHz band repeater is to
(a) call the repeater by its callsign in morse code.
(b) call the repeater on 144·5MHz with a burst of carrier.
(c) transmit a carrier on the repeater input frequency accompanied by a burst of a specified audio tone.
(d) do nothing as the repeater is always on.

40. A bleeder resistor is often used as a safety measure; it is
(a) a resistor used in connection with blood tests.
(b) a resistor across a capacitor for discharge purposes.
(c) a resistor in the emitter circuit of a transistor amplifier.
(d) the series resistor used in a voltmeter.

41. The graph below shows the relationship between current and voltage in a dc circuit.

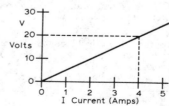

The resistance of the circuit is
(a) 5Ω.
(b) 20Ω.
(c) 0·2Ω.
(d) 80Ω.

42. The "time constant", T, of a resistor R and a capacitor C connected together is given by the formula
(a) $T = C \div R$
(b) $T = \sqrt{C} \times R$
(c) $T = C \times R$
(d) $T = (C \times R)^2$

43. The resonant frequency of the series tuned circuit shown below is

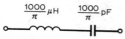

(a) 0·5MHz.
(b) 1MHz.
(c) 5MHz.
(d) 100kHz.

44. In the circuit given below, what is the potential difference (voltage) between points A and B?

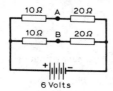

(a) 2V.
(b) 4V.
(c) 1V.
(d) 0V.

45. The most suitable way to measure the voltage across R2 would be by

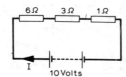

(a) a moving coil voltmeter.
(b) an oscilloscope.
(c) an electronic voltmeter.
(d) a 1,000Ω/V multi-range meter.

46. The current flowing in the circuit below is

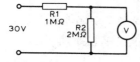

(a) 6A.
(b) 3A.
(c) 1A.
(d) 10A.

47. The power dissipated in the 3Ω resistor of the circuit in question 46 is
(a) 3W.
(b) 0·3W.
(c) 10W.
(d) 1W.

48. The unit of inductance is the
(a) farad.
(b) hertz.
(c) newton.
(d) henry.

49. The total effective capacitance of the circuit below is

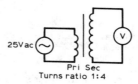

(a) 7·5μF.
(b) 3μF.
(c) 4·5μF.
(d) 2μF.

50. In the transformer circuit shown below the secondary voltage will be

(a) 400V.
(b) 100V.
(c) 6·25V.
(d) 50V.

51. The reactance X_c of a capacitor C at a frequency f is given by the formula
(a) $X_c = 2\pi \sqrt{fC}$
(b) $X_c = f^2 C$
(c) $X_c = 2\pi fC$
(d) $X_c = \dfrac{1}{2\pi fC}$

52. A transistor rf amplifier is operating in Class C, initially with no drive. If the drive power is then increased, the collector current will
(a) slightly decrease.
(b) considerably decrease.
(c) stay the same.
(d) considerably increase.

53. The diagram below shows a semiconductor diode. The direction of easy flow of current is

(a) from A to B.
(b) from B to A.
(c) equally A to B or B to A.
(d) neither A to B or B to A.

54. The intended function of a varactor diode is
    (a) to vary the resonant frequency of a tuned circuit.
    (b) to rectify an alternating voltage.
    (c) as a demodulator in a receiver.
    (d) to generate an agc voltage.

55. "Gate", "source" and "drain" are the names given to the connections to
    (a) a varactor diode.
    (b) an npn transistor.
    (c) a germanium transistor.
    (d) a field-effect transistor.

56. The circuit below is a transistor audio amplifier. By by-passing the emitter resistor R_E

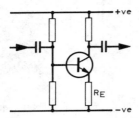

    (a) the gain is increased.
    (b) the gain remains constant.
    (c) the gain is reduced.
    (d) the hum is reduced.

57. The collector current of a transistor is the base current
    (a) multiplied by β.
    (b) divided by I_{CO}.
    (c) divided by β.
    (d) multiplied by V_{BE}.

58. The transistor in the circuit below is connected in a configuration called

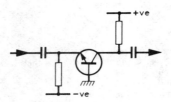

    (a) common emitter.
    (b) common collector.
    (c) common base.
    (d) push-pull collector.

59. The major part of the selectivity of a superheterodyne receiver resides in the
    (a) rf amplifier.
    (b) power supply filter.
    (c) i.f. amplifier.
    (d) local oscillator.

60. In a superheterodyne receiver the intermediate frequency is 455kHz and it is tuned to a frequency of 1,000kHz with the local oscillator frequency set above the signal. The second channel or image frequency will be
    (a) 545kHz.
    (b) 1,455kHz.
    (c) 1,910kHz.
    (d) 910kHz.

61. In an intermediate frequency amplifier employing coupled tuned circuits the bandwidth may be altered by
    (a) varying the coupling between the circuits.
    (b) altering the collector current.
    (c) bypassing the emitter resistor.
    (d) screening the amplifier.

62. Superheterodyne receivers have replaced tuned radio frequency receivers because they are
    (a) cheaper.
    (b) more selective.
    (c) more reliable.
    (d) consume less current.

63. Compared with an ordinary amplitude modulated signal an ssb signal
    (a) occupies a wider bandwidth.
    (b) occupies half the bandwidth.
    (c) is distorted.
    (d) is easier to tune in.

64. In a superheterodyne receiver image frequency interference is reduced by
    (a) using a diode mixer.
    (b) the rf tuned circuits.
    (c) having the local oscillator below the signal frequency.
    (d) reducing the local oscillator level.

65. In the block diagram below, which represents a superheterodyne receiver, the block marked "X" is

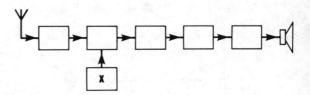

    (a) an rf amplifier.
    (b) a mixer.
    (c) an audio amplifier.
    (d) a local oscillator.

66. The circuit shown below is

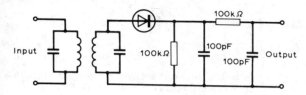

(a) a mains power supply.
(b) a frequency changer.
(c) a frequency discriminator.
(d) an a.m. detector.

67. In the transistor rf amplifier circuit shown below the semiconductor device itself is called

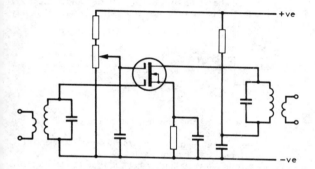

(a) a unijunction transistor.
(b) a varactor.
(c) a dual-gate mosfet.
(d) an npn transistor.

68. The frequency of a vfo is determined by
(a) the supply voltage.
(b) the inductance and capacitance of the tuned circuit.
(c) the type of transistor used.
(d) the particular circuit used.

69. Which of the following factors is most likely to cause frequency drift in a transmitter master oscillator (vfo)?
(a) battery operation.
(b) using a germanium transistor.
(c) heat from a nearby source.
(d) using an npo ceramic capacitor in the tuned circuit.

70. In the simple cw transmitter block diagram shown below the block marked "X" is called a

(a) buffer amplifier.
(b) frequency changer.
(c) frequency multiplier.
(d) frequency modulator.

71. The frequency of a crystal oscillator depends *primarily* on
(a) the output circuit tuning.
(b) the transistor gain.
(c) the ambient temperature.
(d) the dimensions of the crystal.

72. The output of the balanced modulator in an ssb transmitter is
(a) full carrier and both sidebands.
(b) full carrier and one sideband.
(c) suppressed carrier and both sidebands.
(d) no carrier and one sideband.

73. In an amateur cw transmitter the input power to the pa stage is measured by
(a) adding the collector current of the pa to the collector voltage.
(b) multiplying the collector current of the pa by the collector voltage.
(c) multiplying the total transmitter input current by the supply voltage.
(d) dividing the collector current of the pa by the collector voltage.

74. The diagram below shows a Clapp type of variable frequency oscillator (vfo). When used in an amateur transmitter the frequency of oscillation (tuning) is usually controlled by adjusting

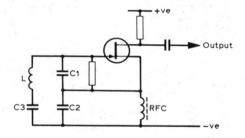

(a) C1.
(b) C2.
(c) C3.
(d) C1 and C2.

75. Which of the four fm modulator circuits shown below is correct?

(a)

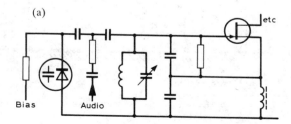

(b)

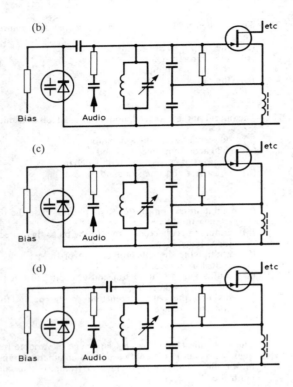

(c)

(d)

76. The velocity of propagation of radio waves is
    (a) 3×10^{10} cm/s.
    (b) 100km/s.
    (c) 10,000mile/h.
    (d) 3×10^6 km/s.

77. Relative to a half-wavelength in free space, the length of a half-wave wire antenna is
    (a) the same length.
    (b) slightly longer.
    (c) slightly shorter.
    (d) three-quarters of the length.

78. A Marconi antenna shown in the diagram below has a physical length of 110ft. Inside the box "X", which component will be needed to tune it to quarter-wave resonance at 1·9MHz?

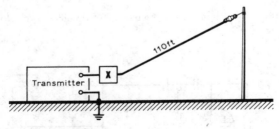

    (a) A capacitor.
    (b) A resistor.
    (c) An inductor.
    (d) A transformer.

79. A station in the UK is working a station in the eastern part of the USA on the 14MHz band. The mode of propagation would be
    (a) sky-wave.
    (b) tropospheric.
    (c) ground wave.
    (d) free space.

80. Which of the following antennas will have a substantially omnidirectional horizontal radiation pattern?
    (a) A Yagi antenna.
    (b) A cubical quad antenna.
    (c) A horizontal dipole antenna.
    (d) A ground plane antenna.

81. The block diagram below shows an amateur transmitter feeding an antenna via a 50Ω coaxial cable. A standing wave ratio meter (same Z_0 as the cable) is connected between the cable and the transmitter and indicates a swr of 3:1. The swr in the cable can be reduced to unity (1:1) by

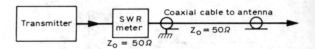

    (a) improving the match between the transmitter and the cable.
    (b) inserting a matching transformer between the transmitter and the cable.
    (c) using a low-pass filter between the transmitter and the cable.
    (d) improving the match between the antenna and the cable.

82. Which of the following regions or layers of the ionosphere is essentially an absorber (attenuator) of radio frequency electromagnetic waves?
    (a) The D region.
    (b) The F layer.
    (c) The F2 layer.
    (d) The E layer.

83. The critical frequency is
    (a) the highest frequency on which it is possible to contact a station.
    (b) the highest frequency at which waves sent vertically are returned to earth.
    (c) the frequency at which the skip distance is greatest.
    (d) the highest frequency with which a desired station can be reached by the ground wave.

84. An amateur transmitter is sending on a frequency of 145MHz. The wavelength of the emission will be
    (a) 2·9m.
    (b) 2·07m.
    (c) 2·0m.
    (d) 1·9m.

85. In a vertically polarized electromagnetic wave
    (a) the magnetic field is in a vertical plane.
    (b) the magnetic field is at 45° to the electric field.
    (c) the electric field is in a vertical plane.
    (d) the electric field is at right angles to the antenna wire.

86. The input impedance of a vertical quarter-wave antenna is
    (a) 50Ω.
    (b) 75Ω.
    (c) 300Ω.
    (d) very high.

87. A half-wave dipole antenna has a length of 0·33m. This antenna will resonate for signals at a frequency of
    (a) 33MHz.
    (b) 145MHz.
    (c) 220MHz.
    (d) 432MHz.

88. A horizontal full-wave antenna can be expected to have which of the following horizontal radiation patterns

(a) 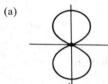   (b)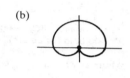

(c)    (d)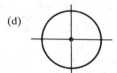

89. The optimum value of swr is
    (a) zero.
    (b) unity.
    (c) 75.
    (d) 300.

90. Besides a voltmeter measuring the ht voltage applied to a transmitter output stage, which additional meter should be connected in the circuit to enable the dc input power to be measured?
    (a) A collector current meter.
    (b) A base current meter.
    (c) An emitter bias meter.
    (d) An rf ammeter.

91. Which type of meter would you use to measure the rf current in a dummy load?
    (a) A thermocouple meter.
    (b) A moving iron meter.
    (c) A moving coil meter.
    (d) An swr meter.

92. An oscilloscope is connected to monitor the rf output of an ssb transmitter. With a two-tone input an rf output of 100W (rms) causes a deflection on the screen of 2cm peak. When working with speech and into the same load the peaks of the ssb signal read 2·8cm. The peak envelope power output is then
    (a) 200W.
    (b) 400W.
    (c) 150W.
    (d) 100W.

93. Which of the following types of wavemeter is the *least* accurate?
    (a) Heterodyne wavemeter.
    (b) Frequency counter.
    (c) Interpolation-type wavemeter with crystal check points.
    (d) Absorption wavemeter.

94. An unknown frequency is fed into a heterodyne wavemeter and the audible beat note is 1kHz. The unknown frequency is then
    (a) Exactly equal to the wavemeter frequency.
    (b) 1kHz below the wavemeter frequency.
    (c) 1kHz above or below the wavemeter frequency.
    (d) 1kHz above the wavemeter frequency.

95. A 0–1mA moving coil meter is to be used as the basis of a voltmeter. If the resistance of the meter is 100Ω what series resistance will be needed if the meter is to read 1V full scale?
    (a) 1,000Ω.
    (b) 900Ω.
    (c) 1,100Ω.
    (d) 9,900Ω.

SECOND SAMPLE TEST PAPER

Part 1. Licence conditions and transmitter interference

1. The mandatory entries which the log must contain in respect of a contact with another amateur station are
    (a) date, time of commencement, frequency used, station called.
    (b) date, frequency band, emission, station called, times of commencement and ending operation.
    (c) date, frequency band, emission, station called, power input, time of commencement and duration of operation.
    (d) date, time of commencement and finishing operation, frequency used, power input, station called.

2. You have installed a 144MHz transceiver on your small boat to operate as a mobile station. Under which of the following conditions is operation permitted?
    (a) Not at all.
    (b) Anywhere, provided the boat remains in British territorial waters.
    (c) On inland waterways and lakes but not in docks, estuaries or harbours.
    (d) Only with special permission of the Home Secretary.

3. Which of the following amateur bands is shared with other services (not on a secondary basis)
    (a) 1·8–2·0MHz.
    (b) 3·5–3·8MHz.
    (c) 7·0–7·1MHz.
    (d) 14·0–14·35MHz.

4. You have a cottage in the country which, within the meaning of the licence conditions, you wish to use as your "alternative premises". Before operating your station there you need to
   - (a) inform the local Telephone Manager at least seven days before you wish to start operation.
   - (b) do nothing.
   - (c) inform the local Telephone Manager before you wish to start operation.
   - (d) inform the nearest police station.

5. You are the holder of an Amateur Licence B and wish to install and use a 144MHz transceiver in your car. Before you do this you need to
   - (a) inform the local Telephone Manager.
   - (b) do nothing.
   - (c) inform the Ministry of Transport.
   - (d) apply for a mobile licence from the Home Office.

6. In addition to sending to and receiving messages from other amateur stations, your licence allows you to receive
   - (a) BBC broadcasts.
   - (b) overseas short-wave broadcasts.
   - (c) ship and shore stations.
   - (d) standard frequency service stations.

7. You are going for a trip in your private aeroplane and ride to the aerodrome on a bus. You are carrying a hand-held 144MHz transceiver. Your licence allows you to operate it
   - (a) in the bus.
   - (b) in the aeroplane.
   - (c) in neither bus nor aeroplane.
   - (d) in the bus and aeroplane.

8. Within a given frequency band your station may only be used with emissions which are
   - (a) specified in the Radio Regulations.
   - (b) at a power not exceeding that specified in the schedule.
   - (c) of the classes of emission specified in the schedule.
   - (d) of the classes of emission specified in the schedule and at a power level not exceeding that appropriate to the class of emission.

9. When the station is used for radio teletype (rtty) transmission it shall be used with
   - (a) International Telegraph Code No 2.
   - (b) the Moore ARQ code.
   - (c) the ASCII code.
   - (d) the Bell System code.

10. Which type of message is not allowed?
    - (a) One mentioning another station's callsign.
    - (b) One mentioning the weather.
    - (c) One which is of an indecent character.
    - (d) One mentioning a friend who is in the station.

11. As an international requirement the licensee shall comply with the relevant provisions of
    - (a) the North Atlantic Treaty Organization.
    - (b) the Telecommunication Convention.
    - (c) the European Economic Community.
    - (d) the United Nations Educational Scientific and Cultural Organization.

12. Measuring equipment is required to verify that the frequency of emission is
    - (a) within the authorized frequency bands.
    - (b) not closer than 20kHz to the edge of the bands 1·8 to 28MHz.
    - (c) correct to an accuracy of one per cent.
    - (d) correct to an accuracy of 10 parts in a million.

13. Entries in the log in respect of contacts made from a vehicle (mobile operation) shall be made
    - (a) as soon as practical after the end of the journey.
    - (b) at the end of each contact.
    - (c) at the commencement of each contact.
    - (d) at intervals of half an hour during the journey.

14. If a visiting, practising, radio amateur who is properly authorized by the Home Office operates your station he needs to
    - (a) do nothing.
    - (b) sign the log.
    - (c) write his callsign in the log.
    - (d) do both (b) and (c).

15. All times written in the log shall be in
    - (a) local time.
    - (b) British Summer Time.
    - (c) Central European Time.
    - (d) Greenwich Mean Time.

16. The callsign prefix and current number for a station in Scotland with a Class A licence is
    - (a) GM8——.
    - (b) GS8——.
    - (c) GM4——.
    - (d) GD5——.

17. If you are operating your station with hand-held equipment as a pedestrian, which would be the correct callsign to use if your main address callsign is G2XXX?
    - (a) GP2XXX.
    - (b) G2XXX/M.
    - (c) G2XXX/P.
    - (d) G2XXX/W.

18. When sending your callsign by telegraphy the speed shall not exceed
    - (a) 10wpm.
    - (b) 12wpm.
    - (c) 15wpm.
    - (d) 20wpm.

19. The correct way to spell the callsign GM7ABD using the recommended phonetic alphabet is
    - (a) Golf Mike Seven Alpha Bravo Delta.
    - (b) George Mike Seven Ack Bravo Don.
    - (c) Great Many Seven Awful Brown Dogs.
    - (d) Golf Mike Sierra Echo Victor Echo November Alpha Bravo Delta.

20. If your licence has expired or has been revoked you need to
    - (a) keep it safely for inspection.
    - (b) return it to the Secretary of State.
    - (c) return it to the local Telephone Manager within seven days.
    - (d) return it to the Secretary of Sate within seven days.

21. It is permissible to use in your transmission "remarks about matters of a personal nature" if the following is not included in the above category
    (a) your address.
    (b) your family's personal activities.
    (c) your business affairs.
    (d) your travel arrangements.

22. If your station is situated within half a mile of the boundary of an aerodrome the height of any antenna or mast shall
    (a) not exceed 100ft.
    (b) not exceed 50ft.
    (c) not exceed 33ft.
    (d) not be above the highest point of the house.

23. If you change your "main address" you need to
    (a) inform the local post office.
    (b) inform the local police station.
    (c) inform the Home Office.
    (d) do nothing.

24. If your transmitter is set to a frequency of 7,000kHz and it drifts up in frequency by 10 parts in a million the frequency will be
    (a) 7007·000kHz.
    (b) 7000·700kHz.
    (c) 7000·070kHz.
    (d) 7000·007kHz.

25. If you are transmitting on a frequency of 21·4MHz your second harmonic on 42·8MHz may cause tvi. What piece of equipment could you use between your transmitter and the antenna to reduce the possibility of interference?
    (a) A low-pass filter.
    (b) A high-pass filter.
    (c) A balanced-to-unbalanced transformer.
    (d) A matching transformer.

26. Which of the following filter circuits would be suitable for inclusion in a radio mains lead to reduce mains-borne interference?

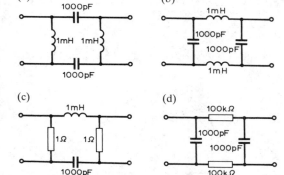

27. Why should the audio bandwidth of an amateur ssb transmitter be restricted to 2 to 3kHz?
    (a) To save power.
    (b) To conserve bandwidth.
    (c) To improve speech quality.
    (d) To increase output.

28. Which of the following circuits would be suitable as a key click filter?

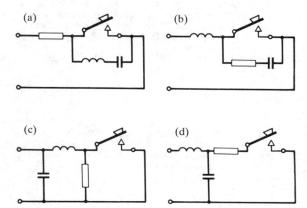

29. Concerning frequency control and unwanted frequencies of emission, a licensee must be able to
    (a) verify the emission is within the authorized band, use a vfo having a frequency stability of one part in 1,000 and ensure that the transmissions do not contain unwanted frequencies.
    (b) check the frequency to an accuracy of one part in a million, use a satisfactory method of frequency control and avoid harmonic radiation.
    (c) verify the emissions are within the authorized band, use a satisfactory method of frequency control and keep spurious emissions to a level not more than 30dB below the main emission.
    (d) verify the emissions are within the authorized band, use a satisfactory method of frequency control and ensure that his transmissions do not contain unwanted frequencies.

30. Why does the use of a balanced-to-unbalanced transformer sometimes help in reducing interference with nearby television receivers when inserted between the centre of a dipole antenna and its coaxial feeder cable?
    (a) It reduces the harmonic radiation for the dipole.
    (b) It tunes out the interference.
    (c) It balances out the interference.
    (d) It avoids an unbalanced feeder being connected to a balanced antenna.

31. Which of the following instruments is useful in detecting the presence of harmonic radiation from an antenna?
    (a) A simple field strength meter tuned to the harmonic frequency.
    (b) A standing wave ratio meter in the feeder cable.
    (c) An acceptor circuit across the output of the transmitter.
    (d) An oscilloscope monitoring the rf signal in the feeder cable.

32. A neighbour's television set is interfered with when you are transmitting at full power on any of the hf bands, and your emissions are free of harmonics. If it has been checked that the interference is getting into the tv set via its antenna what piece of equipment would you insert between the tv feeder cable and the set?
    (a) A low-pass filter.
    (b) A parallel tuned circuit.
    (c) A series tuned circuit.
    (d) A high-pass filter.

33. If f_o is the local oscillator frequency in a receiver, f_s is the wanted signal frequency and the oscillator frequency is higher than the signal frequency, then the second channel (or image frequency) will be
    (a) $f_o - f_s$
    (b) $f_o + f_s$
    (c) $2f_o - f_s$
    (d) $2f_s - f_o$

34. Which of the four circuits below would be used to restrict the modulating frequency range of an amateur transmitter?

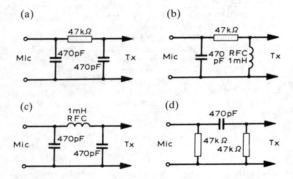

35. Which of the following filtering arrangements would be most effective at stopping leakage of radio frequencies from a screened box containing an oscillator?

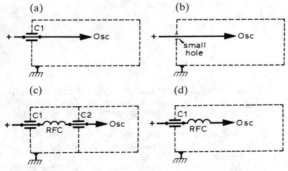

Dotted lines represent the screened boxes

Part 2. Operating practices and procedures, and technical part of syllabus

36. When a call is made to a specific station, and replies are not desired from other stations, which signal is sent at the end of a cw transmission?
    (a) $\overline{AR}$ K
    (b) $\overline{KN}$
    (c) $\overline{VA}$
    (d) K

37. If you hear somebody calling you but cannot exactly make out his callsign, which is the Q-code signal you would send?
    (a) QRZ?
    (b) QRS
    (c) QRK?
    (d) QRZ

38. Which of the following signal reports would be appropriate for a signal which is readable with practically no difficulty, moderately strong and a good dc note, but with a trace of ripple?
    (a) 599
    (b) 487
    (c) 578
    (d) 478

39. The main reason for the use of satellites in amateur radio is to
    (a) increase the range possible at vhf
    (b) improve signal strength at the receiver.
    (c) reduce transmitter power.
    (d) reduce size of the antenna required.

40. The meaning of the Q-code signal "QTH?" is
    (a) "what is the name of your station?"
    (b) "the location of my station is . . ."
    (c) "what is the location of your station?"
    (d) "what is the distance between our stations?"

41. If V is the voltage, I the current, and R the resistance, the Ohm's Law equation can be expressed as
    (a) $V = I \times R$
    (b) $V = I^2 \times R$
    (c) $R = I \div V$
    (d) $R = V \times I$

42. What is the total current in the circuit shown below?

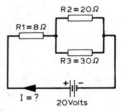

    (a) 1·5A.
    (b) 1·3A.
    (c) 0·8A.
    (d) 1A.

43. What wattage rating resistor would you choose for use in the case indicated below?

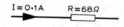

(a) 10W.
(b) 1W.
(c) 5W.
(d) ½W.

44. The reactance X_c of a capacitor C at a frequency f is given by which formula?

(a) $X_c = \dfrac{1}{2\pi fC}$

(b) $X_c = \dfrac{1}{2\pi\sqrt{fC}}$

(c) $X_c = 2\pi fC$

(d) $X_c = \dfrac{1}{\pi fC}$

45. What is the total effective capacitance of the three capacitors shown in the circuit below?

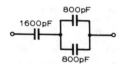

(a) 3,200pF.
(b) 2,000pF.
(c) 400pF.
(d) 800pF.

46. What is the impedance at resonance of the series circuit shown below?

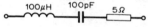

(a) 25Ω.
(b) 205Ω.
(c) √5Ω.
(d) 5Ω.

47. Two inductors L1 and L2 are connected in series aiding as shown in the diagram and the mutual inductance between them is M. What is their total effective inductance?

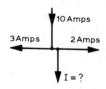

(a) 3·5mH.
(b) 4mH.
(c) 5mH.
(d) 7mH.

48. The relationship between the rms and peak values of a sinusoidal current is
(a) rms value = √(peak value)
(b) rms value = (peak value) ÷ √2
(c) rms value = (peak value) × 2
(d) rms value = (peak value) × √2

49. The diagram below shows a transformer having a turns ratio of 10 connected to a load resistor of 100Ω. Between the input terminals A and B the measured impedance would be

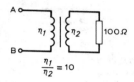

$$\frac{n_1}{n_2} = 10$$

(a) 1Ω.
(b) 100Ω.
(c) 1,000Ω.
(d) 10,000Ω.

50. When the switch in the circuit below is switched over from A to B, the current will vary with time in which of the ways shown?

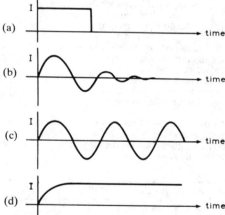

51. In the circuit shown below what is the current I?

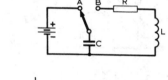

(a) 15A.
(b) 10A.
(c) 1A.
(d) 5A.

52. What type of semiconductor device is represented by the diagram below?

(a) A tunnel diode.
(b) A zener diode.
(c) A varactor diode.
(d) A pin diode.

53. The transistor shown in the diagram below is connected in a

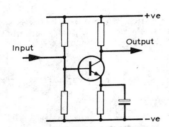

(a) common-emitter configuration.
(b) common-collector configuration.
(c) common-base configuration.
(d) cascode configuration.

54. A transistor is connected in a common-collector configuration (emitter follower). The circuit will have a
(a) low input impedance.
(b) low I_{co}.
(c) high input impedance.
(d) high emitter current.

55. In the semiconductor rectifier circuit shown below the peak ac voltage across the secondary of the transformer is 10V. What will be the dc output voltage across the terminals A and B?

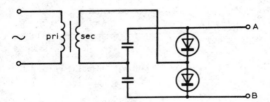

(a) 0V.
(b) 10V.
(c) 20V.
(d) 40V.

56. The output impedance of a power transistor is likely to be in the order of
(a) 10Ω.
(b) 0.1Ω.
(c) $1,000\Omega$.
(d) $10,000\Omega$.

57. Varactor diodes are used for
(a) supply voltage regulation.
(b) altering the effective capacitance of a circuit.
(c) limiting the amplitude of oscillation in an oscillator circuit.
(d) automatic gain control.

58. If a transistor pa is used in an amateur transmitter on 144MHz which of the following output circuits would be suitable?

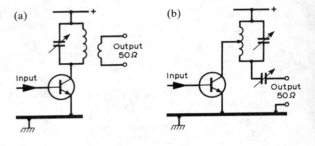

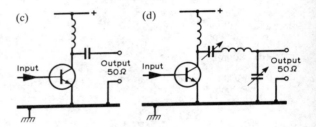

59. The stage marked "X" in the superheterodyne receiver block diagram below is called a
(a) local oscillator.
(b) beat frequency oscillator.
(c) i.f. amplifier.
(d) first mixer.

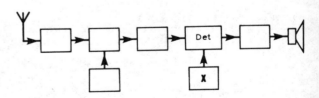

60. The purpose of the radio frequency tuned circuits in a conventional superhet receiver is to
(a) provide sensitivity.
(b) improve adjacent channel selectivity.
(c) reject second-channel interference.
(d) improve the noise factor.

61. The circuit below is that of a detector in a superhet.
     When receiving a steady cw signal the output across the
     terminals A and B will be

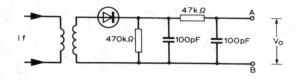

(a)

(b)

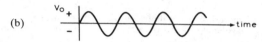

(c)

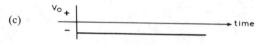

(d)

62. The advantage of a high intermediate frequency in a
     superheterodyne receiver is:
     (a) high selectivity.
     (b) high stage gain.
     (c) good image rejection.
     (d) low background noise.

63. Which of the following circuits would be suitable for use
     as an fm detector?

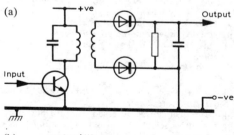

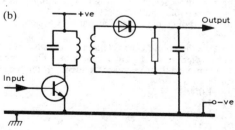

(c)

(d)

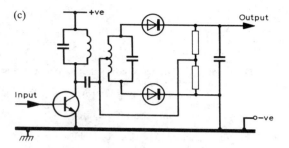

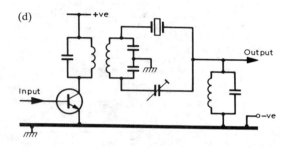

64. The dynamic resistance (R_D) of a parallel-tuned circuit
     would be about
     (a) 40,000Ω.
     (b) 4,000Ω.
     (c) 400Ω.
     (d) very low indeed.

65. What is the main shortcoming of a trf receiver at higher
     frequencies?
     (a) Lack of sensitivity.
     (b) High noise level.
     (c) High power consumption.
     (d) Poor selectivity.

66. In a superheterodyne receiver, agc is used to
     (a) maintain a constant current.
     (b) maintain a constant output level.
     (c) reduce the noise level.
     (d) keep the local oscillator level constant.

67. What is the name of the variable-frequency oscillator
     shown below?

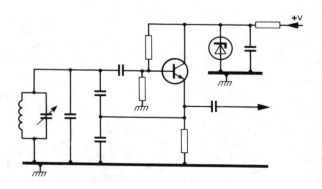

(a)   Clapp oscillator.
(b)   Vackar oscillator.
(c)   Colpitts oscillator.
(d)   Franklin oscillator.

68.   The advantage of a crystal-controlled oscillator is that
(a)   no ht supply is required.
(b)   the frequency stability is improved.
(c)   it may be keyed.
(d)   very few components are required.

69.   The vfo of a transmitter uses a coil which is wound on a ceramic coil former and has a *positive temperature coefficient*. Neglecting the effects of other components in the circuit, if the coil is heated up you would expect the frequency of oscillation to
(a)   increase in frequency.
(b)   stay the same.
(c)   decrease in frequency.
(d)   increase and then decrease in frequency.

70.   What is the purpose of the stage marked "X" in the simple ssb transmitter block diagram shown below?

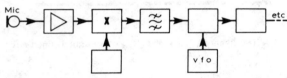

(a)   Balanced modulator.
(b)   Sideband filter.
(c)   Carrier oscillator.
(d)   Down converter.

71.   Why is it not advisable to key the master oscillator (vfo) stage of a transmitter?
(a)   It reduces the output.
(b)   It produces a spacer or backwave.
(c)   It causes sparking on the key contacts.
(d)   It causes chirp.

72.   The circuit shown below is the "equivalent circuit" of a

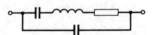

(a)   pi-tank circuit.
(b)   low-pass filter.
(c)   Marconi antenna.
(d)   quartz crystal.

73.   The collector current of an amplifier stage consists of half-cycles of sine-wave form. The stage is therefore biassed in
(a)   Class A.
(b)   Class AB.
(c)   Class B.
(d)   Class C.

74.   Two non-harmonically related audio tones are fed into the microphone input of an amateur transmitter. An oscilloscope connected across the transmitter rf output terminals displays the waveform shown below. The transmitter is working with class of emission

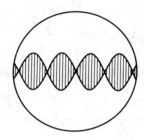

(a)   F3E.
(b)   J3E.
(c)   A3E.
(d)   A2A.

75.   The relationship between velocity of propagation v, wavelength λ, and frequency f, is given by the formula
(a) $v = f \times \lambda$
(b) $v = f \div \lambda$
(c) $v = \sqrt{f \times \lambda}$
(d) $v = f^2 \times \lambda^2$

76.   The F layer in the ionosphere varies in degree of ionization and this has a marked effect on short-wave propagation. When the degree of ionization is high
(a)   there is severe fading.
(b)   the noise level increases.
(c)   the higher frequencies pass through the ionosphere into space
(d)   the higher frequencies are reflected back to earth more readily.

77.   Which of the following layers of the ionosphere is primarily instrumental in allowing very long distance (dx) communication on the 1·8–2·0MHz band by night?
(a)   D.
(b)   Sporadic-E.
(c)   F.
(d)   E.

78.   A 14MHz signal will fade to a minimum at a point 4,000km away when
(a)   two sky waves arrive in phase.
(b)   the sky wave and the ground wave arrive in phase.
(c)   the sky wave and the ground wave arrive out of phase.
(d)   two sky waves arrive out of phase.

79.   Why is an audio tone signal used in order to access a 144MHz band repeater?
(a)   So that it can be accessed from further away.
(b)   To allow selective calling from a number of cars.
(c)   To enable nets to be set up.
(d)   To reduce the chance of spurious access.

80.   An antenna is half a wavelength long and is cut in the centre where it is fed from a transmitter. The impedance of the antenna at its resonant frequency at the feed point will be of the order of
(a)   1,000Ω.
(b)   75Ω.
(c)   5,000Ω.
(d)   10Ω.

81. What is a significant advantage of a quarter-wave vertical ground-plane antenna for dx working on 21MHz?
     (a) Small size.
     (b) All-round radiation.
     (c) Good matching to the feeder.
     (d) Low radiation angle.

82. The advantage of the trap dipole antenna compared with the usual dipole is that
     (a) it has more gain.
     (b) it operates on several bands.
     (c) it is omni-directional.
     (d) it is a broadband antenna.

83. In a three-element Yagi antenna the rods are not of equal length. In order of decreasing length the elements are
     (a) reflector, driven element, director.
     (b) driven element, reflector, director.
     (c) director, driven element, reflector.
     (d) reflector, director, driven element.

84. Long-distance contacts (dx) on the 70cm band are sometimes possible. This is caused by a special condition of the
     (a) troposphere.
     (b) stratosphere.
     (c) ionosphere.
     (d) bathysphere.

85. Which of the diagrams shown below would be the horizontal radiation pattern (polar diagram) of a collinear antenna array consisting of two half-wave elements fed in phase?

(a) 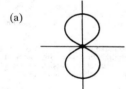   (b)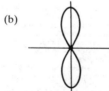

(c) 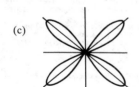   (d)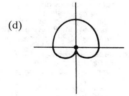

86. You need to cut an electrical quarter-wave length of solid polythene insulated coaxial cable to act as a matching transformer in your 144MHz band antenna system. The physical length of the piece of cable would be approximately
     (a) 25cm.
     (b) 66cm.
     (c) 33cm.
     (d) 50cm.

87. The diagram below shows a folded dipole (length λ/2) in which the diameter of the wires are the same everywhere. The impedance looking into the terminals A and B can be expected to be

     (a) 75Ω.
     (b) 50Ω.
     (c) 600Ω.
     (d) 300Ω.

88. A Marconi antenna is 100ft long and is to operate in the 3·5MHz band. In order to tune the antenna to resonance which component should be inserted between the transmitter output terminal and the end of the antenna?
     (a) A variable inductor.
     (b) A variable capacitor.
     (c) A variable resistor.
     (d) A tapped transformer.

89. The type of antenna shown below is called a

     (a) Windom antenna.
     (b) ground-plane antenna.
     (c) Yagi antenna.
     (d) trap dipole.

90. Moving coil meters in connection with a thermocouple unit are often used to measure radio frequency currents in dummy loads, feeders and antennas. A major disadvantage of such meters is that
     (a) they are expensive.
     (b) they are easily damaged by overload.
     (c) their frequency of operation is too low.
     (d) they are too sluggish.

91. A moving coil meter has a 1mA full scale deflection and an internal resistance of 90Ω. What value of shunt resistor would be needed to make the meter read 10mA full scale?
     (a) 9Ω.
     (b) 11Ω.
     (c) 10Ω.
     (d) 10·9Ω.

92. The input to the power amplifier stage of an amateur transmitter is 50W. If the efficiency of the stage is 65 per cent the output power will be
    (a) 32·5W.
    (b) 27·5W.
    (c) 13W.
    (d) 35W.

93. When you are doing the initial adjustment of a piece of radio equipment it is most helpful to roughly check the frequencies to which the various tuned circuits are tuned. Which of the following instruments would be most appropriate?
    (a) An absorption wavemeter.
    (b) A grid dip oscillator.
    (c) A signal generator.
    (d) A heterodyne frequency meter.

94. A 50Ω dummy load is connected to the output of an amateur cw transmitter and a thermocouple rf ammeter is connected in series as shown in the diagram below. If the meter reads 1·2A, the output power of the transmitter will be

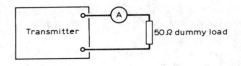

    (a) 72W.
    (b) 60W.
    (c) 40W.
    (d) 87W.

95. An oscilloscope is connected across the dummy load of question 94. With two-tone input the deflection on the screen is 2cm and the power in the load is measured as 72W. What is the peak envelope power output when peaks of speech cause a deflection of 3cm?
    (a) 400W p.e.p.
    (b) 144W p.e.p.
    (c) 324W p.e.p.
    (d) 216W p.e.p.

Note: Questions 4, 10 and 24 in Paper 1 and Question 78 in Paper 2 appear in the set of 40 sample questions issued by the City and Guilds of London Institute, and are reproduced here with permission.

The UK Class A licence schedule
(continued from p89)

F1B   Automatic telegraphy by frequency-shift keying without the use of a modulating audio frequency.

F2A   Telegraphy by on-off keying of a frequency-modulating audio frequency or frequencies, or by on-off keying of a frequency-modulated emission.

F2B   Automatic telegraphy by on-off keying of a frequency modulating audio frequency or frequencies, or by on-off keying of a frequency-modulated emission.

F3E   Telephony.

F3C   Facsimile transmission.

F3F   Slow-scan television and high-definition television.

Phase modulation

G1A   Telegraphy by phase-shift keying without the use of a modulating audio frequency.

G1B   Automatic telegraphy by phase-shift keying without the use of a modulating audio frequency.

G2A   Telegraphy by on-off keying of a phase-modulating audio frequency or frequencies, or by on-off keying of the phase-modulated emission.

G2B   Automatic telegraphy by on-off keying of a phase-modulating audio frequency or frequencies, or by on-off keying of the phase-modulated emission.

G3E   Telephony.

G3C   Facsimile transmission.

G3F   Slow-scan television and high-definition television.

Pulse modulation

K1A   Telegraphy by on-off keying of a pulsed carrier without the use of a modulating audio frequency.

K2A   Telegraphy by on-off keying of a modulating audio frequency or frequencies or by on-off keying of a modulated pulsed carrier—the audio frequency or frequencies modulating the amplitude of the pulses.

L2A   Telegraphy by on-off keying of a modulating audio frequency or frequencies or by on-off keying of a modulated pulsed carrier—the audio frequency or frequencies modulating the width (or duration) of the pulses.

K3E   Telephony, amplitude-modulated pulses.

L3E   Telephony, width (or duration) modulated pulses.

M2A   Telegraphy by on-off keying of a modulating audio frequency or frequencies or by on-off keying of a modulated pulsed carrier—the audio frequency or frequencies modulating the position or phase of the pulses.

Q2A   Telegraphy by on-off keying of a modulating audio frequency or frequencies or by on-off keying of a modulated pulsed carrier—the audio frequency or frequencies modulating the angle of the carrier during the pulses.

V2A   Telegraphy by on-off keying of a modulating frequency or frequencies or by on-off keying of a modulated pulsed carrier—which is a combination of the foregoing, or is produced by other means.

Classification of emissions
Basic characteristics
The basic characteristics of a radio emission are described by three symbols as follows:
(i) First symbol—type of modulation of the main carrier.
(ii) Second symbol—nature of signal(s) modulating the main carrier.
(iii) Third symbol—type of information to be transmitted.

Interpretation
(i) *Carrier power of a radio transmission.* The average power supplied to the antenna from a transmitter during one radio frequency cycle under conditions of no modulation. This interpretation does not apply to pulse-modulated emissions.
(ii) *Peak envelope power of a radio transmitter.* The average power supplied to the antenna by a transmitter during one radio frequency cycle at the highest crest of the modulation envelope, taken under conditions of normal operation.
(iii) *Effective radiated power (erp)* (in a given direction). The product of the power supplied to the antenna and its gain relative to a half-wave dipole in a given direction.

APPENDIX 5

Calculations in the RAE

The basic mathematical processes are: addition, subtraction, multiplication, and division. As long as only "whole" numbers are involved, such sums are simple. However, very often we must consider quantities which are less than one (unity), for instance, ½, ⅓, ⅛ etc. Here ⅛ means one-eighth part of the whole.

⅛ is called a *vulgar fraction* and has two parts; the "8" (the bottom part) is called the *denominator* and the "1" (the top part) is the *numerator*. The magnitude of a fraction is not changed if we multiply top and bottom by the same number, ie

$$\frac{3}{16} \times \frac{4}{4}$$

As the "4" is on the top and the bottom we can "cancel" it thus:

$$\frac{3}{16} \times \frac{4}{4} = \frac{3}{16}$$

A fraction should always be cancelled down to its simplest form:

$$\frac{12}{16} = \frac{3 \times 4}{4 \times 4} = \frac{3}{4}$$

Here top and bottom have been divided by 4.

Fractions can be

(a) *Multiplied*

$$\frac{1}{2} \times \frac{3}{4} \times \frac{5}{8} = \frac{1 \times 3 \times 5}{2 \times 4 \times 8} = \frac{15}{64}$$

(b) *Divided*

$$\frac{3}{4} \div \frac{1}{2}$$

Dividing by ½ is the same as multiplying by $\frac{2}{1}$, ie

$$\frac{3}{4} \div \frac{1}{2} = \frac{3}{4} \times \frac{2}{1} = \frac{6}{4} = 1\frac{2}{4} = 1\frac{1}{2}$$

In other words, dividing by a fraction is the same as multiplying by that fraction "upside down". Another example is:

$$\frac{7}{8} \div \frac{3}{4} = \frac{7}{8} \times \frac{4}{3} = \frac{7}{2} \times \frac{1}{3} = \frac{7}{6} = 1\frac{1}{6}$$

Here we divide top and bottom by 4.

(c) *Added*

$$\frac{2}{3} + \frac{2}{3} = \frac{2+2}{3} = \frac{4}{3}$$

If the denominators are different, we must make them the same, ie "bring them to a common denominator". For example

$$\frac{2}{3} + \frac{5}{6} = \frac{4}{6} + \frac{5}{6} = \frac{9}{6} = \frac{3}{2} = 1\frac{1}{2}$$

Here we have multiplied top and bottom of $\frac{2}{3}$ by 2, making it $\frac{4}{6}$. Hence we can add it to $\frac{5}{6}$, making $\frac{9}{6}$, which is then simplified to $1\frac{1}{2}$. Another example is

$$\frac{1}{3} + \frac{5}{6} + \frac{7}{8} = \frac{8}{24} + \frac{20}{24} + \frac{21}{24} = \frac{8+20+21}{24}$$

$$= \frac{49}{24} = 2\frac{1}{24}$$

It is generally preferable to divide out fractions greater than 1 as we have done above.

(d) *Subtracted*

Exactly the same rules apply to the subtraction of fractions.

We can also express parts of the whole as "decimals" or $\frac{1}{10}$ parts, written as 0·1, 0·2, 0·3 etc (these are equivalent to $\frac{1}{10}, \frac{2}{10}, \frac{3}{10}$ etc). The "full stop" is known as the *decimal point*. In a decimal, the "nought" before the decimal point should never be omitted.

The denominator of any fraction can be divided into the numerator to give a decimal, eg

⅛ = 0·125
⅜ = 0·375

The more common fractions and decimal equivalents should be memorized, eg

$$\frac{1}{10} = 0\cdot1 \qquad \frac{1}{8} = 0\cdot125$$

$$\frac{2}{10} = \frac{1}{5} = 0\cdot2 \qquad \frac{2}{8} = \frac{1}{4} = 0\cdot25$$

$$\frac{3}{10} = 0.3 \qquad \frac{3}{8} = 0.375$$

$$\frac{4}{10} = \frac{2}{5} = 0.4 \text{ etc} \qquad \frac{4}{8} = \frac{1}{2} = 0.5 \text{ etc}$$

Numbers can be expressed to "so many significant figures" or "so many decimal places".

Thus 12345 is a number to five significant figures
1234 is a number to four significant figures
123 is a number to three significant figures

Note also 1·23 is a number to three significant figures (the decimal point is ignored).

12·345 is a number to three decimal places
12·34 is a number to two decimal places
12·3 is a number to one decimal place

Decimals may be "rounded".

3·3267 to three decimal places is 3·327
(the 7 is greater than 5, so 6 becomes 7)
3·327 to two decimal places is 3·33
(the 7 is greater than 5, so 2 becomes 3)
3·33 to one decimal place is 3·3
(the 3 is less than 5, so is ignored)

Powers of numbers

A number is said to be "raised to a power" when it is multiplied by itself so many times. Thus $2 \times 2 = 4$ means that 2 raised to the power 2 is 4. In this case we would say 2 "squared" is 4 and write it as $2^2 = 4$. The "little 2 up in the air" is called an *index*. Similarly $2 \times 2 \times 2 = 8$ means that 2 raised to the power 3 is 8, or 2 "cubed" is 8, written as $2^3 = 8$. Also $2 \times 2 \times 2 \times 2 = 16$. Here we have no alternative but to say 2 "to the power 4" = 16 or $2^4 = 16$.

The use of indices or the index notation is a very convenient way of expressing the large numbers which often occur in radio calculations, eg

$$100 = 10 \times 10 = 10^2$$
$$10,000 = 10 \times 10 \times 10 \times 10 = 10^4$$
$$1,000,000 = 10 \times 10 \times 10 \times 10 \times 10 \times 10 = 10^6$$

Note that $10 = 10^1$ (the index here is taken for granted). Similarly

$$\frac{1}{100} = \frac{1}{10 \times 10} = \frac{1}{10^2} \text{ (written as } 10^{-2})$$

$$\frac{1}{10,000} = \frac{1}{10 \times 10 \times 10 \times 10} = \frac{1}{10^4} \text{ (written as } 10^{-4})$$

$$\frac{1}{1,000,000} = \frac{1}{10 \times 10 \times 10 \times 10 \times 10 \times 10} = \frac{1}{10^6}$$

$$\text{(written as } 10^{-6})$$

Numbers expressed in the index notation are multiplied and divided by adding and subtracting respectively the indices.

$$10^2 \times 10^3 = 10^{2+3} = 10^5$$

$$10^4 \div 10^2 = 10^{4-2} = 10^2$$
$$\frac{10^5 \times 10^7 \times 10^{-2}}{10^3 \times 10 \times 10^{-3}} = \frac{10^{5+7-2}}{10^{3+1-3}} = \frac{10^{10}}{10^1} = 10^9.$$

We can do this as long as the "base" is the same in each case. In the above examples, the "base" is 10. For example $10^2 \times 2^2 = 100 \times 4 = 400$, which is neither 10^4 or 2^4!

Roots of numbers

The root of a number is that number which when multiplied by itself so many times equals the given number; the "square" root of 4 is 2, ie $2 \times 2 = 4$, and this is written $^2\sqrt{4} = 2$.

Similarly the "cube" root of 8 is 2, ie $2 \times 2 \times 2 = 8$, and $^4\sqrt{16} = 2$ etc. Note the little 2 in the sign for square root is normally omitted so that $\sqrt{}$ signifies the square root.

Numbers like 4, 16 and 25 are called *perfect* squares because their square roots are whole numbers, thus

$$\sqrt{49} = 7 \qquad \sqrt{121} = 11 \quad \text{etc}$$

It is most unlikely that other square roots will be needed in RAE calculations; however, the following should be memorized as they can often be very useful.

$$\sqrt{2} = 1.41 \qquad \sqrt{3} = 1.73 \qquad \sqrt{5} = 2.24 \qquad \sqrt{10} = 3.162$$

For example

$$\sqrt{200} = \sqrt{2 \times 100} = \sqrt{2} \times \sqrt{100} = 1.41 \times 10 = 14.1$$
$$\sqrt{192} = \sqrt{3 \times 64} = \sqrt{3} \times \sqrt{64} = 1.73 \times 8 = 13.5$$

It is always worth checking to see if the number left after dividing by 2, 3 or 5 is a perfect square.

The square root of a number expressed in the index notation is found by dividing the index by 2, thus $\sqrt{10^6} = 10^3$ and $\sqrt{10^{12}} = 10^6$ and so on. Similarly $\sqrt{10^{-6}} = 10^{-3}$ etc. Should the index be an odd number, it must be made into an even number as follows.

$$\sqrt{10^{-15}} = \sqrt{10 \times 10^{-16}}$$

$$= \sqrt{10} \times 10^{-8}$$
$$= 3.162 \times 10^{-8}$$

The constant term "π" occurs in many calculations; π can be taken to be 3·14 or 22/7. The error in taking π^2 as 10 is less than 1·5 per cent and is acceptable here. $1/\pi$ can be taken as 0·32 and $1/2\pi$ as 0·16 (the error in calling this $\frac{1}{6}$ is really somewhat too high). $1/2\pi = 0.16$ is particularly useful.

Typical calculations

We will now apply these rules to the solution of problems likely to be met in radio work as a lead-in to some typical numerical multiple-choice questions.

Answers to three significant figures as given by a slide

rule or four-figure logarithm tables are satisfactory for most radio purposes and the eight figures given by the electronic calculator should certainly be rounded off.

The most important aspect is to remember that the units met with are most likely to be the practical ones such as microfarads, picofarads, milliamperes, millihenrys etc. These must be converted to the basic units of farads, amperes and henrys before substituting them into the appropriate formula. This involves multiplying or dividing by 1,000 (10^3), 1,000,000 (10^6) and so on. Therefore the important thing is to get the decimal point in the right place or the right number of noughts in the answer. The units, symbols and abbreviations given in Table 2.2 (p6) must be thoroughly understood. The commonest conversions are as follows:

There are 10^6 microfarads in 1 farad, hence $8\mu F = 8 \times 10^{-6}$ farads

There are 10^{12} picofarads in 1 farad, hence $22pF = 22 \times 10^{-12}$ farads.

(The use of "nano" or 10^{-9} is now fairly common; there are 10^9 nanofarads in 1 farad so $1nF = 1 \times 10^{-9}$ farads, but such a capacitor may well be marked "1,000pF".) Similarly other conversions are

$$50\mu H = 50 \times 10^{-6} \text{ henrys}$$
$$3mH = 3 \times 10^{-3} \text{ henrys}$$
$$45mA = 45 \times 10^{-3} \text{ amperes}$$
$$10\mu A = 10 \times 10^{-6} \text{ amperes}$$

Problem 1
What value of resistor is required to drop 150V when the current flowing through it is 25mA?

This involves Ohm's Law which can be expressed in symbols in three ways:

$$R = \frac{V}{I} \qquad I = \frac{V}{R} \qquad V = I \times R$$

where R is in ohms, V in volts and I in amperes. Clearly the first, $R = V/I$, is needed. First of all, we must express the current (25mA) in amperes.

$$25mA = \frac{25}{1,000}A \quad (\text{or } 25 \times 10^{-3}A)$$

Substituting values for V and I

$$R = \frac{V}{I}$$

$$= 150 \times \frac{1,000}{25}$$

(we are dividing by $\frac{25}{1,000}$, ie multiplying by $\frac{1,000}{25}$)

hence
$$R = \frac{150 \times 1,000}{25}$$

25 "goes into" 150 six times, so

$$R = 6 \times 1,000$$
$$= 6,000\Omega$$

Problem 2
What power is being dissipated by the resistor in Problem 1?

The power dissipated in the resistor is power (watts) = V (volts) $\times I$ (amps). By Ohm's Law, power can be expressed in two other forms.

$$W = \frac{V^2}{R} \text{ and } W = I^2R$$

because we know V, I and R we can use any of the above relationships, say

$$W = \frac{V^2}{R}$$

$$W = \frac{150 \times 150}{6,000}$$

Two "noughts" can be cancelled top and bottom, leaving

$$= \frac{15 \times 15}{60}$$

Cancelling 15 into 60 leaves

$$= \frac{15}{4} = 3\frac{3}{4}W$$

The other two forms will, of course, give the same answer—try them!

Problem 3
Resistors of 12Ω, 15Ω and 20Ω are in parallel. What is the effective resistance?

$$\frac{1}{R} = \frac{1}{R_1} + \frac{1}{R_2} + \frac{1}{R_3}$$

$$= \frac{1}{12} + \frac{1}{15} + \frac{1}{20}$$

120 is the common denominator of 12, 15 and 20, so

$$= \frac{10}{120} + \frac{8}{120} + \frac{6}{120}$$

$$\frac{1}{R} = \frac{10 + 8 + 6}{120}$$

$$\frac{1}{R} = \frac{24}{120}$$

This is a simple equation "in R", and the first step in solving it is to "cross-multiply", thus

$$R \times 24 = 1 \times 120$$

Hence, dividing each side by 24

$$R = \frac{120}{24}$$

$$R = 5\Omega.$$

Problem 4
Capacitors of 330pF, 680pF and 0·001μF are in parallel. What is the effective capacitance?

The first step is to express all the capacitors in the *same* units which can be either picofarads or microfarads.

$$0\cdot001\mu\text{F} = 0\cdot001 \times 1{,}000{,}000\text{pF}$$

(there are 1,000,000pF in 1μF) and hence

$$0\cdot001\mu\text{F} = 1{,}000\text{pF}.$$

Effective capacitance is therefore

$$330\text{pF} + 680\text{pF} + 1{,}000\text{pF} = 2{,}010\text{pF}.$$

Problem 5
What is the reactance of a 30H smoothing choke at a frequency of 100Hz?

$$X_L = 2\pi f L$$
$$X_L = 2\pi \times 100 \times 30\Omega$$
$$= 6{,}000\pi \text{ ohms}$$

We take π to be 3·14 so

$$X_L = 6{,}000 \times 3\cdot14$$
$$= 18{,}840\Omega$$

Problem 6
What is the reactance of a 100pF capacitor at a frequency of 20MHz?

$$X_C = \frac{1}{2\pi f C}$$

(X_C is in ohms when f is in hertz and L in henrys)

$$f = 20\text{MHz} = 20 \times 10^6\text{Hz} = 2 \times 10^7\text{Hz}$$
$$C = 100\text{pF} = 100 \times 10^{-12}\text{F} = 10^{-10}\text{F}$$

(it is much more convenient here to use the index notation) hence

$$X_C = \frac{1}{2\pi \times 2 \times 10^7 \times 10^{-10}} \text{ ohms}$$

$$= \frac{1}{2\pi} \times \frac{1}{2 \times 10^{-3}}$$

Note that we have kept $\frac{1}{2\pi}$ intact because $\frac{1}{2\pi} = 0\cdot16$, thus

$$X_C = 0\cdot16 \times \frac{1}{2 \times 10^{-3}}$$

$$= \frac{0\cdot16 \times 1{,}000}{2}$$

$$= 80\Omega$$

Problem 7
What is the impedance (Z) of an inductance which has a resistance (R) of 4Ω and a reactance (X) of 3Ω?

$$Z = \sqrt{(R^2 + X^2)}$$
$$= \sqrt{(4^2 + 3^2)}$$
$$= \sqrt{16 + 9}$$
$$= \sqrt{25}$$
$$= 5\Omega$$

Problem 8
At what frequency do a capacitor of 100pF and an inductance of 100μH resonate?

At resonance

$$2\pi f L = \frac{1}{2\pi f C}$$

hence

$$f = \frac{1}{2\pi \sqrt{LC}}$$

(f is in hertz, L is in henrys, C is in farads)

$$100\mu\text{H} = 100 \times 10^{-6}\text{H}$$
$$100\text{pF} = 100 \times 10^{-12}\text{F}$$

$$f = \frac{1}{2\pi \sqrt{LC}}$$

$$= \frac{1}{2\pi \sqrt{100 \times 10^{-6} \times 100 \times 10^{-12}}}$$

$$= \frac{1}{2\pi \sqrt{10^2 \times 10^{-6} \times 10^2 \times 10^{-12}}}$$

$$= \frac{1}{2\pi \sqrt{10^{-14}}}$$

$$= \frac{1}{2\pi \times 10^{-7}}$$

$$= \frac{1}{2\pi} \times 10^7$$

$$= 0\cdot16 \times 10^7$$

$$= 1\cdot6 \times 10^6\text{Hz}$$

$$= 1\cdot6\text{MHz}$$

Problem 9
What quantity of electricity is stored in a 100μF capacitor when it is charged to 500V?

Quantity (coulombs) = capacitance (F) × voltage (V)

$$Q = 100 \times 10^{-6} \times 500$$
$$= 1 \times 10^2 \times 10^{-6} \times 5 \times 10^2$$
$$= 5 \times 10^{-2}\text{C}$$

Numerical multiple-choice questions in the RAE

The numerical multiple-choice questions set in the RAE involve quite simple calculations in order to decide which of the four answers given is correct. The questions are likely to be similar to the problems just worked through and generally the answer comes out without the need for any aid to calculation. As in solving the previous problems, the most important thing is to "get the units right". The way to solve these questions should be clear from the following worked examples.

Question 1

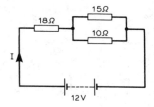

The current I is
  (a) 0·67A.
  (b) 0·5A.
  (c) 0·43A.
  (d) 0·25A.

The effective resistance of the two resistors in parallel is

$$R_{eff} = \frac{15 \times 10}{25} = 6\Omega$$

The effective resistance of the whole circuit is

$$R_{eff} = 18 + 6 = 24\Omega$$

$$I = \frac{12}{24} = 0·5A$$

Answer (b) is therefore correct.

Question 2

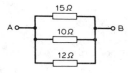

The effective resistance between points A and B is
  (a) 37Ω.
  (b) 17Ω.
  (c) 6Ω.
  (d) 4Ω.

The effective resistance must have a value less than the value of the smallest resistor, so neither answers (a) nor (b) are correct. Take the top two resistors and apply the formula

$$R_{eff} = \frac{R_1 \times R_2}{R_1 + R_2} = \frac{15 \times 10}{25} = 6\Omega$$

Again apply the formula to include the 12Ω resistor.

$$R_{eff} = \frac{6 \times 12}{18} = \frac{72}{18} = 4\Omega$$

Answer (d) is therefore correct.

Question 3

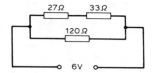

The current flowing through the 27Ω resistor has a value of
  (a) 100mA.
  (b) 60mA.
  (c) 33mA.
  (d) 27mA.

The current flowing through the 120Ω resistor has no bearing on the answer. The current through the 27Ω resistor will be the same as that through the 33Ω resistor. The current through the two resistors in series

$$= \frac{6}{27 + 33} = \frac{6}{60} = \frac{1}{10} \text{ A}$$

The correct answer is (a).

Question 4
The voltage across the 33Ω resistor in the previous question is
  (a) 4·5V.
  (b) 3·3V.
  (c) 1·2V.
  (d) 0·6V.

$$V = I \times R = \frac{1}{10} \times 33 = 3·3V$$

The correct answer is (b).

Question 5
A λ/2 dipole has a length of just under 7·5m. It will be resonant at a frequency of approximately
  (a) 15MHz.
  (b) 20MHz.
  (c) 25MHz.
  (d) 30MHz.

$$\lambda = 15m \quad f = \frac{c}{\lambda} = \frac{300 \times 10^6}{15} = 20 \times 10^6 Hz$$

Therefore (b) is the correct answer.

Question 6
An oscilloscope shows the peak-to-peak voltage of a sine wave to be 100V. The rms value is
  (a) 70·7V.
  (b) 50V.
  (c) 35·35V.
  (d) 27·28V.

$$V_{rms} = V_{peak} \times 0\cdot707$$
$$= 50 \times 0\cdot707 = 35\cdot35V$$

The correct answer is (c).

Question 7
The internal capacitance between the base and emitter of a transistor is 2pF. The reactance at a frequency of 500MHz will be approximately
  (a) 16kΩ.
  (b) 1·6kΩ.
  (c) 160Ω.
  (d) 16Ω.

$$X_C = \frac{1}{\omega C} = \frac{1}{2\pi \times 500 \times 10^6 \times 2 \times 10^{-12}} = \frac{1}{2\pi \times 10^{-3}}$$
$$= 0\cdot16 \times 10^3 = 160\Omega$$

The correct answer is (c).

Question 8
A loudspeaker speech coil has a resistance of 3Ω. If the voltage across it is 3V, then the power in the speech coil is
  (a) 9W.
  (b) 6W.
  (c) 3W.
  (d) 1W.

$$P = \frac{V^2}{R} \text{ watts} \quad P = \frac{3^2}{3} = 3W$$

Answer (c) is therefore correct.

Question 9
A smoothing choke has an inductance of 0·2H. Its reactance at a frequency of 100Hz is approximately
  (a) 1,250Ω.
  (b) 400Ω.
  (c) 125Ω.
  (d) 40Ω.

$$X_L = 2\pi f L = 2\pi \times 100 \times 0\cdot2 = 40\pi \quad \text{or about } 125\Omega.$$
Hence (c) is the correct answer.

Question 10
A coil has a reactance of 1,000Ω and a resistance of 10Ω. Its approximate impedance is
  (a) 10kΩ.
  (b) 1,100Ω.
  (c) 1,000Ω.
  (d) 990Ω.

$$Z = \sqrt{R^2 + X_L^2} = \sqrt{100 + 10^6} = \sqrt{1,000,000} = 1,000\Omega$$

The effect of the resistance is so small that it can be neglected, so (c) is the correct answer.

Question 11

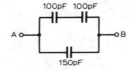

The capacitance measured between terminals A and B will be
  (a) 350pF.
  (b) 200pF.
  (c) 50pF.
  (d) 37·5pF.

The capacitance must be greater than 150pF. The two 100pF capacitors in series have an effective capacitance of 50pF. Therefore the answer is 150 + 50 = 200pF, ie answer (b).

Question 12

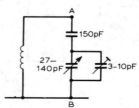

When the variable capacitor and the trimmer capacitor of a local oscillator tuned circuit are adjusted to their maximum values, the effective capacitance between points A and B will be
  (a) 300pF.
  (b) 200pF.
  (c) 75pF.
  (d) 50pF.

The tuning and trimmer capacitors will have an effective capacitance of 140 + 10 = 150pF. Therefore capacitance between A and B will be 75pF, and (c) is the correct answer.

Question 13
When the variable capacitor and the trimmer are set at minimum, the effective capacitance between points A and B will be
  (a) 180pF.
  (b) 120pF.
  (c) 75pF.
  (d) 25pF.

Using the same calculations, (d) is the correct answer.

Question 14

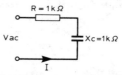

The current I leads the applied voltage by an angle of
  (a) 180°.
  (b) 90°.
  (c) 45°.
  (d) 30°.

Because $R = X_C$ the phasors are equal in magnitude, ie

$V_R = I \times R$ and $V_C = I \times X_C$.

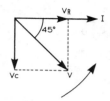

The answer is (c).

Question 15

The peak-to-peak value of a sine wave having an rms voltage of 14·1V is approximately

(a) 56·4V.
(b) 40V.
(c) 28·2V.
(d) 20V.

The peak value for the positive half-cycle is $14\cdot1 \times \sqrt{2}$ = 20V. Therefore the peak-to-peak voltage = $2 \times 20 = 40$V.

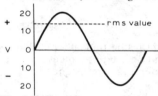

(b) is the correct answer.

Question 16

A quarter-wave antenna is resonant at 10MHz. Its approximate length will be
(a) 30m.
(b) 20m.
(c) 15m.
(d) 7·5m.

$$\lambda = \frac{C}{f} = \frac{300 \times 10^6}{10 \times 10^6} = 30\text{m}$$
$$\lambda/4 = 7\cdot5\text{m}$$

(d) is the correct answer.

Question 17

A charge of 300μC is stored in a capacitor. If the voltage across it is 200V, its capacitance is
(a) 1·5μF.
(b) 5μF.
(c) 6μF.
(d) 15μF.

$$300\mu\text{C} = 300 \times 10^{-6}\text{C}$$
$$\text{Capacitance (farads)} = \frac{Q \text{ (coulombs)}}{V \text{ (volts)}}$$
$$C = \frac{300 \times 10^{-6}}{200}$$
$$= 1\cdot5 \times 10^{-6} \text{ farads}$$
$$= 1\cdot5\mu\text{F}$$

Hence (a) is the correct answer.

Summary of formulae

Ohm's Law $R = \dfrac{V}{I}$ $V = IR$ $I = \dfrac{V}{R}$

Power $W = V \times I$ $W = I^2R$ $W = \dfrac{V^2}{R}$

Reactance $X_L = 2\pi fL$
$$X_C = \frac{1}{2\pi fC}$$

Resonance $f = \dfrac{1}{2\pi\sqrt{LC}}$

Resistors (series) $R = R_1 + R_2 + R_3 + \ldots$

Resistors (parallel) $\dfrac{1}{R} = \dfrac{1}{R_1} + \dfrac{1}{R_2} + \dfrac{1}{R_3} + \ldots$

Capacitors (series) $\dfrac{1}{C} = \dfrac{1}{C_1} + \dfrac{1}{C_2} + \dfrac{1}{C_3} + \ldots$

Capacitors (parallel) $C = C_1 + C_2 + C_3 + \ldots$

Wavelength (metres) $= \dfrac{300}{f(\text{MHz})}$

For a sine wave, rms value = 0·707 × peak value
Charge $Q = CV$.

Supplementary information

Knowledge of the band plans, decibel notation and most of the amateur telegraphy abbreviations listed in this appendix is not called for in the RAE syllabus but they are included here for the sake of completeness.

The decibel notation

The decibel notation is the most realistic way to define a change in power level in an electrical circuit. The following notes are included as an introduction for those readers who have a knowledge of logarithms.

Consider the statement "the power level has increased by 1W". What does this mean? Obviously an increase in power from 0·25W to 1·25W is vastly different from an increase from 10W to 11W or from 100W to 101W, yet in each case the power level has increased by 1W.

The effect of a 1W increase in power in each case may be compared by the use of the decibel notation. The difference between a power level W_1 and a power level W_2 when expressed in decibels is

$$\text{Number of decibels} = 10 \log_{10} \frac{W_2}{W_1}$$

In the above examples

(a) 0·25W to 1·25W

increase in decibels $= 10 \log_{10} \frac{1 \cdot 25}{0 \cdot 25} = 7\text{dB}$

(b) 10W to 11W

increase in decibels $= 10 \log_{10} \frac{11}{10} = 0 \cdot 4\text{dB}$

(c) 100W to 101W

increase in decibels $= 10 \log_{10} \frac{101}{100} = 0 \cdot 04\text{dB}$

The advantage of this notation is therefore obvious. Voltages may also be compared in this way, since

$$W = \frac{V^2}{R}$$

$$\frac{W_2}{W_1} = \frac{V_2^2}{R_2} \div \frac{V_1^2}{R_1}$$

$$= \frac{V_2^2}{R_2} \times \frac{R_1}{V_1^2}$$

Power and voltage ratios in terms of decibels

Decibels	0	3	6	10	20	40	60
Power ratios	1	2	4	10	100	10^4	10^6
Voltage ratios	1	1·4	2	3·16	10	10^2	10^3

if, and only if, $R_1 = R_2$ then

$$\frac{W_2}{W_1} = \frac{V_2^2}{V_1^2}$$

hence number of decibels $= 10 \log_{10} \dfrac{V_2^2}{V_1^2}$

$$= 20 \log_{10} \frac{V_2}{V_1}$$

It must always be remembered that the decibel is a ratio and can be used as a measure of magnitude only when the reference level is quoted.

IARU Region 1 HF Band Plan

Band		Type of emission
3·5–3·6MHz 3·6 3·6–3·8	±20kHz	cw [2] rtty [1] cw and phone [2,3]
7-–7·04MHz 7·04 7·04–7·1	±5kHz	cw rtty [1] cw and phone
10·1–10·15MHz 10·145	±5kHz	cw rtty [1]
14–14·1MHz 14·09 14·1–14·35	±10kHz	cw rtty [1] cw and phone
21–21·15MHz 21·1 21·15–21·45	±20kHz	cw rtty [1] cw and phone
28–28·2MHz 28·1 28·2–29·7	±50kHz	cw rtty [1] cw and phone

Notes
1. For rtty, recommended section of operation shared with cw.
2. 3,500 to 3,510kHz and 3,790 to 3,800kHz reserved for intercontinental working.
3. 3,635 to 3,650kHz is used by USSR stations for intercontinental working.
4. For sstv, recommended operating frequencies are: 3,735, 7,040, 14,230, 21,340, 28,680kHz, all ±5kHz.
5. For beacons, 28·2 to 28·3MHz is recommended.

6. For the downlink of amateur satellites, 29·3 to 29·51MHz is recommended.
7. The transmitter power on the 10MHz band should not exceed 250W mean output power.
8. No contests should be organized on the 10MHz band.
9. Credit for awards or diplomas should be accepted for contacts made on the 10MHz band.
10. SSB may be used on the 10MHz band during emergencies involving the immediate safety of life and property, and only by stations actually involved in the handling of emergency traffic.

UK 144MHz Band Plan

	144·000		
	144·000		Spot frequency (UK use forbidden)
CW only	144·000–144·015		Moonbounce
	144·050		CW calling frequency
	144·100		CW ms reference frequency
	144·150		
	144·250		Used for GB2RS and slow morse transmissions
SSB and cw only	144·260±		Used by Raynet
	144·300		SSB calling frequency
	144·400		SSB ms reference frequency
	144·500		
	144·500		SSTV calling frequency
	144·540		Spot frequency (UK use forbidden)
	144·600		RTTY calling frequency
All modes non-channellized	144·600±		RTTY working (fsk)
	144·675		Data transmission calling
	144·700		FAX calling frequency
	144·750		ATV calling and talkback
	144·775		Raynet
	144·800		Raynet
	144·825		Raynet
	144·845		
Beacons			
	144·990		
	145·000	R0	
	145·025	R1	
	145·050	R2	
FM repeater inputs	145·075	R3	
	145·100	R4	
	145·125	R5	
	145·150	R6	
	145·175	R7	
	145·200		
	145·200	S8	Raynet
	145·225	S9	Used by Raynet
	145·250	S10	Used for slow morse tone modulated transmissions
	145·275	S11	
	145·300	S12	RTTY-afsk
	145·325	S13	
	145·350	S14	
FM simplex channels	145·375	S15	
	145·400	S16	
	145·425	S17	
	145·450	S18	
	145·475	S19	
	145·500	S20	FM calling channel
	145·525	S21	Used for GB2RS fm newscasts
	145·550	S22	Used for rally/exhibition talk-in
	145·575	S23	
	145·600		
	145·600	R0	
	145·625	R1	
	145·650	R2	
FM repeater outputs	145·675	R3	
	145·700	R4	
	145·725	R5	
	145·750	R6	
	145·775	R7	
	145·800		
Satellite service			
	146·000		

NOTES
MS operation can take place up to 26kHz higher than the reference frequency.

The beacon and satellite service bands must be kept free of normal communication transmissions to prevent interference with these services.

The use of the fm mode within the ssb/cw section and cw or ssb in the fm-only sector is not recommended.

Repeater stations are primarily intended as an aid for mobile working and they should never be used for dx communication. FM stations wishing to work dx should use the all-mode section, taking care to avoid frequencies allocated for specific purposes.

UK 432MHz Band Plan

	432·000		
CW only	432·00–432·015		Moonbounce
	432·050		CW calling frequency
	432·150		
SSB and cw only	432·200		UK ssb calling frequency
	432·300		IARU ssb calling frequency
	432·500		
	432·600±		RTTY working (fsk)
All modes non-channelized	432·600		RTTY calling frequency
	432·675		Data transmission calling
	432·700		FAX calling frequency
	432·800		
Beacons			
	433·000		
	433·000	RB0	
	433·025	RB1	
	433·050	RB2	
	433·075	RB3	
	433·100	RB4	
	433·125	RB5	
	433·150	RB6	
	433·175	RB7	
FM repeater outputs in UK only	433·200	RB8/SU8	Used by Raynet
	433·225	RB9	
	433·250	RB10	
	433·275	RB11	
	433·300	RB12/SU12	RTTY repeater and rtty afsk working
	433·325	RB13	
	433·350	RB14	
	433·375		
	433·375	SU15	
	433·400	SU16	
FM simplex channels	433·425	SU17	
	433·450	SU18	
	433·475	SU19	
	433·500	SU20	FM calling channel
	434·600		
	434·600	RB0	
	434·625	RB1	
	434·650	RB2	
	434·675	RB3	
	434·700	RB4	
	434·725	RB5	
FM repeater inputs in UK only	434·750	RB6	
	434·800	RB8	
	434·825	RB9	
	434·850	RB10	
	434·875	RB11	
	434·900	RB12	RTTY repeater–afsk
	434·925	RB13	
	434·950	RB14	
	435·000		
	434–440		Sub-band devoted to UK atv—frequencies chosen so as to avoid interference to other band users and in particular, the amateur satellite service
	435–438		Amateur satellite service sub-band
	440·000		

UK 70MHz Band Plan

	70·025		
Beacons only			
	70·075		
CW only			
	70·150		
SSB and cw only	70·200		SSB calling frequency
	70·260		
	70·260		National mobile calling frequency
All modes	70·300		RTTY calling frequency
	70·350–70·400		Raynet
	70·400		
FM simplex only	70·450		FM calling frequency
	70·500		

Amateur abbreviations

AA	All after . . .(used after a question mark to request a repetition)	**CUAGN**	see you again	**OC**	old chap
		CUL	see you later	**OM**	old man
AB	All before . . .(see AA)	**CW**	continuous wave	**OP**	operator
BK	Signal used to interrupt a transmission in progress	**DF**	direction finding	**OT**	old timer
		DR	dear	**PSE**	please
BN	All between . . .and . . .(see AA)	**DX**	long distance	**PWR**	power
		ELBUG	electronic key	**RCVR**	receiver
C	Yes	**ENUF**	enough	**RPRT**	report
CFM	Confirm (or I confirm)	**ES**	and	**RX**	receiver
CL	I am closing my station	**FB**	fine business	**SA**	South America
CQ	General call to all stations	**FM**	frequency modulation	**SED**	said
DE	Used to separate the callsign of the station called from that of the calling station	**FER**	for	**SIG**	signal
		FONE	telephone	**SKED**	schedule
		FREQ	frequency	**SN**	soon
		GA	go ahead, or good afternoon	**SRI**	sorry
NIL	I have nothing to send you			**SSB**	single sideband
NW	Now	**GB**	goodbye	**STN**	station
OK	We agree (or it is correct)	**GD**	good day	**SUM**	some
R	Received	**GE**	good evening	**SW**	short-wave
RPT	Repeat (or I repeat)	**GG**	going	**SWL**	short-wave listener
TFC	Traffic	**GLD**	glad	**TKS**	thanks
W	Word(s)	**GM**	good morning	**TMW**	tomorrow
WA	Word after (see AA)	**GN**	good night	**TNX**	thanks
WB	Word before	**GND**	ground (earth)	**TRX**	transceiver
		GUD	good	**TV**	television
		HAM	amateur transmitter	**TVI**	television interference
Informal amateur abbreviations		**HI**	laughter	**TX**	transmitter
ABT	about	**HPE**	hope	**U**	you
ADR	address	**HR**	here or hear	**UR**	your
AFR	Africa	**HRD**	heard	**VFO**	variable frequency oscillator
AGN	again	**HV**	have		
ANI	any	**HVY**	heavy	**VY**	very
ANT	antenna (aerial)	**HW**	how	**W**	watts
BCNU	be seeing you	**INPT**	input	**WID**	with
BD	bad	**LID**	poor operator	**WKD**	worked
BFO	beat frequency oscillator	**LSN**	listen	**WKG**	working
BK	break-in	**MNI**	many	**WL**	will or well
BLV	believe	**MOD**	modulation	**WUD**	would
BUG	semi-automatic key	**MSG**	message	**WX**	weather
CANS	headphones	**MTR**	meter (or metres)	**XMTR**	•transmitter
CK	check	**NA**	North America	**XYL**	wife
CLD	called	**NBFM**	narrow band frequency modulation	**XTAL**	crystal
CNT	cannot			**YL**	young lady
CONDX	conditions	**ND**	nothing doing	**73**	best regards
CRD	card	**NR**	number	**88**	love and kisses
CUD	could	**OB**	old boy		

Answers to practice multiple-choice RAE questions

FIRST PAPER

Part 1

1	c	13	d	25	a
2	b	14	a	26	b
3	d	15	d	27	b
4	b	16	a	28	a
5	d	17	a	29	d
6	b	18	c	30	d
7	b	19	b	31	a
8	d	20	a	32	b
9	c	21	d	33	c
10	c	22	c	34	a
11	c	23	c	35	c
12	a	24	b		

Part 2

36	b	56	a	76	a
37	a	57	a	77	c
38	d	58	c	78	c
39	c	59	c	79	a
40	b	60	c	80	d
41	a	61	a	81	d
42	c	62	b	82	a
43	a	63	b	83	b
44	d	64	b	84	b
45	c	65	d	85	c
46	c	66	d	86	a
47	a	67	c	87	d
48	d	68	b	88	c
49	b	69	c	89	b
50	b	70	a	90	a
51	d	71	d	91	a
52	d	72	c	92	b
53	b	73	b	93	d
54	a	74	c	94	c
55	d	75	d	95	b

SECOND PAPER

Part 1

1	b	13	a	25	a
2	c	14	d	26	b
3	b	15	d	27	b
4	a	16	c	28	b
5	b	17	c	29	d
6	d	18	d	30	d
7	c	19	a	31	a
8	d	20	b	32	d
9	a	21	c	33	c
10	c	22	b	34	a
11	b	23	c	35	c
12	a	24	c		

Part 2

36	b	56	a	76	d
37	a	57	b	77	c
38	d	58	d	78	d
39	a	59	b	79	d
40	c	60	c	80	b
41	a	61	a	81	d
42	d	62	c	82	b
43	b	63	c	83	a
44	a	64	a	84	a
45	d	65	d	85	b
46	d	66	b	86	c
47	b	67	c	87	d
48	b	68	b	88	b
49	d	69	c	89	d
50	b	70	a	90	b
51	d	71	d	91	c
52	c	72	c	92	a
53	a	73	c	93	b
54	c	74	b	94	a
55	c	75	a	95	c

Index